THIRTY BULLIES

A Celebration of Twenty Years of the Rugby World Cup

ALISON KERVIN

SIMON &
SCHUSTER

London · New York · Sydney · Toronto

A CBS COMPANY

First published in Great Britain in 2007
by Simon & Schuster UK Ltd
A CBS COMPANY

Copyright © 2007 by Alison Kervin

PICTURE CREDITS
pp. 2, 6, 7, 8, 9, 11, 12, 13, 15, 17, 19, 21, 31: Getty
pp. 1, 4, 10, 14, 16, 20, 22, 25, 26, 27, 30, 32: Offside
pp. 5, 23, 24: PA Photos
p. 28: Action Images
pp. 18, 29: Mirrorpix
p. 3: Popperfoto

The right of Alison Kervin to be identified as the author of this
work has been asserted by her in accordance
with sections 77 and 78 of the Copyright,
Designs and Patents Act, 1988.

1 3 5 7 9 10 8 6 4 2

Simon & Schuster UK Ltd
Africa House
64–78 Kingsway
London WC2B 6AH

www.simonsays.co.uk

Simon & Schuster Australia
Sydney

A CIP catalogue for this book is available
from the British Library.

Hardback ISBN: 978-1-84737-012-9
Trade Paperback ISBN: 978-1-84737-013-6

Typeset in Palatino by M Rules
Printed and bound in Great Britain by
Mackays of Chatham Ltd

THIRTY
BULLIES

*For Charlie and Edward Walker, and Macey and Poppy
Cubbage. But most of all for George Kervin-Evans –
the little dynamo whose vivid imagination, questioning
mind and constant analysing know no bounds.*

'Rugby is a good occasion for keeping thirty bullies far from the centre of the city'

Oscar Wilde

CONTENTS

ACKNOWLEDGEMENTS

Thanks to everyone who helped me track down players from the past and reminded me of the stories, lifestyle and the world of rugby 20 years ago. I made a million phone calls and spoke to a million people – thank you all. Thanks, too, to the spouses who called back to correct things and remembered events, people and matches more clearly. A particularly huge thank you to Jason Leonard and Florent Rossigneau – the men with the biggest rugby address books in the country.

Thanks to Alan Pearey for his fine research skills, and to Peter Kervin and Jeremy Sayers for their magnificent red-pen wielding at the editing stage. Thanks, too, to Daniel Evans for all his help.

Many thanks to everyone at Simon & Schuster, especially Andrew Gordon and Rory Scarfe, but also to all the people whose unseen work has made everything run so smoothly . . . from the marketing people to the sales people to the cover designer. It's much appreciated. Thanks, as always, to my lovely agent, Sheila Crowley, and to all at AP Watt.

Thanks, too, to all at the RFU library, particularly Jed Smith; to everyone at Sports Statistics & Information Systems Ltd; Jeremy Duxbury in Fiji and to all those he put me in touch with. Thanks to the government of Fiji for their help. Many thanks to David Kirk, Pat Lam, Brian Lima, Rory Underwood, Geoff Cooke, Mike Harrison, Gareth Rees and Peter Winterbottom. To all at SARFU, IRB, the Australian Institute of Sport, the Australian Rugby Union, the New Zealand Rugby Union, the France Rugby Union, Japan Rugby Union, the Zimbabwe Rugby Union, the communications department of the government of South Africa and the kind man who helped me with a host of papers about the Mandela story but wanted to remain anonymous. To all at the New Zealand library of rugby, Sean Fitzpatrick, Clive Woodward and Paddy Lund. Also thanks to Brian Smith, Keith Wood, Gavin Hastings, Bob Dwyer, Francois Pienaar, Rod Macqueen and Alex Wyllie.

Thanks to Don Rutherford, Jim Blair, Tom McNab, Paddy Lennon at London Irish, Olivier Magne, Robbie Russell and the lovely Brian Moore. To all in Ivory Coast rugby who tried valiantly to understand what on earth I was talking about. Indeed, thanks to all the unions – I spoke to every one of them at some stage.

Final thanks to everyone in Amida who sent over coffees while I bashed away on my laptop like a loony from morning to night. And thanks to my family, especially Mum who never seems to get a mention – I don't know why. To Sue Bence, Louise Voss, Jayne Kearney, Lisa, Steph, Sally, Lee, Julie, Yvonne, the two Michelles, Julia, Gaby, Charlie, Catherine, Lisa, Dan, Paul, Andy, Oliver, Sebastian, Rupert, Rene, Yorkie and all my friends . . . for keeping me sane.

INTRODUCTION

Terry Davies is a man of simple beliefs and tastes. The sprightly septuagenarian leans back in his worn armchair, takes a sip of sugary tea, and reiterates his long-held view that *Countdown* is the best television programme ever made, English summers were designed for watching cricket, and the winters are for mixing with rugby folk.

He has a lovely tale, does Mr Davies, about the time that he and his wife, Pam, travelled to Brisbane in 1987 to meet their new grandchild for the first time. The long-haul travel did not agree with him, so, naturally enough, on his first morning on the other side of the world, he was up, dressed and shaved by 4 a.m. In his head it was time for lunch, in England it was time for *Countdown* and in Australia it was too early for breakfast. He decided to go for a walk – away from his hotel and the other big glittering international establishments in the vicinity, and over to the rougher side of town, where the hotels for the financially less advantaged were situated.

Through the dirty window of one such hostelry, he thought he saw movement. When he peered more closely, he was greeted by the sight of three young men – lying on the floor in the reception area by the window. 'They were in a terrible state,' recalls Davies. 'One had boot polish on his face that had rubbed off on to his shirt and was all over his hands. Another had a plant in his back pocket and it looked as if he'd been trying to eat it. They were all big, unshaven and really messed up. I thought they'd been beaten up. I wondered how big the blokes who'd hit them must have been.'

Our valiant, jet-lagged hero decided to check the men were okay. 'My goodness, I couldn't believe it when I walked in there. It was three England players. They were lying on the floor, drunk.

They couldn't get their keys to fit in any of the doors, and couldn't find their rooms.'

Davies called the manager and the two of them tried unsuccessfully to herd the three drunk international rugby players into the lift. It was no good. The men wanted to sing to the picture of Sophia Loren on the noticeboard and wouldn't be moved. Davies left.

'The next time I saw the players, they were running out to play against Wales in the quarter-final. "There they go!" I said to my wife. "They're the men I told you about." She shook her head when they lost the game and said, "No wonder they can't play properly if they're out getting drunk," but I just thought "Ah, leave them alone – at least they enjoyed themselves while they were here. That's what rugby's all about."'

Sixteen years later, and it is four in the afternoon in the England team's hotel. Again, the players are in Brisbane, and again they are preparing to face a quarter-final match against Wales. This time it is the 2003 World Cup, and England are favourites to lift the trophy. A group of journalists has gathered in the bar – beyond the reception area's sweep of marble floor that dazzles and gleams like an ice rink in the stunning Australian sunshine. There are vast windows, grand pillars and a small forest of sub-tropical plants. It is elegant in that modern, summery, minimalist way of a million design magazines. Huge, squashy, butter-coloured sofas are everywhere, all of them covered in piles of small, fluffy white cushions – like a litter of kittens curled up in the midday sun. In the corner of one sofa sits Prince Harry, chatting to Clive Woodward about the England team's prospects. The coach is explaining the importance of homeostasis, biomechanics, nutrition, precision fitness and psychological state.

The men at the bar order pints. 'Did you hear what happened to us this morning?' asks one.

The journalists, it transpires, had returned to their hotel at around 6 a.m. and, rather hampered by the amount of wine they'd consumed, were unable to find their keys. They collapsed on to the sofas and fell asleep. Blind drunk, they lay there until, at

7 a.m., barely an hour after they had settled down, they awoke to the sound of heavy footsteps. They looked up to see the England players collecting in the reception area to go for their morning training session. Martin Johnson looked down at the prone journalists – a look of disgust creeping across his face. The famously furrowed brow had furrowed further. 'What are you doing?' he enquired, with a naivety unique to modern international players. Mickey Skinner would have known what the men were doing there, and Derek Stark and Richard Webster and Martin Bayfield, Robert Norster, Rob Henderson . . . all of them. They would have known exactly what they were doing there, and chances are they'd have been coming back in from a drinking session themselves. 'Hadn't you better get up?' asked England's captain, as he led his men out of the hotel. 'Yes,' said the journalists, obediently stumbling to their feet.

Never, in the entire history of sport, has there been a transformation as fundamental as that which blasted through rugby union during the first twenty years of the World Cup. The past, where rugby is concerned, is not so much a foreign country as a distant planet. The average international player in 2007 is over two stone heavier than the average player in 1987, with less body fat and greater muscle mass – faster, stronger, fitter, more powerful and with quicker reaction times. The average match contains twice as much time in which the ball is in play (from twenty-two minutes in 1987 to forty-four minutes in 2003). According to a poll of the world's leading fitness advisers, the players eat around 40 per cent more food now and drink around 200 per cent more water. Alcohol consumption has dropped by an amazing 70 per cent.

That is not to say that every player in 1987 was staggering around the pitch in a drunken frenzy, nor is it to suggest that every player in 2007 is teetotal and a perfect physical specimen – that is patently not the case; we've seen them in their skintight Lycra shirts! What is undeniable, though, is that there have been vast, sweeping changes in terms of the physical condition and lifestyle of rugby players in the last twenty years and the result of the changes is a much faster, more power-packed game. The players' expectations of the sport have altered as much as the sport's expectations of them.

In Brisbane in 1987, the England players complained that their beds were so short that Wade Dooley's feet were hanging off the end of them; the food was so bad that half the players took to living off chocolate and they had a daily allowance of Aus$35. By 2003, the England team were travelling first-class, they took a chef with them wherever they went and the players were all on six-figure salaries, with agents, book deals, newspaper columns and huge public profiles.

'We didn't take it seriously in 1987,' says Paul Rendall, England's prop. 'I can remember thinking "as long as we have a good time – everything will be okay". Then we got to the World Cup and we couldn't believe it – the New Zealanders had been training. Bastards! Bloody cheats. They had matching training tops and proper coaches and everything. We'd never seen anything like it. It was as if they'd let us down – broken ranks.'

While the New Zealand team of 1987 went about showing why they were regarded as the greatest side in the world, with stars like Michael Jones – the stunning player of the tournament who refused to play on Sundays because of his religious beliefs – England had a different approach. This is best illustrated by Rendall, who set about organising beauty pageants for the players in order to keep them from getting bored. I have seen the photos, and no amount of therapy will ease the shock of the pictures that were taken during the swimming costume section. Brian Moore won the contest in style – having squashed his ample frame into a high-cut swimming costume, which revealed parts of his anatomy that only a wife should see. He looked quite touched when they lay the winner's tiara on his shiny bald head. If only he'd had front teeth, and hadn't had a black eye from the match the day before – he'd have looked quite charming.

Such antics occur in clubs around the country all the time. One of the fascinating and delightful things about rugby union in the past was that the international players did it too – they behaved in exactly the same way as the lowly club players did. If your contribution to world rugby was to run out for the local thirds every weekend, you had a similar lifestyle to the men who represented their country. You all shared tales of try-scoring hero- ism – more elaborated and embellished with every pint – then you all got up and went to work the next morning. All that separated the best at rugby from the worst was God-given talent.

World Cups changed all that. They changed rugby players' images of themselves and their fundamental understanding and interpretation of what it was to be an international sportsman. World Cups triggered the transformation of their very con- sciousness of themselves as rugby players.

> The major thing that happened when the World Cups started [says Brian Moore, England hooker for the first three World Cups] was that we started to think of ourselves as proper sportsmen, and we'd never seen ourselves like that before. Even when we were playing league rugby for the first time – we were still just having a laugh, being rugby players. We'd always thought of rugby as being not quite like other sports. Once the World Cups got going, we became athletes. We started to think about winning, and it was the winning that became the enjoyment rather than the pranks.

But winning, and the striving for international success, demanded a revolution in another area, because what soon became apparent was that winning World Cups was about much more than having good players. Those players had to be pre- pared, mentally and physically, and they had to know what they were doing tactically: defensively and in attack. You still needed good players in order to win, but suddenly the realisation hit that you could have good players and still not win.

Winning was, paradoxically, more complex than just being the best. Strength of purpose, a clear vision, intelligent thinking, con- fidence and belief can push a team of less talented individuals to victory. Good coaching was needed, and so began a revolution in rugby coaching. The art began to grow, and it became less didac- tic – more about thinking and understanding, challenging and questioning as experts from outside the sport came in, and the narrow but rigid boundaries of rugby were pushed back to accommodate fresh thinking and new ideas. Their arrival in the sport prompted further redefinition of rugby, as fitness was over-hauled to ensure that players were physically able to make the changes that the new coaches were insisting on, and perform as was expected of them.

Issues like mental preparation, psychological advantage and decision-making were on the agenda. Rugby union was becoming, in all but name, a professional sport. In the new climate, it became inevitable that amateurism would wither and die. The noose was already around the neck of amateurism by the time the 1980s started, and leagues had loosened the trapdoor below it. Once the World Cup became a regular fixture – providing a massive commercial opportunity to companies and, most pertinently, to television – the trapdoor was opened and amateurism was gone for ever. Then, of course, the sport's progress gained further momentum and took a giant leap into the future.

Thirty Bullies marks the first twenty years of the rugby World Cup with the players' stories of the tournaments. From the funny and irreverent, to the tragic and brilliant – the fascinating tale of the World Cup from the perspective of those who played in it.

The book contrasts and evaluates across countries and across generations – looking at the fitness programmes of England in 1987, and the fitness work undertaken by New Zealand in 1987; then, looking later at the fitness work undertaken by England in 2003, to get a sense of how teams compared across the world and how they compare across time.

There are all the fun stories from the players – from Victor 'once more into the mouth, dear feet' Ubogu, who declared, during his run along the beach in Durban in the 1995 World Cup, 'Christ, this altitude is killing me!' to former England manager Jack Rowell's comment to Ubogu when the two met. 'Jack, why did you take an instant dislike to me?' asked Ubogu. 'Because, Victor, it saved time,' said Rowell.

Simon Shaw, the England second-row, recalls one particularly funny story when his club, Bristol, was trying to raise funds for an under-19 tour in the days when everything was funded by raffles. 'Derek Eves was organising one of those race nights where they screen old horse and greyhound races. He asked me if I wanted a dog and what I wanted to call it. "Okay," I said, "I'll have Number 5, Shawsy's Surprise." He moved on to a worried-looking Ronnie [Mark Regan], who said he'd let him know. Next day Derek asked whether he'd come to a decision. "I've had a word with my mum," replied Regan, "but she says our Alsatians are enough and we don't need a greyhound".'

Regan is the butt of many of the modern England jokes. Such as the time the England team were invited to the celebratory tea party at Buckingham Palace after the 2003 World Cup victory. Regan was met by a royal attendant as he entered the room. The attendant bowed and said: 'Earl Grey, sir?' Pause. 'Er, no. Mark Regan, Leeds Tykes,' came the reply.

Thirty Bullies is divided into Parts – with one for each of the World Cups. As well as featuring the stories, anecdotes, results and challenges of the star players and major international teams, there is also a chapter on the minnow side that made the biggest splash – from Fiji who had to overcome a coup to get there in 1987, to Western Samoa in 1991 and the tragedy of Côte d'Ivoire's appearance in 1995.

There is also a special study of the winning side in each World Cup Part. What does it take to win a World Cup? What did the winning side in each World Cup do to prepare for the tournament? What is winning World Cups all about? What separates winners from losers? In each Part, a list of ten major reasons why the winners triumphed is produced. At the end of the book, the lists are compared. What similarities exist between the sides that have won? In the conclusion of *Thirty Bullies* there is a summary of the attributes that every World Cup winning side has had. It makes fascinating reading, and implies that there is a formula for success that does not change much, even as the sport itself has changed dramatically.

Why do the northern hemisphere sides fare less well than their southern counterparts? Only one northern side has won (England 2003), but there has been a team from the northern hemisphere in every final except 1995 (France 1987, 1999 and England 1991, 2003). Also, in third-place play-offs, there is an equal split – with five southern and five northern sides contesting them. So, what appears to be missing from the northern hemisphere sides is that crucial drive to actually win the thing. There are lots of theories as to why this is. The scientists at the Australian Institute of Sport have their theories and the coaches and captains of the winning sides have theirs. Again, their thoughts make for interesting and challenging reading.

Success in sport is a fascinating subject to get to grips with because of the central role of 'winning' in sport's very make-up. Rarely in sport do you have the traditional business solution of a win/win situation. Sport loves winners. In other fields competition has to be manufactured – competitions are created to find the greatest writers (Booker Prize, Orange Prize), greatest actors (Oscars, Baftas), greatest musicians, journalists, artists, television presenters, soap stars, salesmen, marketing campaigns . . . the list goes on. No such manufactured competitions are needed in sport because it has competition at its soul. Competition is what sport's very design is based on and existence has depended on. When there's no natural winner at the end, they play extra time. If a winner still doesn't emerge, they play golden goals. If a winner still doesn't emerge they kick penalties. A winner will be found. That's why it's so uniquely compelling, absorbing and thrilling.

The issue of why some teams win and why some teams don't, why some people succeed and why some don't, forms the basis of a million bar-room debates. Why do Australia do so well in World Cups? They manage to do what no other teams do, and be consistently good. They are the only team to have made it to the final two World Cups running, and the only team to have won it twice. Why? What is the role of the highly acclaimed Australia Institute of Sport in all this? Is their ability to talent-spot and nurture young players a crucial element in the continuing success of the Australian sides? Or do they just have better coaches? Better players?

Then, on the other side of the coin, there is the ever-present question of why New Zealand isn't more successful. As the 2007

World Cup approaches, the All Blacks are once again favourites to win. They are favourites going into most World Cups because they are so damned good. Why, then, have they not won the competition for twenty years? They have made it to the semi-final or the final of every World Cup. They have scored 50 per cent more tries than any other team across the World Cups, and they have accumulated 50 per cent more points. Yet they have only won once – in the first World Cup when none of the other teams knew what they were doing! Why? Is it, paradoxically, because they were too good to start with? All Black history is filled with success, but they learned how to achieve that success before the World Cup changed all the rules of competition. New Zealand were awesome on the extended three-month tours where the better side would emerge triumphant by the end, and they remain awesome in the Tri Nations competitions where they utterly dominate – New Zealand have won eight of the twelve championships that have taken place since it started while Australia have won two and South Africa two. The top four try scorers in the competition are all New Zealanders, as are three of the top five all-time points scorers in the competition. Astonishing, isn't it? Added to this is the fact that on the occasions that New Zealand have won the Tri Nations they have obliterated the opposition, whereas when Australia and South Africa have won, the tournament has been much closer.

The difference between the great, big world tours and the Tri Nations competition with its home and away element, versus the World Cup, is the knockout factor. This means that an ability to win by a huge margin – racking up ten victories out of thirteen on tour by playing brilliant rugby, is not as valuable as stringing two victories together by the skin of your teeth to get to the final of a World Cup. New Zealand have struggled more than most sides to come to terms with rugby's new definition of winning because they had so perfected the art of winning in 'old rugby'. The essential differences between winning a traditional tournament and winning a knockout competition should not be underestimated.

Victory in World Cups demands the adoption of a more ruthless, scientific approach to victory. It's about working out specifically in this match which opposition players you need to target and what you have to do to throw them off the scent. It's less 'pure' in many respects – less about building yourself into a great team and more about working out how to blow everyone else out of the way en route to the final. That is not to say that World Cup winning sides aren't great, but they are perhaps more streetwise. To use a cricket analogy – the old rugby tours were more like Test cricket, while rugby World Cups are arguably more like a series of one-day games.

All Black legend Zinzan Brooke, who played in New Zealand's 1987 victory, said:

> The difference between rugby before there were World Cups and afterwards is massive. I was lucky to play in both eras and the whole of international sport has changed. I think that the guys now do miss out on the touring experience and the friend-ships that come with it. These days, they just fly in for a game and then head straight out again. That's a shame. When I first started playing for the All Blacks, a simple tour to Australia would take in sixteen matches. Now, it's just a couple of Tests and home, and save yourself for the big one – the rugby World Cup. Every other match is a stepping stone on the way instead of being valuable in itself. The rugby World Cups have become everything and winning them means everything. Part of me thinks that's a shame.

Thirty Bullies looks in some detail at what it takes to win World Cups, but more than anything, the book looks at the play-ers whose skills, pain, fun, joy and plain ridiculousness has made the first twenty years of rugby World Cups such a triumph.

My thanks to all of the players for their co-operation with the book, and for years of entertaining company. I hope you enjoy sharing their memories as much as I have.

Alison Kervin
Hampton Court, May 2007

PRELUDE

How and why did the World Cup start?

In football we have had foul play, cheating, ultra-nationalism and every sort of ill that you don't want in sport. You rugger fellows would be best advised to stick to your international tours and matches and forget all about the flummery of a World Cup.

Sir Stanley Rous of the Football Association

A glance through the minutes of the International Rugby Board (IRB) meetings reveals a terrible truth – more time at their exalted get-togethers was given to the design of IRB ties than was afforded discussion on the hosting of an international tournament.

Such was the dislike of anything approaching a World Cup that on the occasions when one was suggested, the idea would be dismissed immediately, without further discussion. In 1969 the Board went so far as to declare categorically that 'approval not be given to participation by teams from member unions in any competition or tournament, at whatever level, or wherever taking place, in which teams from several countries take part' – thus eliminating in one sentence any prospect of a World Cup.

Luckily, the officials of the Australian Rugby Union and the New Zealand Rugby Football Union did not give up easily, and in 1983, after dozens of failed attempts, they both wrote to the IRB seeking to hold a World Cup tournament in their separate countries for separate reasons. New Zealand were the world's premier rugby nation and eager to expose themselves to competition on the world stage, while Australia had an eye on the bicentennial celebrations of 1988 and were keen to mark them with a major international tournament. Neither was aware of the other's letter until the meeting at which both proposals were turned down.

The two countries offered to pool resources to conduct a feasibility study, to be presented at the IRB's annual meeting in March 1985, and the IRB finally, miraculously agreed. Were they drunk? No, it seems that their positive response was down to the fact that a terror greater even than the thought of a World Cup tournament was lurking on the touchlines, in the shadowy shape of David Lord, an Australian entrepreneur. It was news of Lord's approaches to key players in the southern hemisphere in his bid to organise an independent tournament that moved the members of the IRB to sanction the feasibility study.

Andy Haden, the former New Zealand player, was one of those approached by Lord. 'It was explained to me that the eight teams would meet each other on a round-robin basis, giving a total of twenty-eight matches,' he said. 'The winnings would be carved up between the teams in the competition, depending on where they finished but ensuring that all were adequately compensated.'

Tournaments would be played in each of the participating countries (the eight founder members of the IRB, with South Africa replaced by Argentina), with each tournament lasting two months, followed by two months off before the next one. All players, coaches, administrators and referees would be guaranteed salaries for the first two years of the professional tournament's duration.

'Throughout New Zealand, twenty-eight players were approached and only two refused to sign,' adds Haden. 'The initial letters of intent signed by New Zealand players were held, for safety, at my bank in Auckland.' Haden says that most European players also signed up to the professional tournament. 'Lions manager Willie John McBride told the press that if he received evidence that any member of his team had negotiated with David Lord, he would be obliged to send him home. I wonder if Willie appreciated that, in view of the vast numbers of British players involved, the chances were that any replacement player called would also have signed. How could anyone turn down the offered $250,000 for two years?'

The arrival of Lord created a real threat for the British and Irish officials. They recognised that whatever their fears about the prospect of a World Cup tournament run under the jurisdiction of their organisation, it was nothing compared to the prospect of a moneyed entrepreneur taking over. The combination of increased pressure from the southern hemisphere representatives and the growing threat of a rival rugby competition prompted the IRB to think more seriously about a World Cup.

On 1 December 1984 they commissioned the feasibility study, and in March 1985 it was voted for by the eight IRB members – Australia, New Zealand, South Africa, France, England, Scotland, Ireland and Wales. They came down in favour of a Rugby World Cup by six votes to two. Ireland and Scotland were against the proposal as it appeared to threaten the amateur status of the sport, while France were in favour only if countries from outside the IRB were invited to take part.

The eight founder members were invited to participate. South Africa declined their invitation, and Zimbabwe was invited in its place to make sure there was representation from Africa. Also invited were Italy, Romania, Canada, Argentina, USSR, Japan, Fiji and Tonga. The USSR never accepted its invitation, instead a host of financial demands arrived that could not be met, so the USA was invited instead. For this first tournament, there were no qualifying rounds, and the rather arbitrary system for inviting teams annoyed countries like Western Samoa which had a good rugby reputation and had hoped to be invited. The World Cup was planned for May and June of 1987.

PART ONE: 1987

Cheers, beers and cauliflower ears

1

Fooling the fat testers and drinking 'til dawn

I think Brian Moore's gnashers are the kind you get from a DIY shop and hammer in yourself. He is the only player we have who looks like a French forward.

Paul Rendall, England prop, 1987

O h, how I wish I'd been there . . . in that room, on that day, just to see those faces. It was August 1986 and the cream of English rugby was crammed into a small room at Bisham Abbey Training Centre in Buckinghamshire. Dean Richards and Peter Winterbottom lolled across the tables, struggling to stay awake. The bright fluorescent lighting swam before their red-rimmed eyes, as sweat prickled on their greying skin. The morning meeting had come hot on the heels of a taxing evening training session, lasting approximately an hour, and a taxing drinking session, lasting approximately eight. Significantly more pints had been drunk than press-ups had been pushed, and the effects were beginning to show. Richards and Winterbottom had led the charge – valiantly disposing of far more alcohol than was strictly necessary . . . or wise. Now they just had to get through this quick meeting, then stumble back home to bed.

Rory Underwood, the only non-drinker in the group, had every reason to feel more alert than his hungover teammates, but he was lost in his own sugar-induced trance – the England wing and RAF pilot had an ability to eat chocolate, sweets and crisps with a speed more commonly associated with six-year-olds on Christmas morning. 'What are we here for?' he asked.

Brian Moore, a young hooker, shrugged. No one really knew. The team had just been told to assemble, so assemble they did.

Moore was a man who was not averse to a drink himself – like some superhero in reverse, he was a quite brilliant, incisive and belligerent solicitor by day, reduced to world-class drinker by night – hanging out at The Sun in Richmond, talking nonsense at the bar with anyone who'd listen. The Sun was scene for many of the England team's less sophisticated moments back in the 1980s, such as when John Olver fell over the bar and landed up in the salad cart in the early hours of the morning. Those who know Olver best claim that it was the first and last time the man ever went near a lettuce leaf. Certainly the sight of him emerging half covered in tomatoes and a delicate garlic mayonnaise lives on in the minds of all who witnessed the moment.

Olver was the team joker of the 1980s – he and Mickey Skinner were the men at the centre of a million pranks and wind-ups. When Merlene Ottey found herself unlucky enough to be in a room opposite Olver during one training camp in Lanzarote – with just a rooftop balcony separating them, she must have known that it was only a matter of time before her fluorescent green training leotard disappeared from her balcony for the night – to be replaced, stretched beyond all recognition, the next morning.

One of Olver's front row comrades in the 1980s was Paul Rendall, who was also sitting in that small, airless room on that auspicious day in 1986. Rendall was a man respected and admired by his peers. He was team judge at the kangaroo courts that formed such an unrelenting feature of life on tour back in the amateur days. In fact, such an overwhelming influence did he exert in this role, that he is still referred to as 'judgey' today – some twenty years after he was doling out sentences and convictions. His punishments are remembered with a mixture of fondness and downright terror ... like the time he ordered

players to shave off their moustaches and made Brian Moore
drink out of a dog bowl and wear a collar. Then there was the
time when John Bentley was tied to a tree and made to sing
'Chanson d'Amour' every ten minutes for three hours. 'It was
hysterical!' says Moore. Whether Bentley thought it quite so
funny is debatable. He's probably still in therapy. There was a
moment when the players hit back at Rendall, though. They convened a 'Players' Revolutionary Court' and brought Rendall
before it, charged with over-exuberance in his sentencing. He was
found guilty and punished by being forced to spend an evening
dressed as a dusky Fijian maiden – complete with boot-polish,
pink permed wig, straw bra and grass skirt.

'At the time, practical jokes were an important feature of the
sport,' says Moore. 'When someone called "dead ants" halfway
through a match – you didn't stop to wonder whether it was
appropriate to act. Whatever was happening, you dived on to the
floor – end of story. Dead ants, Ralgex on the testicles, rugby
songs . . .'

Moore recalls how the players would be out drinking until
4 a.m., then meet at the Bank of England ground the next morning for England training. 'The overriding aim of the session, as
most sessions, was to get through it without being sick. That's
pretty much what England training was in the 1980s – all of us
trying not to be sick.'

The sport of rugby union in the 1980s was a world unto itself.
While the 1980s generally was the decade in which many other
sports had become glamorous, multi-million-pound entertain-
ment industries, rugby became the sport that time forgot.
Coaches were considered an unnecessary extravagance, training
was cheating, fitness was a waste of time and diets consisted of
eating deep-fried, small farm animals and drinking your body
weight in beer. Hoorah! Rugby players were real men and had no
need for the obsessions which consumed other sportsmen.

In 1986, a year before the first World Cup, an analysis of
sportsmen by Dr Craig Sharp, a sports scientist working at
Leicester University, found rugby union forwards to be the least
fit of all sportsmen in the country (they came fiftieth behind

bowls players and archers). Rugby union backs came in fortieth place. No one in the sport cared. Indeed, there was a secret pride in the fact that the sport had not succumbed to this new overly competitive spirit which seemed to have distracted so many other sportsmen. Rugger was still a gentlemanly, leisurely and social sport – and thank the Lord for that.

These were the days, remember, of men like Dean Richards – a fine player, but training, my God, training? As Will Carling explains: 'While the rest of the team were stretching or jogging to loosen up, Dean would sit in the corner reading the match programme. If he needed to warm up, he'd pat his stomach and see how long it took for the wobbles to subside.'

Richards' drinking capacity was legendary. Players recall how they would do half-hour stints with him at the bar because to drink along with him for any longer would render a man unable to walk, speak or remember his name.

And the England players weren't alone. Willie Duggan, the former Irish back-row player, famously swore that a cigarette before running out on to the pitch served as a lovely warm-up on match days. On colder training nights, he claimed that the best warm-up was to make sure that the heater was on full blast as he drove to the ground. On the subject of food, he was unshakeable. 'Big food,' he said, 'makes big players. And there's never any harm in a drink.'

Alan Tait of Scotland recalls that tours were for fun and for enjoying yourself and getting to know other players around the world: 'The diet was completely different back then; for example, we had whatever we wanted off the sweet tray, so players helped themselves to gateaux, cheesecake, ice cream. Everybody ploughed in and everybody put on masses of weight on tours. You didn't think about the consequences of it all.'

That's the way it always had been in rugby union, and many believed it was the way it always would be.

Then, it was decreed that there would be a World Cup tournament, and everything would change forever. The tournament was scheduled for 1987 so, in August 1986, England's finest players had been brought screaming and kicking from the pubs of west London to Bisham Abbey to discuss preparation for the tournament.

'Okay,' said Don Rutherford, entering the stuffy room and looking with alarm at the state of the players before him. 'Everyone listen,' he shouted.

The Rugby Football Union's Technical Director was a man advanced enough in his thinking to recognise that this rabble in front of him, though fine and upstanding men, and supremely talented rugby players, were in no fit state to contest a rugby World Cup tournament the following year. 'I have someone to introduce to you,' he said. The players rolled their eyes and continued to focus on not being sick.

In walked Tom McNab – a genial Scotsman with a terrible reputation for making grown men cry with his agonising fitness drills. 'I'm here to get you fit,' he said, sternly.

A few smiled and thought to themselves 'that'll never happen'. A few raised their eyebrows. Rendall raised his eyebrows so far into his hairline that they haven't been seen since. Moore sat forward and smiled, as did Underwood. In that moment, old rugby and new rugby went their separate ways.

'We need to get you weight training, sprint training, and we need to take a look at your diets,' he added.

Underwood sat back, surreptitiously wiping the greasy chocolate stains from round his mouth, and contemplating a life without crisps and Mars bars.

'You are all going to get fitter,' reiterated McNab. 'I'm not a man to take "no" for an answer.'

Rendall shuffled in his chair as he had one of those awful morning-after flashbacks. Had he really been dancing with a chair? It was hard to remember.

McNab had been working in athletics when Rutherford met him and asked him to help out with the England team. He was national athletics coach in the 1960s and 1970s, and Olympic coach for the Games in 1972 and 1976, as well as writing highly acclaimed books and acting as a consultant on *Chariots of Fire*. Now, here he was – facing an entirely new challenge.

The England rugby team . . . [says McNab, with a shake of his head and a smile in his voice as he recalls his time with England in the 1980s]. In all honesty, when I first turned up at training, I could hardly believe it. I was a fifty-year-old man and I swear to you, I was fitter than any of them. They didn't train at all – they did nothing. They just used a basic fitness that they already had because they played rugby on a regular basis and worked off that.

They'd train Tuesday and Thursday with their clubs at the most – but training did not involve any fitness work. I'm sure some of them had never lifted a weight in their lives. I'm not exaggerating. I really think that they hadn't. I could lift heavier weights than they could. Even compared with an average club athlete, they were woeful . . . woeful. You would imagine that rugby players would at least be weight training, wouldn't you? I would have understood if their flexibility or fine motor skills hadn't been worked on, but I didn't expect to find that they'd done no fitness at all.

An athlete, at the time, would have been doing four or five times as much. There were some good physical specimens in there – but almost by default. So much needed to be done, that I wasn't sure where to start.

To be fair to the players, this was a totally different rugby culture. It may have been just twenty years ago, but it might as well have been five hundred. Players simply didn't think about the impact of fitness on their game. There was no shortage of competitive players – men who were prepared to fight tooth and nail for a place in the team and to give everything on the pitch in pursuit of victory for their country, but fitness? Hello? What was that all about?

'After we'd met Tom, people were asking what the ability to do a vast number of push-ups or a fast 400 metre time had to do with international rugby,' says Moore. 'It seemed odd to be doing things away from the pitch to make you better on it. Gym work? In the past, we'd just gone from the rugby field to the bar for a couple of quiet drinks.'

Or, as Gareth Chilcott memorably remarked on his retirement from Bath, 'I thought I would have a quiet pint . . . and about seventeen noisy ones.'

Drink was always a major part of rugby union at international level, but it is the 1984 tour to South Africa that is believed to have set new standards in drunkenness. The England players partied from night till noon. 'I remember Chris Butcher telling me that all the England players had been on the beer for four weeks solidly,' says Moore. 'People went missing, missed flights and missed games – they just drank and partied all the time.'

Peter Winterbottom was on that tour: 'It went a bit off the rails,' he admits. 'The whole tour was pretty much a shambles. The lads went out all the time and had a great time. It was rugby in the old days. We were never going to beat the Springboks, or even play any decent rugby; we were a pretty average side.'

So, if you can't beat 'em, you might at least enjoy yourselves while losing to them. Rugby in the northern hemisphere in the mid-1980s was desperately amateur – in every sense of the word. John Gallagher, a promising young full back, left London for New Zealand in March 1984 claiming that rugby in England and particularly the structure of rugby in England, would not allow his talent to be fulfilled. 'It's hard to be a success there,' he lamented to newspaper journalists, when he touched down in New Zealand. His move paid off, and in 1986 he was named as full back for the All Blacks tour to France. 'You could take the sport seriously in New Zealand,' he said. 'In fact, people expected you to. You weren't odd if you wanted to win and wanted to improve. In England they thought it was odd if you didn't want to get drunk all the time.'

The difference between the way the sport was treated in New Zealand and England was staggering, but there was no real measure of how big the gulf had become because the players met so rarely, and on the occasions that they did travel down under, their efforts lacked the sophistication that one might expect of an international tour. In 1985 England toured New Zealand and got off to a less than glorious start when Andy Simpson hit his head getting on the plane, and was forced to endure being stitched up by

Derek Morgan, who'd brought with him the emergency kit from his dental practice in Newbury. Wade Dooley recalls that the tour was another big drinking extravaganza, particularly when England lost and needed to drown their sorrows, or when they won and needed to celebrate . . . or even if they drew. 'There was, pretty much, always a reason to get drunk.'

One evening, in Gisbourne, in the north-east corner of New Zealand's north island, Steve Brain, the England hooker (who would later vie for a place with Moore) started to look for candidates to out-drink him. Players took bets on whether such a thing was possible or likely, as two stools were laid out in the middle of the bar, and rules for the contest were established. Wade Dooley was thrust forwards and gamely climbed on to the stool. The two men then had to nominate drinks from a nearby table. 'We drank and drank,' recalls Dooley. 'And just as I thought I was about to die, Brain toppled off his chair and into the drinks table. There was a clatter of glasses then in walked [Martin] Green [the manager]. I've done it, I thought, though I was almost at the collapsing stage myself.'

McNab had much work to do to get England fit for the 1987 World Cup, but he knew that it would be a mistake to rush headlong into transforming every part of their fitness, so he started slowly, lest he scare them off completely. 'I had to prioritise – I couldn't do loads of things at once, so I decided to improve their running straight away. I knew that would have a direct impact on how they played. I did simple running practices with them. Some of them got quite good, actually.'

Next, Sunday and Wednesday training sessions were introduced.

'And I did make huge inroads,' says McNab. 'But it was rather a case of too little, too late.'

The team went on a training camp to Portugal, and Judy Oakes, the shot putter, was brought into the group to teach weightlifting.

'I remember Richards was fooling around and Judy couldn't believe it,' says McNab. 'She'd come to help out and they weren't listening to her. She said "if you don't want to train here – bugger off." I had to explain to her that all this was totally alien to the players, and I think she was as surprised by the whole thing as I had been.'

Moore recalls those training camps in Portugal, designed to get the players used to playing on the hard grounds that they would face in Australia. 'It was odd because, from very little training, we were suddenly doing loads, but it was quite chaotic because we hadn't stopped the drinking and partying, so we were absolutely exhausted all the time. The England management had us out all day, every day, training in the midday sun, then we'd party all night. We were training hard – running into each other, beating each other up – really going for it. I remember there were loads of athletes there watching us in amazement. They were resting all day and having physio, then coming out to train at 5 p.m. when it was cooler. By that time, we were all in the bar.'

One of the athletes they befriended in Portugal was a young Steve Backley. The javelin thrower was watching them one evening as they played a game called 'Pass It On'.

> Basically, that involved us all standing in a circle, punching each other and shouting 'pass it on' [explains Moore]. Steve Backley said 'Can I join in?' 'Okay,' we said. John Hall and Richards were either side of him. 'What do I do now?' he asked, after he'd been punched by Hally. 'Pass it on to Richards!' we all shouted. But he wouldn't punch Richards so, in the spirit of the game, Hall kept hitting him, which was the punishment for not passing it on. Eventually, after he'd been hit about twenty times, he said 'I want to go now' and left.

Some players embraced the new fitness regime. Moore, who had been battling with Brain for the hooker position, realised that the difference between the two hookers could be fitness. 'Moore just got his head down and worked at it. The men started on equal footing but Brian was 20 to 30 per cent higher fitness than Steve by the end. It was a very sensible approach and that's why Brian ended up in the England shirt through three World Cups,' says McNab.

Jeff Probyn and Chilcott were two other men who took to the training. Chilcott realised if he lifted his fitness levels, his game would improve dramatically. 'Slowly they began to accept me,' says McNab. 'I knew what I was doing was for the best and they came to realise it too, and welcomed me, which was nice.'

'There was lots of technical advice, like how to use weights properly or how to get props sprinting with high knees. The front row didn't take to that, as you can imagine,' recalls Mike Harrison, England captain for the 1987 World Cup.

One man, though, excelled. McNab declared that Underwood was the greatest natural athlete he had ever seen.

'And that includes Daley Thompson,' says the fitness guru. 'He was a shining athlete in his physical capacities. He didn't want to train, of course, but what he had, naturally, was quite unbelievable. Even the most dedicated of men – like Allan Wells – don't have such thigh-muscle development.'

Rutherford also recalls Underwood's physical abilities:

He was the most powerful player of all. One of the tests involved throwing a 16 lb shot two-handed over your head. To everyone's surprise, Rory threw it at least one metre further than anyone else. It was a simple equation: speed times strength equals power. McNab would try to illustrate that, though the England squad may have been pretty good rugby players, they were not power-ful athletes. It wasn't down to size, as Underwood showed. Pound for pound he was the most powerful athlete we had.

Another test was called the Sergeant Jump. You'd have a marked board and put chalk on your fingers. You'd measure the difference between a standing stretch and a jumping stretch and that would indicate power in your thighs.

'It was a shock for all the forwards,' says Underwood. 'They thought "Bloody winger, beating us all." But Tom knew what he was doing. He had studied the relative amounts of time in which forwards pushed and shoved and rucked and mauled, and that backs spent in sprinting various distances, and he told all of us what it would take to make ourselves better.'

While Underwood was delighting in the discovery that he was infinitely fitter than he had expected, or indeed than he had any right to be, considering most of his food shopping was done in Cadburys, he was hit with some bad news – he was to share a room with Rendall on the trips to Portugal. 'There were complaints from Rory all the time,' says Moore. 'He complained that Paul left a ring round the bath and didn't make his bed.' That was nothing, though, compared to the time when Rendall came into his room at 4 a.m. with some of the players from the bar, insisting that there was a party going on, and Rory was throwing it.

Rendall had a reputation for his kindnesses towards his fellow players, such as the time he offered comforting advice to Probyn when the newcomer won his first cap. Rendall leaned over and whispered to him: 'Don't worry, stay calm. Just get on with your game, forget the stadium, forget the 50,000 crowd, just think of the ten million watching at home on television.'

Rendall and Probyn would go on to room together at the 1987 World Cup, which doesn't really bear thinking about. 'I was impressed with him, to be fair,' says Probyn. 'His ability to drink all night long, sleep for an hour and then train for four hours in ninety degrees was quite something. The coaches were worried about how he'd play, I was worried about whether he'd live.'

Once the players had started training, McNab wanted to assess their fitness to illustrate the changes they were making, and thus motivate them further.

'But, my goodness, it was hard to get them to go to be tested. I tried to send them to Loughborough University for fitness testing but they just wouldn't go. The guys would call from Loughborough and say no one had turned up. Even when I insisted that they all went, we got a 30 per cent return. They simply didn't want to know how fit they weren't.'

Because of these logistical problems, McNab realised he'd have to devise a test that could be done at training sessions, and didn't need additional equipment or facilities. He opted for the bleep test: an analysis of VO2 max (aerobic fitness – the ability to run around without getting tired). The bleep test involves running between two points, aiming to reach each point before a bleep. Through the test, the bleeps get progressively closer together making it harder to complete as you fatigue. It is an absolute killer. The test would become the scourge of generations of players ... and now they know who to blame – those boys from 1987 who wouldn't turn up to the testing centres!

'They absolutely hated the bleep test,' says McNab. 'But it proved very useful for us, and we did see real improvements.'

The test was done on the cobblestones outside Twickenham because there was nowhere else to do it, and the backs scored 10s and 11s, with the forwards struggling behind, with a lowest score of seven. Just to compare, in the bleep tests done before the 2003 World Cup, the forwards were scoring around the 16 mark, with Neil Back scoring 17.

'It was all hard work, and like nothing we'd ever done before,' says Dooley. 'Tom introduced a running drill called jelly jaw which involved players sprinting, keeping the jaw as loose as possible. Then there was the dreaded test for body fat content which became more challenging as percentages were reduced.'

In the first year, the acceptable body fat level was 15 per cent, and Dooley was 19 per cent. 'But I was amazed at how quickly it dropped. The lowest number I recorded was 11 per cent.'

Of course, not everyone treated the tests with deadly seriousness, and Rendall worked out that if you didn't drink anything for three days before the test, your body fat would be considerably reduced. Rendall is not sure how he figured this out, but is adamant, to this day, that he came up with a way to fool the testers.

Linked to body fat testing, of course, was an overhaul of the players' diets. 'No nutrition advice was being given to the players at the time,' recalls McNab. 'They were still drinking in the week of a competition. They'd all come from a drinking culture so it was very hard to explain that the drinking had to stop. In the end, it was about reaching compromises.'

McNab produced diet sheets to show the players which foods were good for them and which were not. It was all quite a shock. 'The boys always had a few beers in the build up to internationals,' says Dooley. 'It was quite normal to dine on steak on the Friday evening before a game. He tried to get us to eat chicken instead.'

'We were hanging on to the shirt-tails of amateurism,' says

Harrison. 'They talked about diet, which was unheard of before then, about keeping alcohol down to moderate levels. We were told what to eat – pasta and chicken, etc. – but there was no monitoring. I eat like a horse. I used to have a couple of beers on the eve of Internationals, to help me sleep.'

But Harrison and the others did find that the increase in workload as a result of the World Cup preparations was having a real impact on their lives. 'From January to May in 1987 I had about two weekends at home,' said Harrison. 'We had these fitness schedules and had to keep to them.'

Harrison had three young children by this stage and found it difficult. 'There was a dramatic change when we started preparing for the World Cup. Looking at what the guys do today, we didn't do that much training, but for us at the time, it felt like a huge amount. It really affected your ability to do your job and I think in that moment the sport moved a big step towards professionalism because the whole thing was becoming unsustainable.'

Moore agrees: 'The coaches wanted us to change everything – the way we trained, the way we ate and how much we drank. We did start eating better . . . in front of the coaches. We'd eat as much as we could of the bland, healthy food put before us, then head off to McDonald's for some proper food. We kind of figured that it was what you were seen eating that counted – not what you actually ate.' That was nothing compared to England lock John Orwin, who insisted on eating a fillet steak the morning before a game.

While the players focused on getting themselves into the peak of physical condition, the managers of the sixteen sides around the world that had been selected to compete in the tournament gathered in New Zealand and Australia for a managers' conference. They travelled round all the venues and hotels and discussed how the tournament would work.

It was all quite intriguing [says Moore]. The coaches went off on this jolly to have a look at where we'd be playing and what the tournament would involve, and they seemed to come back none the wiser. There was this overriding feeling from all in official capacity at the RFU that the World Cup would never work, so there was really no point in trying too hard.

I can remember feeling excited by the prospect of the tournament, but when something has no history, it's hard to understand what it is and what it represents, what its true purpose is. I think we were all pretty relaxed and excited about the tournament . . . then we arrived in the southern hemisphere and saw how well prepared they were. Then, I think we all got it, we all understood that the World Cup would become the very peak of the game, and the most important tournament in the rugby world.

2

Journey into the unknown

Gee, you gotta have guts to play that kinda football. In boxing, you know the punch will come from the guy in front of you, so you're prepared. In rugby, you know it could come from any one of fifteen people, and a whole lotta them could be behind you. You can't prepare for that.

Marvin Hagler, former world middleweight champion

While in England, Rendall was busy continuing his important life's work – finding ever newer and better ways to fool the body-fat testers – and while Underwood kissed a teary goodbye to KitKats and cheese and onion crisps for ever, rugby on the other side of the world was going through a fairly substantial reinvention of its own.

New Zealand, such a powerful force in world rugby since the sport began, were in trouble. After 100 years of domination, the formerly unbeatable All Blacks were suffering setback after setback. The core players in the All Blacks team had alienated themselves from the New Zealand public by taking part in a controversial rebel tour to South Africa in 1986. They couldn't call themselves 'the All Blacks' but nevertheless a squad of established New Zealand players went to the banned country, creating huge resentment and divisions in the New Zealand game. There was a feeling that the players had 'sold their souls' and put their personal financial gain above their individual morality and the good name of New Zealand. They returned to antagonistic scenes at the airport, with demonstrators waving flags condemning their action and the press roundly criticising them.

David Kirk, who along with John Kirwan did not tour, says, 'For New Zealanders, the tour was probably the most powerful national experience since the Second World War. It was deeply damaging to rugby's good name and badly affected popular support for our national game.'

When the rebel players returned, they were banned for two Tests as punishment, forcing Brian Lochore, coach of the All Blacks from 1985 to 1987, to pick ten new players – nicknamed the Baby Blacks – to represent New Zealand against France in a one-off Test match. New Zealand won the match 18–9, but they lost their next game 13–12 to Australia, prompting the selectors to dump ten of the Baby Blacks and replace them with the Cavaliers who had served their two-Test ban. The new side beat Australia 13–12 in Dunedin, but the whole incident had driven a wedge into the heart of New Zealand rugby – separating the Cavaliers from the new, young players who had temporarily replaced them.

Australia won the third and final Test, clinching a series victory on New Zealand soil for the first time in thirty-seven years. There was disbelief among the New Zealand fans. But their most memorable defeat was yet to come. It happened on tour to France, in a game in Nantes that was laced with violence. New Zealand lost 16–3 and returned home feeling demoralised. 'It was a very difficult time for the game in New Zealand,' said Lochore. 'You wondered where on earth they'd go from here.'

Across the Tasman Sea, there cannot have been a starker contrast, as Australia was beginning to emerge as a genuine power in rugby. 'Australia became the team to beat,' says Alan Jones, flamboyant coach of Australia in the 1980s, and the man who should take a healthy dose of praise for the turn-around in fortunes. 'We started doing the unexpected,' he said. 'And as soon as we did that, we started winning.'

The 1980s was the decade in which Australian rugby came good. In 1980, they won the Bledisloe Cup for only the fourth time in its history of almost fifty years. Then, in 1984, Jones took his young Wallabies side and its blend of fast, running rugby, with its flat back line to Britain and Ireland, and cruised to a 'Grand Slam' of victories – beating England, Ireland, Scotland and Wales, as well as defeating a strong Barbarians side.

Then, in 1986, Australia toured New Zealand, and for the first time won two games away from home, losing the third by one point. The Wallabies were jubilant and hugely optimistic of success in the World Cup. Brian Smith was half-back for Australia in 1987 (he later switched allegiance to Ireland on the strength of an Irish grandmother): 'Alan Jones was a very charismatic coach . . . his attention to detail turned us into a team of athletes, especially with regard to speed and strength and conditioning.'

The New Zealanders recognised that the Australians were looking good, and they knew that they were in disarray – with the team in factions and the dressing room divided.

At the beginning of 1987, there were all these unanswered questions [says Kirk]. Just how good were the Australians? How could we beat them? Which players should New Zealand go for – the new Baby Blacks or the experienced Cavalier players? Would the team gel? Who should be the captain? Had we left it too late to succeed in the tournament against strong teams like Australia and France? And would the people of New Zealand turn out to support us? If a generation of fans turned their backs on rugby, what would be the implications for the future of the sport? There were lots of unanswered questions – some of them quite important and far-reaching.

There were pertinent questions being asked at Heathrow airport, too, though arguably less important and not as far-reaching as those being posed in New Zealand. The England team prepared to board their flight to Australia – their base for the duration of the tournament – with the biggest question mark hanging over what should adorn the faces of Moore and

Richards. 'In the end, we got on the plane with me wearing Elton John glasses,' recalls Moore. 'Then during the flight I changed, and Dean and I wore Gorbachev and Reagan masks for the remainder of the journey.'

The players of Wales, Ireland and Scotland also assembled at Heathrow airport to catch their flight to New Zealand and found themselves on the same flight as one another – spread across the economy section of the plane. Gavin Hastings was Scotland's full back in 1987:

> It was a strange experience. We walked into the airport and there they were – all as confused about the tournament as we were. The World Cup had just sort of arrived and no one quite knew what we were going into. Then we arrived in New Zealand after the most horrific journey with stops in Dubai and Singapore where pretty much everyone had had a drink. I think stopping twice was the cheapest possible way of getting us out there but it didn't do much to help our preparations.

There was great relief when the huge party of players from Britain and Ireland began their descent into New Zealand, but then there were further difficulties to be overcome, as they couldn't touch down in Auckland because of cloud cover, so the plane was diverted to Christchurch where it sat on the runway for an hour and a half, before it was finally given clearance to fly back to Auckland and land.

> We were drained when we arrived [says Hastings]. It felt like we'd been travelling for days. Just as we were all starting to think of getting to the hotel and crawling into our rooms, the Scotland management, in their wisdom, decided we should go out and have a training session. When you have been on a plane for over thirty hours, you become a bit pent-up with frustration and, although we were only supposed to be playing a light game of touch rugby, it suddenly developed into a full-blown physical game. It was the worse thing in the world for

team morale and I don't suppose it did much for our recuperation from the flight either.

Paul Thorburn was on the flight with the Wales team:

It seems odd, looking back, that we would all be on the same plane. Now, we'd all have our separate arrangements for the trip but for that first World Cup, I suppose the countries all got on the flight that they were told to regardless of whether it fitted in with their preparations or not.

Training then was nothing like it is now, but before the tournament, we had special training weekends; we'd be away in hotels for three days at a time. The general activity was raised, we upped the ante. We all had full-time jobs, but we trained hard, too. When we arrived in Auckland, Ray Williams, who was secretary of the WRU [Welsh Rugby Union], called us into the team room for a meeting. He reminded us of our obligations to the amateur code. Then we went upstairs to our rooms and turned on the TV to see New Zealand players doing adverts for things like farm machinery and banana drinks. There was a lot of scepticism among the players, and a feeling that we weren't competing on equal terms. They said they [the All Blacks] weren't being paid but I don't believe you do that sort of thing without some form of reward.

I'd just left university and got my first job, with a security business. I managed to get six weeks off work and they paid me. But six weeks is a long time and it was hard to get the time. A number of players weren't paid. I think they received 'broken-time' payments of £16 a day.

Hooker Colin Deans was Scotland's captain at the 1987 World Cup. He was first capped in 1978, so was a senior player by the time the tournament started nine years later. He remembers the training sessions clearly. 'We did no weight training because the physicality of the matches was enough. Jim [Telfer, the coach] was a hard, hard taskmaster. You'd do your scrummaging and line-outs and mauling and rucking, and then at the end of the session you'd have the "golden gauntlet", which had been introduced by Nairn McEwan, a Scotland coach of the late seventies. So you'd run to the 25, bark ten times, do fifteen press-ups, hop to the halfway line, sprint to the 25. By the time you got to the line everybody would collapse.'

While the Welsh, Irish and Scottish players settled into their New Zealand bases, England adjusted to being away from the action – 'far from the centre of the city' as Oscar Wilde suggested they should be. Far from the centre of bloody anywhere, to be fair, as they were forced to watch most of the tournament unfold on television from Australia. 'Basically,' recalls Probyn, 'it didn't feel like we were at any sort of World Cup.' They stayed at Rushcutters Bay, as Underwood recalls 'bunked up in a travel lodge. It had a low-budget feel to it.' Dooley says: 'The hotel was like something out of the 1950s. My feet were dangling off the end of the bed.'

As soon as the team had checked in to their hotel mid-morning, like their Scottish counterparts, they went straight out to train. 'Just a quick lunch and we climbed into playing kit and got back on to the coach for a training run,' says Probyn. 'It always takes two or three days for the system to work properly, by which time we were back in Sydney to prepare for our opening World Cup match, against Australia. It wasn't the best.'

England's management team for the World Cup was much more professional than ever before. Previously, the team had toured with just a manager and assistant manager, but the arrival of the World Cup had prompted the introduction of a team of people. In addition to coach Mike Weston, there was Martin Green and Des Seabrook – the assistant coaches. McNab was fitness coach. Kevin Murphy was the physio and Ben Gilfeather the doctor.

> I ran three businesses in 1987, but in the twelve months prior to the World Cup, I was only in Durham for six months [said Weston]. I was a stranger to my family and to my businesses. My accountant told me that if I didn't give my estate agency business proper attention, I'd go bankrupt.
>
> When I arrived for the World Cup, I had to set up a bank

account. I had Aus$50,000 and ended up giving Aus$4000 back.
I think the players had a weekly allowance of Aus$35. All the
flights and hotels were paid for. But everything else we paid
for – meals, drinks, trip to the Barrier Reef, taxis, training facilities, gyms, boot repairs, medical bills, dentist, cinema, extra
blazers, hire of a secretary. From leaving Heathrow to returning, I never touched a drop of alcohol all trip. It was my way of
tackling the job.

Many players competing in the World Cup suffered financially as a result of representing their country. Deans was a PVC
window salesman. 'My employer was very supportive but not
everybody had it easy. Roy Laidlaw was an electrician and was
part of a two-man company – him and his boss. He went unpaid
for the World Cup; people lent a hand, the butcher would give
him meat, that sort of thing. On the Lions tour he wasn't paid for
twelve weeks.'

Jonathan Webb, the England full back, won the first of his
thirty-three England caps at the 1987 World Cup.

I was a medical student at Bristol University leading up to the
1987 World Cup and it was manageable. We trained in the
evenings and I did the bookwork around that. Generally, I had
no on-call commitments.

But my medical finals were in May and June 1987 and I just
assumed I couldn't go [to the World Cup]. I was on the point of
telling the RFU that I couldn't go, because medicine was my
career, but a fearsome professor heard about it and said, 'I'll try
and sort it out.' He rang round all the heads of departments
and told them, 'Webb should go.' So I ended up doing my individual finals three weeks before everyone else.

It wasn't ideal doing the exams that way, because there was
no camaraderie, no sense of all being in this together. I was
doing the exams while the normal day-to-day business went on
around me, whereas normally you're shut away. But it was a
great gesture and for me it was amazing, because it made my
[rugby] career.

Rory Underwood had missed England's trips to South Africa (1984) and New Zealand (1985) because of his job in the RAF, so the World Cup was his first tour.

'The Air Force were fantastic. They just said, "Put it on the board." For tours or World Cups I had to apply for leave of absence but it was never a problem. And I'd still be paid.'

Harrison took two weeks' holiday and two weeks' special leave in order to compete. 'You needed an understanding wife [Harrison got married at twenty-one],' he says. 'I took most of my holidays in those days for rugby trips. For home Internationals, I'd have Thursday off as holiday and Friday off as special leave. Not that we were made to feel all that "special" – the players flew out in economy and the committee were in first-class. There was nobody to see us off at Heathrow and nobody to greet us when we came back.'

Alan Tait of Scotland was a roofer in 1987. 'I had to ask my boss for time off and it was nerve-racking having to ask for six weeks. But he liked rugby and was happy to let me go, though of course I didn't get paid. We got a daily allowance of about a tenner at the World Cup, but it didn't bother me. I was just happy to be there.'

Moore was just finishing his articles in 1987, so would train at lunchtimes and in evenings. 'I would love to have had that extra 5 per cent. The New Zealand guys were being paid to play or in jobs which facilitated their playing. It was frustrating that nothing was ever done about it.'

There was a strong feeling among most northern hemisphere players that the southern hemisphere players were being paid to play, a feeling that was exacerbated by the sight of Andy Dalton on television during the tournament advertising a Japanese tractor. The Scottish RFU felt so strongly about it that they lodged a complaint. 'There were other adverts, too,' recalls Deans. 'On the first day I remember seeing some adverts on the sports channel in Auckland. John Kirwan was advertising some ointment for your back; Andy Dalton was advertising a four-wheel drive bike on his farm; Andy Haden was advertising Caltex oil. A lot was happening. The New Zealand guys trained every day, there were rumours that they were being paid or getting Ford cars. It got to you in many ways.'

But John Gallagher says this was not the case.

The game was going global, and 100 million people watched the World Cup final. Everyone was making [money] out of it except the players. Andy Dalton was at the end of his career; he was a farmer and so he made an ad selling farm machinery. It didn't say, 'Andy Dalton, All Black', it said, 'Andy Dalton, farmer'. It was ridiculous the fuss that caused. He wasn't earning money directly from the game but indirectly. He wasn't endorsing the All Blacks. He was a farmer but a famous farmer.

It rankles a bit when people say New Zealand players were getting paid. We were getting an IRB allowance like everybody else, it was 15 dollars a day. People focus more on teams that are winning, they get jealous. It's Tall Poppy syndrome. There was no money in being an All Black, which is why four of us went to rugby league within the space of a month early in 1990. I went to Leeds, Frano Botica went to Wigan, John Schuster went to Newcastle Knights in Australia, and Matthew Ridge went to Manly. There was no money in rugby union unless you went to Europe or Japan. In England there were rich owners who'd say, 'You can work in a pub, I'll make it worth your while.'

I was a policeman then, as was Murray Pierce, our second-row. We were given twenty-eight days' annual leave but if you were selected for Internationals you could get an extra twenty days. The whole World Cup lasted four weeks and so that was my twenty days. Other rugby tours took care of my annual leave.

We won the World Cup on Saturday 20 June and on the Monday morning Murray Pierce and I were on the beat in Wellington. Rather than give us shift work, the New Zealand police decided to stick us on a high-profile job with all the media cameras in tow. It was a way to get their money back!

'I just don't believe that they weren't being paid,' insists Moore. 'We began to feel very bitter about it in 1987 because we were all struggling financially to be able to play.'

The World Cup hadn't started and already the worst fears of the administrators were starting to be realised, as players questioned amateurism more frequently and more thoroughly, and came to the conclusion that it was grossly unfair.

'It was something that niggled,' says Moore. 'It didn't keep you awake at night, it just niggled at you and made you feel quite angry at times. It wasn't that we minded not receiving money, it was just that we minded not being on the same conditions as the teams we were about to compete against.'

Before the World Cup started, the collection of selected teams sat down at the inaugural dinners – held in Auckland and Brisbane simultaneously. All the players took their seats, feeling proud of themselves for getting a place, and pleased that the tournament was finally on the verge of starting. But no players had faced a more arduous route to the first ever rugby World Cup than the gentlemen of Fiji.

3

The incredible Fiji story

We sat at the World Cup opening dinner, feeling so proud of ourselves for getting there, then we heard about the Fiji team and everything they had been through and thought – My goodness, we have had it all so easy.

Jacques Fouroux, France coach

Turtle Island . . . can there be a more alluring name for a place? This beautiful slice of Pacific Ocean paradise sits indulgently, bathed in glorious sunshine, in the Central Yasawas area of Fiji. Like so many of the country's islands, it has breathtaking, long, white, sandy beaches fringed by azure water and an income derived from coconut farming. But there is something that distinguishes this island from the rest of Fiji – it is an hour ahead. It has been operating on its own unique time system since *Blue Lagoon* was filmed there in 1980, and everyone involved in the shooting had to get up an hour earlier to catch the sunrise. Such is the way with these small Fijian Islands, that no one really thought it worth bothering to change things back once the filming was over, so Turtle Island has kept *Blue Lagoon* time ever since, and the villagers still get up sixty minutes before the rest of Fiji. They call it 'Bula Time' – meaning time for 'health', 'life' and 'vibrancy'.

Turtle Island was home to Nik Qoro and Kavaia Salusalu, Fiji
internationals in 1987, who were part of the first wave of top-class
rugby players to emerge from the Central Yasawas area after the
sport arrived there in the 1960s. In their youth, they ran around
using coconuts and empty plastic bottles as substitutes for a ball,
while the beautiful beach substituted as a field. They played at
school, and in the long evenings after school, but rarely against
other islands. Such are the limitations of Fiji island life, that to do
so would demand quite staggering feats of organisation and considerable time. So, islanders enjoyed the sport for what it was –
running around on the sand, barefoot, playing a version of the
sport more like sevens than fifteen a side, but involving up to
twenty people and few laws.

This, in a nutshell, is the problem that faced Fiji in the 1980s.
There was shortage of neither skill nor enthusiasm, but geogra-
phy, transportation and communication difficulties rendered
competition between the islands extraordinarily difficult. Jeremy
Duxbury is the sponsorship and marketing director of the Fijian
Rugby Union.

> Logistically, Fiji is the most complicated rugby side to put
> together because Fiji consists of 300 islands, some of them tiny,
> many of them without transportation or communication sys-
> tems. Some of the players in 1987 came from Matuku, an island
> which consists of just three small villages and no landline.
> Getting hold of someone from there was virtually impossible.
> You had to book a radio telephone call – like a radiogram –
> but arranging when to phone was hugely difficult.

So, once a player had been identified – no mean feat in itself –
the coach would have to track him down to tell him about training sessions. This involved ringing the police station on the island
and getting the one policeman stationed there to cycle through
the fields looking for the player. This strategy demanded that
there was a police station on the island in the first place. Many
times the police officer would come back to the phone hours later
and say he could not find the player concerned.

'The boat goes past the islands once a month bringing food, so that was the only other way to reach players – put letters on the boat and hope they get to the right guy and that he has the skills to write a letter back and put it back on the boat to you.' Considering the logistical difficulties, it is astonishing that Fiji ever got any sort of international side together at all.

One of Fiji's star players in the 1980s was full back Severo Koroduadua, nicknamed 'Big Foot'. He is the second highest scorer in Fiji rugby history, and became one of the most famous players in the country in 1987 when, after making a superb break in the World Cup quarter-final against France, he dropped the ball in open field. Koroduadua is from Galoa, which means 'black swan' in Fijian. It is one of the remotest places on earth – off the north coast of the long sprawling island of Vanua Levu. It is just a couple of kilometres long and a few hundred metres wide. From the village, you can see the sun rise and set over the Pacific Ocean. Getting to the island involves getting a boat from Suva that takes around six hours, and then it's a two-hour trek across Vanua Levu to the remote town of Lekutu from where the local boat goes down the Lekutu river for twenty minutes to the island. It makes jumping on the train to Bisham Abbey sound like child's play.

Fiji were one of the sixteen sides chosen to contest the 1987 World Cup, and the task of getting them ready fell to George Simpkin – a coach who had worked with the side since 1985, after visiting the country on a two-week coaching stint from his native New Zealand and deciding to stay.

'Getting the players together was difficult enough, given that they were all out working on the different islands, but the next task after that was trying to persuade them to work on any kind of forward play. They hated it. All their strength lay in their lower body, so while they could run well and had strong muscle definition in their legs, they had nowhere near enough upper body strength for the international game.'

Once Simpkin began work, he found that he had a very receptive and appreciative audience. Rugby is a national sport in Fiji, and the most popular sport in the indigenous community.

There are an estimated 86,990 registered players from a population of around 950,000, which means roughly one in ten plays the sport. Compare this to England, where there is a population of 60,094,648 and the number of registered players is 634,460, meaning that around one in ninety-five plays the sport, and you get an impression of the extent to which rugby has become part of Fijian culture. People play primarily for the love of the game, but they delight in winning. When they won the 2005 Sevens World Cup, Prime Minister Laisenia Qarase allocated a day for national celebration.

> When rugby games are on, it's massive in Fiji [says Duxbury]. No one's allowed to speak if there's a match on television. One of the problems here is that the signal varies a lot, so the sort of reception you get is unpredictable. Add to this the fact that there are some islands without any television sets on them, and there's something of a panic as people try to get themselves in front of a television that works. It can mean rowing for miles to another island. You often see people dragging their television equipment up to the top of the hill to get a signal, and the rowing boats going between the islands are so full, they look as if they are about to sink. The situation, when there are matches being played in Fiji, is even more manic. The grounds are packed, and there are people hanging out of the trees to watch.

Rugby in Fiji began in around 1920, and the first match was against Western Samoa in 1924. None of the players wore boots, and it was played at 7 a.m. to allow Samoan opponents time to get to work afterwards. For reasons not immediately evident, it was played on a pitch with a large tree on the halfway line. Fiji won 6–0. By 1938, Fiji rugby had moved on so far that players wore boots for the first time. They did this in honour of the New Zealand Maori team but many Fiji players found them too restrictive, and by the end of the match, dozens of discarded boots lay along the side of the pitch. It wasn't until the 1960s that Fiji toured Europe for the first time, and in 1970 they destroyed the Barbarians 29–9. It was a Fiji side containing Sitiveni Rabuka – a man who would one day be Prime Minister of Fiji and an important character in getting Fiji to the 1987 World Cup.

Simpkin decided to take his players to a military base to train before they left for New Zealand in 1987 to work on their set-piece play. 'Once I'd got them all together in one place, I breathed a sigh of relief,' said Simpkin. 'Nothing could go wrong now.'

On the morning of 14 May, just over a week before the start of the 1987 World Cup, a squad of ten masked, armed soldiers entered the Fijian House of Representatives in Suva. They were led by Colonel Sitiveni Rabuka, a high-ranking military officer, protesting at the election of the country's first Indian leader. Rabuka approached Prime Minister Timoci Bavadra from the public gallery, and ordered Members of Parliament to leave the building. They did so without resisting. It was the first of two military coups to reassert ethnic Fijian supremacy. During the coup, and immediately following it, there was swift international condemnation, with Australia, New Zealand, United States and Britain refusing to recognise the new government. All flights in and out of the country were grounded.

In the Suva Army Barracks, the Fijian team continued to train. Simpkin had no idea that the government had been overthrown. He recalls hearing a great deal of marching, and the sound of raised voices and soldiers preparing themselves to leave the base, but he largely dismissed these as training exercises. 'Many of the officers involved in the coup were friends,' he says. 'They told me that reservists were being brought in and that's what the frenzied activity was. I didn't think it was anything to worry about, but asked "Why do they need reservists?" That's when I was told about the coup. I was also told that all phone lines to the outside world had been cut and no planes were flying.'

In New Zealand, concern was starting to mount about the Fijian team. Nothing had been heard from them, and requests from the NZRFU for them to confirm that they would be attending had not been answered. It was just over a week until kick-off. If they weren't coming, the World Cup organisers needed to approach the Western Samoans – the reserve team – and invite them to compete instead. NZRFU officials tried to call Fiji to ask whether the players were likely to be on the plane, but there were no phone lines in operation.

Dick Littlejohn of the NZRFU decided that, since it was increasingly unlikely that Fiji would show up, he ought to try and start getting things ready for the Western Samoan team.

> The first problem I had was that no one seemed to have any idea what the Western Samoa shirt looked like. It was secret that Western Samoa might be called, because we did not know for definite what Fiji's situation was, so we could not ask Western Samoa outright what they wore – we needed to find out. Ivan Vodanovich, the gear man, could not find a copy of the Western Samoa shirt anywhere. Then one day he was walking down the street and saw a youngster in a strange blue footy jersey with a national monogram. Ivan asked the boy what shirt it was, as he'd taken to asking everyone in an unusual shirt what country they were from, just in case. The lad said 'Samoa' and explained that he'd won it playing for Western Samoa colts. Ivan persuaded him to swap it for an All Black jersey. Finally, we had a Western Samoa jersey to copy if we needed to.

Simpkin was becoming slightly worried about whether the team would get to New Zealand after all. He decided to speak to the officers again, to check whether there was any development and whether planes were flying. 'The message came back the same day that Colonel Rabuka himself would guarantee that a plane would be available to fly us to New Zealand.' Simpkin relaxed and went back to teaching forward play to Fijians, but the outside world still had no idea whether the Fijians would be in New Zealand.

Sri Krishnamurthi, sports editor of the *Fiji Times* newspaper, arrived at his desk to be told by the editor that rumours were circulating that Fiji were going to be replaced by Western Samoa at the World Cup. 'Is that right?' asked the editor. Krishnamurthi said he didn't think so but would find out for definite. He headed down to the military base and told Simpkin that there were huge concerns in New Zealand.

'We will be there,' said Simpkin.

'Are you sure?' asked the journalist.

'Yes,' said Simpkin.

'Leave it to me. I'll tell them.'

Krishnamurthi rushed back to phone his friend Dean McLachlan at *Rugby News* in Auckland, but he could not get a line out of the country. He dialled the operator and explained that he needed to get a message to New Zealand urgently to say the Fijian team would be at the World Cup.

She opened a line, and put him through to Auckland. Krishnamurthi duly spoke to McLachlan who passed the message to NZRFU that the Fijians were coming.

'I was very pleased to hear they were coming,' says Littlejohn, 'but was still concerned because the coup was still being featured on the news. The day Fiji were due to arrive I could not make contact and I was worried that something had happened. I shot up to Auckland airport and found an obliging chap who could talk to the pilot of the plane en route from Nadi. He came back with the word that the Fijians were on the plane. We were all enormously relieved.'

4

The beginning of a new era in world rugby

This team looks good on paper, let's see how it looks on grass.

Nigel Melville

The first rugby World Cup was played in May and June 1987 between sixteen nations. The teams were divided into four pools of four nations, with the top two in each pool moving on to the quarter-final stage. The scoring system was: two points for a win; one point for a draw; zero points for a loss.

Officials in New Zealand had managed, at terrifyingly short notice, to secure sponsors for the tournament. Dick Littlejohn, who was clearly working hard for the money he wasn't being paid, had managed to fit in a flying trip to Japan in the weeks leading up to the tournament, and returned clutching a sponsorship deal. 'I spoke in English and my interpreter turned my words into Japanese,' said Littlejohn, indicating that the interpreter had added flourishes of his own to the translation. 'To the extent that I'm not entirely sure what I said to the businessmen, but they did seem to smile an awful lot and seem terribly happy with everything.' The flourishes worked, and the couple returned to New Zealand with a deal for US$3.25 million from KDD broadcasting firm.

The opening ceremony was on 22 May 1987, held in Eden

Park in Auckland. The 'extravaganza' was prepared in three weeks by the late Lew Pryme, then executive director of Auckland RFC, and, let's be honest, the limitations of time and money showed rather ferociously as schoolgirl go-go dancers and young gymnasts cavorted across the pitch, looking tired and fed up in the drizzling rain. It was too damp even to attempt to light the rather feeble-looking clump of fireworks that sat alongside the young dancers, so it was left to a few strips of bunting and a cluster of national flags to announce that the World Cup had arrived. They hung forlornly in the rain while the goose-pimply teenagers leapt around to the sounds of a brass band and Highland pipers. That, ladies and gentlemen, was the opening ceremony for the biggest, most extravagant tournament in the history of rugby union.

There were flaws, of course, as there were bound to be – perhaps the most fundamental of which was the decision to organise the opening ceremony on a Friday, instead of at the weekend, when people might actually be able to go to it. It meant the ground, which had a 46,000 capacity, was only half-full. Added to the 'Friday' issue was the residual bitterness which still hung over the country after the All Blacks' decision to tour South Africa the year before. In this climate, few saw any reason to take the day off work to watch the New Zealand team play Italy in the rain, and as the All Blacks fired to a 70–6 victory in front of a small cluster of fans, it wasn't hard to see why. The game was a complete mismatch, leading Marzio Innocenti (the Italian captain) to look into the camera lens with the shell-shocked appearance of one who has just been through a major trauma, and declare: 'We tried, but they always have the ball.' Perhaps someone had omitted to tell Innocenti and his team that it was their job to try and get the ball off the marauding New Zealanders. John Kirwan was the star of the match, scoring a magnificent solo try. Over a decade later he became coach of the Italian side. Officials in Italy have confessed that it was on that rainy day in 1987 that they first became captivated by him, and wanted him, one day, to coach their side.

For New Zealand, getting the opening game out of the way

was a relief. They were under immense pressure to perform in the tournament, not least the captain, Kirk. 'We were carrying the hopes and expectations of three and a half million people,' says the former All Blacks captain. 'It was a relief to get out and play but also a great fulfilment of expectation. We were hungry and grateful it had come around.'

Gallagher agrees: 'There was unbelievable pressure on us to win the World Cup. It wasn't so much a desire to win, more a fear of failure. We simply couldn't contemplate defeat.'

The potential barriers to victory in the pool stages were their co-inhabitants in Pool 3 – Argentina, Italy and the magical, dancing Fijians. Fiji beat Argentina 28–9, offering the first surprise result of the tournament but, rather more predictably, they fell to New Zealand 74–13. Fiji lost 18–15 to Italy, but went through on try count. The pool was dominated by the young, dynamic New Zealand team which featured Zinzan Brooke, a star of the future. 'The 1987 World Cup saw my first cap, against Argentina. I was nervous about it because a couple of days before the game I was told that as the only Maori in the side I'd be leading the haka. That scared the crap out of me. I was up at five on the morning of the game, mentally rehearsing what I had to do. I concentrated more on the haka than on the match itself.'

While New Zealand were having an easy start to their World Cup campaign, things were a little tougher for Scotland, who were in Pool 4 with France, Romania and Zimbabwe. Their start to the tournament was not helped by the fact that the French players were on the same flight to Christchurch as them. 'We were fortunate enough to be at the airport first so most of us were sitting together,' says Deans. 'But there were exceptions – namely myself and Iain Milne. We had the pleasure of Jean-Pierre Garuet's company for the flight. As is usual in front-row combinations, very little was said but a few grunts. It made it a very difficult flight for both parties.'

When Scotland arrived, they trained in the grounds of a prison. Then, on the day of the game, they assembled in Derrick Grant's room to have a last-minute discussion, and a healthy lunch of omelette, chips and Mars bar, the last being what Deans describes as a 'tradition' before a big match.

At the ground, Deans recalls that the player heard a pipe band playing outside – giving all the players lumps in their throats. They won the toss and elected to play with the low sun on their backs – it couldn't have been more perfect. Suddenly things were looking good for the Scots.

'Our approach was deadly serious,' says Deans. 'We went with the intention of winning it; that was the plan. We stumbled and stuttered at times, but we had world-class players in key positions and we played what was in front of us. We knew we had to top the group, but lost out on try difference after a cracking 20–20 draw with France.'

The Scots were bitterly disappointed to lose after drawing the match, a feeling that was only compounded when the French walked into the after-match reception. As Alan Tait recalls: 'We had Number 1s, Number 2s and Number 3s. Number 1s were old blazers and ties; Number 2s were chinos and polo shirt; Number 3s were casuals. I remember the French players were wearing blue leather jackets, nice suede shoes and jeans. Typical French, we thought.'

The French may have been leading the pack sartorially, but they were not without their problems – in the form of their accommodation which Serge Blanco described as being 'like Club Med: great for having a good time but not so good for concentration'. The manager of the France team, Yves Noe, was more explicit about his concerns. 'There is too much desire at Mon Désir,' he said, referring to the fact the piano bar was full of attractive young women. He moved the players to somewhere 'more suitable'.

Having lost their opening encounter, Scotland knew they would come second in the pool, as long as they beat Romania and Zimbabwe – the other two teams in Pool 4. 'But it was difficult,' said Deans. 'Because no one had any experience of playing three internationals in ten days. That was something that only came in to rugby in the World Cup tournaments, and it's what led to the development of bigger squads of players to cope.' In the event, Scotland beat both sides with ease.

'Colin Deans won his fiftieth cap in the match against Zimbabwe,' recalls Gavin Hastings. 'We came back into the changing room and we were pretty euphoric. Roy Laidlaw made a wonderful, emotional speech about Colin's contribution to Scottish rugby – it was very moving. When he said he would like to present Col with a small memento on behalf of the team, we looked around and realised Colin wasn't in the changing room. He was upstairs doing an interview, and had missed the whole thing.'

On the same day that France and Scotland had played the opening game in Pool 4, over in Australia, England were preparing to take on Australia in the first game of Pool 1 at the Concord Oval in Sydney. 'England knew that the primary match was the one against Australia,' says Underwood. 'Our big game.'

Australia won, but in somewhat controversial circumstances, as eleven minutes into the second half, Keith Lawrence, the referee, awarded a try to David Campese, the Australia wing, even though he had knocked on. England never recovered and lost the game 19–6. England's second game produced a vastly different result, as they beat Japan 60–7; then Australia beat Japan 42–23. It was desperately disappointing for the Japanese fans who have a huge love of rugby. It is the third most popular sport behind baseball and sumo wrestling, and Japan has the fourth largest rugby-playing population in the world. The players in Japan are known for their speed, but have sometimes been at a disadvantage because of their relatively smaller size compared to southern hemisphere and European players. Shiggy Konno was Chairman of the Japanese RFU and a real champion of the sport. He died while this book was being written. Japanese players described his death as 'the greatest catastrophe in Japanese rugby. The father of the sport has gone.' Konno summed up the problems of Japanese rugby in 1987, when he declared helplessly: 'Whenever we discover a 6 ft 3 giant, the western world invariably responds with a new breed of 6 ft 8 locks.' All the big guys in Japan head for sumo wrestling where there is serious money and prestige awaiting.

When I began work on *Rugby World* magazine in 1995, I came across a letter from a passionate Japanese rugby fan.

'He writes in to us all the time,' said the staff on the magazine. The letter said how much he liked the sport and looked forward to *Rugby World* arriving every month. Limitations in his use and understanding of English were clear from the start. He'd send 'Happy Easter!' cards and 'Happy Birthday' cards – randomly through the year, when they bore no connection to any events taking place. Clearly, his delight at discovering a card with English printed on it overshadowed any consideration of what the English might mean. I thought him delightful and looked forward to his monthly missives that were pretty much a collection of words that had no right to be joined together in the same sentence.

'Hey rugby like me I. Yes, play plenty. Magazine I see. Great! Is win now works team good I try. Goal!'

The photographs, invariably enclosed, showed him playing rugby in mud-splattered glasses that had been taped to the side of his head. He was usually being chaired off the pitch with a great big beaming smile.

'Don't you ever write back?' I asked. They looked askance. 'What? And encourage him with his mad and inappropriate birthday and Christmas cards? No.'

I decided I knew best. I sent a *Rugby World* T-shirt and a note introducing myself and thanking him for his lovely cards.

It took two weeks for the deluge of letters, cards, photos, posters, grass (!) and gifts to arrive.

Some days, I'd be confronted by cards arriving with every postal delivery (three times a day). The rest of the staff smiled and shook their heads in a 'we told you so' sort of way. Then, in one letter, there was a photograph of him in the *Rugby World* T-shirt ... with his son, and his wife ... and his daughter in the same shirt. 'It big shirt!' ran the caption, referring to the 'one size fits all' shirt I had sent. It rather summed up Japanese rugby for me – boundless enthusiasm hampered by physical size.

England's final game in the pool was against USA – a team hoping that a major world tournament would do much to lift the sport in America. Coach Ron Mayes, a New Zealander, said: 'The World Cup has had a tremendous effect. It is the most exciting thing to happen since I entered the game.' On the two occasions that rugby union was an Olympic sport, the USA won indicating, perhaps, that the lure of a glamorous world tournament did much to galvanise players into action in America. 'Certainly,' said Mayes. 'Eyes will be opened by this event and the sport will be taken more seriously.' England beat USA, thus ending their World Cup dream prematurely. 'We'll be back,' declared Mayes. 'Next time. We'll be back.' Much the same could be said of the departing Japanese.

The final games were played in Pool 2, which featured Wales and Ireland, along with Canada and Tonga. It was these latter two teams who kicked off the group – with Canada beating Tonga 37–4, much to the dismay of the Tongans, who resented being asked to play a match on Sunday, strictly a religious day of rest in Tonga. It was a great result for the Canadians, though, who had come into the tournament 'blind' – with no idea what to expect at the World Cup since they had no Five Nations or Bledisloe Cup competition. In the Canadian team was a young man who would go on to make a huge impression on the World Cup, and become a talismanic figure in the Canadian team – Gareth Rees. He was just nineteen in 1987, and arrived in New Zealand with little knowledge or understanding of his opponents or what would be required in a competitive tournament. He says:

We'd never even seen a video of Tonga. I remember that Tonga's prop – I think he was one of their chiefs, actually – wouldn't bind properly. His head wasn't interlocked with the other front row, and he was standing up all the time. We just found it really annoying. Now, of course, you'd never get away with it.

I remember watching Ireland play Wales on television the day after the Tonga game, and it was abysmal rugby. I had always thought of the Five Nations teams as being in a different league to us, but suddenly I got a sniff that perhaps we could do something here. That was a wonderful feeling . . . suddenly thinking that you might have a chance against them was the stuff of dreams.

Hans de Goede, Canada's captain in 1987, rates the victory over Tonga as the most significant moment in Canada's rugby history, and Rees as the most significant player in the sport's history. Sadly for the Canadians, they were beaten 46–19 by Ireland, and 40–9 by Wales, so failed to qualify.

Indeed, from the start of the tournament, it was clear that it would be Wales and Ireland that would go through from this pool – the question was, in what order? The winner of the pool would be likely to face a quarter-final against England, while the team finishing in second place would meet Australia – considered a far more taxing prospect.

But, before Ireland and Wales kicked a ball, there were health scares for both teams. Glenn Webbe of Wales was badly injured in the team's 29–16 defeat of Tonga and had to get a flight home, along with Stuart Evans, the prop.

In a 'Carry On Rugby'-style moment, John Rawlins came out to replace him, but pulled a hamstring minutes into a training session, and had to go straight home without playing. Wales were in a mess – where could they find a replacement prop with just days to go before one of their most important matches of the tournament? Enter Dai Young, a 19-year-old who was out on holiday in Australia to watch the tournament. 'They asked me if I'd play. "Yeah," I said, and that was that. I was uncapped and suddenly playing for Wales in the World Cup. What a holiday that turned out to be.'

It was the start of Young's international career which would lead to him amassing fifty-one caps, playing on three Lions tours across three decades (1989, 1997, 2001), and being on the receiving end of one rather amusing moment of sledging. 'Do that again,' he was told by Gareth Chilcott, 'and you'll live up to your name.'

Meanwhile, Ireland were having problems of their own, as Mick Doyle was rushed to hospital in Auckland with a suspected heart attack. Medical tests cleared him, but the drama did not help Ireland in the least, as they went down 13–6 to Wales. Mark Ring scored Wales' solitary try.

Ieuan Evans, a player who would one day captain Wales,

found it all a little strange. 'It felt bizarre, really bizarre that Wales should be playing against Ireland 12,000 miles from home, kicking off at something like 3 a.m. British time.'

'The World Cup was enjoyable, but we had a lot of time to fill with home-made games,' said Ring. One such game was pool. They held a tournament at the hotel, the main rule of which was that everyone had to play, whether they wanted to or not. They ran a book on the whole affair, with each player putting in NZ$25 to start things going. Paul Thorburn and Phil Davies were in the final – the best of five frames, with beer mats covering the pockets to save money. 'Cliff' Thorburn and 'Steve' Davies played in dicky bows and shirts. Webbe was referee in his rugby blazer, with white gloves.

There was, in theory, a drinking curfew imposed upon the players during the World Cup, and the management encouraged them to stay in their hotels. One day, Ring and Webbe couldn't stand it any more, so went out for a walk, spotted a light on in a bar, wandered in, and there were the Scotland and Ireland squads having a drink.

They joined them in playing a series of drinking games. 'It was the one where you stroke the face of the person next to you, having rubbed your finger in the ashtray first. Webbe had dirtied his fingers so John Jeffrey of Scotland had soot-black stripes across his face. Not pleased.'

In the break between the pool matches and the quarter-finals, England players went to Hamilton Island for a break. 'By going there, we became chief destroyers of our chances of glory,' said Richards. 'We were preparing for an important quarter-final match against Wales by going paragliding, water-skiing, sunbathing and relaxing on Hamilton Island on the Great Barrier Reef.'

'It was just a great big jolly,' says Moore. 'Everyone just pissed around – they thought it was great. Remember, these were boys who would salivate over a free T-shirt back then. They took the golf buggies and drove them everywhere – they just messed around all the time.'

Hamilton Island was the venue for all manner of player pranks, most of them executed on Martin Green, the coach, who, according to Dooley, was 'blissfully unaware of the tide fluctuations' around the island, so he stripped off and dived into what he believed to be several feet of water . . . only to scrape his entire body across the live coral. He looked as if 'someone had slashed his face and body with a razor'. Because of the danger from infection, he spent the next few days covered in iodine – much to the amusement of the players. Then, as if that were not enough humiliation, Steve Brain decided it would be enormous fun to snip the crotch out of Green's underpants, and the toes of his socks, during a training session. The great amusement derived from this was merely exacerbated by the fact that Green changed into his redesigned underwear after training, and pretended that nothing had happened. 'That made it all so much funnier,' says Dooley.

If the trip to Hamilton Island didn't exactly get the players in the right frame of mind for a crucial rugby match, then neither did holding a birthday party for Winterbottom by a poolside. No prizes for guessing what happened to Winterbottom . . . yes, of course, he fell in. He banged his knee in the fall, and needed stitches, making him doubtful for the quarter-final.

'I suppose, looking back, some of it was a bit daft,' concedes Harrison, the England captain. 'Lots of silly things happened. I remember one time I was being interviewed by Australian television and Mickey Skinner said I had to get "There ain't much meat on a fruit bat" into the interview . . . And I did!'

The eight quarter-finalists consisted of the seven nations of the IRB, as predicted, and Fiji – as not predicted. Hoorah for the World Cup's first surprise result! One of the primary aims of the tournament had been to 'expand' the rugby world, and develop the smaller rugby nations. It had been assumed that Argentina would make it through to the quarter-final stage, but Fiji – with their penchant for running, handling and try-scoring – were rewarded with a place in the final eight. That was the good news. The bad news was that their quarter-final would be against France.

*

The first of the quarter-finals was between Scotland and New Zealand. 'When the death or glory time arrives, you don't mess around,' said Lochore to the All Blacks players. The war of words was certainly being won by New Zealand and Australia. The war on the pitch? Well, yes, that was being won by New Zealand and Australia, too. Against Scotland, the All Blacks showed superior physical presence, power and speed, while Scotland relied on their defence to hold back the black tide. The only answer to New Zealand's thirty points, was a solitary Hastings penalty, as New Zealand won 30–3.

Scotland's case was not helped greatly by the fact that they went out looking for parties the night before the game.

Being Scotsmen, we liked to have a good time [said Deans]. Christchurch was the headquarters of Steinlager and when we were there, we said, 'Any chance of some free beer for the boys?' They said, 'Of course, here you go,' and we became friendly with their sales director. At one point, he said: 'The talk is that you might beat New Zealand tomorrow. Look, if you do, would you like to become the official team of Steinlager?' Of course we said yes! We had the best parties ever out there. We were disappointed to lose to New Zealand, but the All Blacks said we were the hardest team they played in the tournament. It was a backhanded compliment I suppose. They still won by twenty-seven points.

So, Scotland became the first team to be knocked out at quarter-final stage, and prepared to fly home.

Our manager was Bob Munro [recalls Deans]. He had an SRU gold card and it used to annoy us that at the end of tours, we'd play a game on the Saturday, be on a plane on the Sunday, and be back in the UK by the Monday. The All Blacks or Australians would get to spend two or three days in Singapore, so we badgered Bob to give us a couple of days in LA on the way home. He had to give in. We went to Disney World and we took the place over, singing and dancing all

day. I remember Scott and Gavin Hastings wearing funny
duck hats.

The following day, in Auckland, the Fijians played the French –
showing, once again, the joyous abandon that had delighted the
crowds who watched them at the pool stage of the tournament.
Fun, running rugby played with youth and vitality. But, despite
the Fijians' brilliance, panache and exciting play, the French controlled the game and won 31–16. Severo Koroduadua made a
superb break but, holding the ball in one hand, saw it squirt out
of his grasp on the try line. 'People in Fiji still mention that
moment today,' he says. 'It was twenty years ago, but no one has
forgotten. "Ah, you!" they say – "the ball dropper".'

Next it was time for Britain and Ireland to lose two teams, as
Ireland were overpowered 33–15 by Australia, and Wales beat
England 16–3 in one of the worst matches ever seen.

'I have no idea why England performed so poorly,' says
Harrison.

'It was that trip to Hamilton Island,' says Richards.

But Harrison is not convinced. 'We were buoyant and confident beforehand, yet we didn't produce it on the field. Wales
didn't create, they seized on our mistakes – that was the most disappointing feature.'

'After the Wales game, we went to a disco and found the
Welsh there too,' says Underwood. 'That was less than wonderful
in the circumstances. The next day, as our coach sped past the
Mayfair Crest Hotel in central Brisbane, and headed for the airport, we saw Wales climbing on board their own coach; they were
going forward in the competition and we were going home. That
flight to London seemed to go on for ever; some of the team
drowned their sorrows.'

'Eighty-seven was a shame really,' says Winterbottom. 'We
had some reasonable players but the organisation wasn't up to
scratch. There was a very bad period in the mid-Eighties for
England; from 1984 to '88 the team underperformed and it was a
tragedy that England were allowed to be so unsuccessful.'

*

So to the semi-finals, which had developed into a battle between the hemispheres – with France and Wales fighting for the north against the tournament hosts. In order to relax and recouperate a little, the Wales team had two days off in Surfers' Paradise and Lochore took New Zealand to Wairarapa to train, billeting the players out in ones and twos to give them a break from hotels.

New Zealand had drawn a Sunday match for the game, meaning Michael Jones, one of their stars, couldn't play. Not that they missed him too much. Ten minutes into the game, and they had already scored two tries, as their forward power imposed total dominance, and the Wales scrum disintegrated. It was a physical demolition. Wales lost 49–6.

'Ah well,' sighed Keith Rowlands, the Wales team manager. 'The sooner we can get home and continue beating England, the better.'

The Wales players had not lost their ability to have some fun though, and after the match, as John Kendall-Carpenter stood up to address the players, Ring bet Richard Moriaty, Chairman of the rugby World Cup organising committee, that he could pinch Kendall-Carpenter's handkerchief from his top pocket while the official was making his speech. The subject of the handkerchief had come up before among the players who remarked that Kendall-Carpenter always had it – come hell or high water – in his top pocket. Ring went to the salad bar, picked up a pair of tongs and sneaked behind the official, with the rest of the players looking on. Moriarty had given him 6–1 odds, so Ring was determined to succeed. But, just as he pulled out the handkerchief, he discovered that it was sewn in. 'At least we knew why he always wore it,' said Ring. 'Blimey, I nearly pulled his blazer off trying to get the thing out.'

The nature of the defeat by New Zealand was crushing. Wales had been out-powered and outmanoeuvred at every turn. The physical differences between the players were staggering. It was shown most clearly when Wales' second-row, Huw Richards, was sent off for punching Gary Whetton. Ring tried to cheer him up by giving him the shorts that John Kirwan had given him, but they found the shorts were too big for Richards. The New

Zealand wing's shorts were too big for the Wales second-row. The two teams had a post-match dinner after the game, before New Zealand prepared for the final. Thorburn tried to lighten the mood by standing up and singing: 'Always look on the bright side of life,' much to the horror of everyone else in the room. 'It just didn't seem that funny,' said Ring. 'We were all just ready to go home.'

The second semi-final was in great contrast to the first, in that it was a truly great game. Arguably, it was one of the greatest games of all time. Australia had Campese who scored his twenty-fifth try to become the highest try-scorer in international rugby, and France had Serge Blanco – a masterful, natural ball player who was quick-thinking and unpredictable but always brilliant. The two sides combined to produce a breathtaking finale. Australia still had the bulk of their 1984 Grand Slam team and their 1986 Bledisloe Cup team intact for the game. But there was nothing they could do to halt France.

With two minutes to go, France scored one of the greatest tries of all time – they launched an attack inside the Australian half. Eleven players handled the ball before Serge Blanco drifting up from full back then belted for the line and scored in the corner. It ended 30–24 to France, and the disappointment was written all over the faces of the Australian players who had been so confident of reaching the finals, they had already booked their flights to Auckland and hotel accommodation. In contrast, the French were euphoric.

After the final whistle, in the changing room, we were the happiest men in the whole world [says Blanco]. We had accomplished a great feat because the Australians had been out-and-out favourites but we, the French, had done it. Everyone would have liked to have been in our shoes, but not everyone could have played like we did. It was a moment of extreme happiness – an extraordinary moment of rapport and communication. After showering and changing, we gave a press conference, by the end of which time the stadium was in complete darkness. We all went out on to the pitch, we did a lap of honour and we sang! We sang Basque songs for half an hour. It was a way to re-experience the emotions through our voices, because the voice is the instrument of the feelings. There was absolutely no one else there. Just us. It was our little secret. Our special time, a really quite extraordinary moment that was ours alone. It was a moment of sheer magic which is difficult to describe. The feelings, the emotions. So happy, so proud of what we had done. Yes, the happiest men in the whole world.

Blanco is sure that France won because they were absolutely determined to get to the final and prevent the predicted New Zealand v Australia encounter. Interestingly, he adds that he thinks that it was the desire to make it to the final that would ultimately stand in their way, because they had fulfilled their objective so didn't have the motivation in the final game.

The penultimate game of the World Cup is the most disliked in the tournament. Third place play-offs . . . pah! A bun fight for the runners-up medals. No team in the history of international competition has set off for a major tournament with their sights set on third place. To win a play-off is rather like being the fireman who runs into a burning building to save the children and comes out with the dog. In 1987, Wales were so short of numbers for their play-off against Australia that, once again, they were forced to turn to those who had travelled to watch. Richard Webster was such a man – a brickie by trade, he had taken the summer off to travel to New Zealand to watch Wales in the World Cup. He was drinking with friends when a message was passed to him – the manager of the Wales team wanted to talk to him. 'Yeah right,' said Webster. 'Of course he does.'

Webster would become the second holidaying Welshman to be called out of his deck chair and on to the pitch.

We were travelling down to Rotorua three days before the game and stopped after a couple of hours for a break in a café overlooking a reservoir [recalls Thorburn]. Mark Ring asked if

I'd pretend to be Peter Jackson, from the *Daily Mail*, for a wind-up on Richard Webster. So I used the café phone to ring the phone kiosk in the car park, and went through the routine, 'You've been selected for Wales, how does it feel? etc.' Richard fell for it hook, line and sinker. He got quite emotional on the phone. Nobody said a word to him and it wasn't until two years later that he found out about it, when Bleddyn Bowen mentioned it at a dinner at which he was speaking. Richard happened to be there.

Bets were taken on the number of points that Australia would amass during the course of what it was assumed would be a one-sided encounter. 'We'd been written off by the media and we used that as motivation, sticking newspaper cuttings on the changing-room wall.' But Australia were reduced to fourteen men after only four minutes and Wales took advantage to win 22–21 to much cheering from the New Zealand crowd who supported anyone except Australia. Paul Thorburn's conversion in the last minute of the game, from the touchline, won the game. All that was left now, was the final game.

5

The crowning of the first World Champions

The Monday after the Saturday final, I was back at work as a policeman. It was difficult to do my job because I was recognised all the time. Being a World Cup winner had some good spin-offs, but I never did any undercover work again.

John Gallagher, New Zealand full back, 1987

It was the first-ever World Cup final. Thirty men stood proudly in the tunnel leading out onto the Eden Park pitch, pacing from foot to foot as the excitement of the crowd mounted outside. Fifteen of the men wearing the black of New Zealand, fifteen of them in the distinctive blue of France. The men in black determined to prove that they were the greatest rugby side in the world, and the men in blue eager to show that, when it came to battle between a team oozing discipline and commitment and a team showing flair and creativity, the latter would triumph every time.

"Ave you got eet?' asked Denis Charvet.

'I 'ave eet. Of course I 'ave eet,' replied Franck Mesnel.

'Where do you 'ave eet?' enquired Charvet.

'I 'ave eet. Do not worry where I 'ave eet,' mumbled Mesnel, and Charvet smiled to himself.

For Mesnel, that flamboyant centre and darling of the Paris social scene, the World Cup final of 1987 was another event in the year nominated as the Racing Club de Paris 'Year of Living Dangerously', so he had to take to the field with a pink bow tie about his person in his efforts to add style and sophistication to rugby. Racing Club had opened the year by playing Bayonne in Basque Country while sporting 'jaunty Basque berets'. Then, in April, they ran onto the pitch to play Brive in navy blue blazers. A week later, it was natty Bermuda shorts, then black face make-up. In Paris, they played in the national championships wearing pink bow ties. Next it was the World Cup. What would they wear for that?

'There are strict regulations regarding player dress,' came the instruction from the tournament organisers, so Mesnel was pre-vented from running out wearing the tie, as was his preference. His overt peacocking was contained by the regulators but the spirit lived on, as the bow tie made it on to the pitch after all – from the inside of Mesnel's shorts.

It was, alas, one of the few moments of French chic to make its way onto the field that day. The final of the first World Cup was a relatively dull affair, especially when compared to the fireworks of the semi-final. The running rugby spectacle keenly anticipated by the millions watching across the globe was replaced, instead, by a display of fine kicking by Grant Fox. The New Zealand number 10 ended the contest with seventeen points which, added to the three tries scored by Michael Jones, David Kirk and John Kirwan, gave the All Blacks a comprehensive victory. There was scant consolation for France in the latter stages when Pierre Berbizier ran in the only French try.

'We beat the French by playing precisely and relentlessly,' said Gallagher, 'relying on their flair to lead them into errors that would give us the breaks. Our job was to impose our own rhythm and style on the match. It wasn't to negate the opposition – if we played our own way, opposition impotence would be a happy by-product, it would happen automatically.'

Such a clinical approach to the game was backed up by utter self-belief. 'From the first minute in the first match, we found a fluency born of simplicity and confidence. We wove a spell. We were going to win. We believed it,' said Kirk.

After receiving the trophy, Kirk thrust it into the air – his face beaming with delight as a nation applauded, and the team prepared to celebrate.

> We were just so relieved when we won [says Gallagher]. After the final we went back to our hotel – more of a motel – and had one huge party. People were being thrown in the swimming pool at four or five in the morning. I'd agreed to meet John Taylor [ex-Wales player-turned-journalist] at 9 a.m. the next morning to talk about a rugby video. I don't know how I managed to speak, let alone get up at that time. I was lucky I experienced the dying embers of amateurism, and the start of professionalism. Players ten years before me never had that. I feel very privileged.

Much that happened in the 1987 World Cup is so alien to the way we view international rugby today that it's as if it were fished from a golden era centuries past – not from a tournament which took place just twenty years ago. There's an almost sepia-like quality to it. This grand world tournament, seen by millions and making millions, but featuring men who were grateful just to be given the time off work to attend. Frenchmen smoked in their chic blazers and tucked pink bow ties inside their shorts before playing in the biggest match of their lives. The northern hemisphere sides played pranks and met up in bars, while the Japanese arrived cheerfully, got thumped by everyone and left cheerfully, promising that next time it would all be different. The dynamic Fijians sidestepped a military coup to get to the tournament, then surpassed all expectation when they arrived. And New Zealand won.

The aim of this next section is to look at why they won, and how, and to look in some detail at the preparation that New Zealand went through, prior to the 1987 World Cup.

In reality, New Zealand's preparation for the 1987 World Cup began decades before the tournament kicked off. The years of world supremacy had created a crucial 'aura of invincibility' around them. The effect of this should not be underestimated. In

1987, everyone went into a match against the All Blacks expecting to lose. This gave them a massive psychological advantage over rival teams. But there was also a lot of practical preparation that went into getting the New Zealand team right in 1987. Four years before the World Cup, the decision was made to appoint a Scottish fitness trainer called Jim Blair to work with Canterbury rugby club. Blair then moved to Auckland in 1984 when the team started playing 'total rugby' under John Hart. Because he had worked with these two major clubs, by the time the World Cup came along, he had made an impact upon a large proportion of the players who would contest the tournament, especially since eleven of the men in the 1987 squad were Auckland players.

Blair is an important character in understanding why New Zealand won the World Cup. In Hart's words, Blair had two great skills.

> One was devising programmes for individualised training by each man in the team. The other was the presentation of a number of training skills in grid activities, using balls, which improved the agility and speed of players. He attacked every player, assessing his strengths and weaknesses and offering means of improving one and eradicating the other. Bit by bit, you could see the players responding. Their speed improved, in some cases quite remarkably. Their agility grew like a mushroom. When he immersed them in training groups ... their development was extraordinary.

Blair began working with the New Zealand team as soon as they began their preparation for the World Cup. He was given fifty names of players that would make up the initial All Blacks training squad, and was told to get them fitter than they'd ever been. And so he travelled round the country, writing training programmes for the players that they could happily complete in their home environment. For example, one player was a farmer who lived out in the wilds and said he couldn't get to a gym. 'I told him to put dirt into bags and move them from one end of the barn to the other – pushing them, pulling them, lifting them. There's lots of things you can do to get fit at home. It just takes a bit of creative thinking. When I worked with a group of players in Samoa once, there were not enough balls, so we used coconuts – the only limit is your imagination.'

Blair was eager to make sure the players did training that was relevant to their position in the team, so he split the squad up – props and locks worked on one training schedule, the hooker, half-backs and back row worked on another, the centres had a different training plan, and the wings and full backs had a fourth, distinct training plan. He worked on endurance, and controlled the amount of pure weight training the players were doing.

'I wanted to get them strong as a prelude for power, not just "strong" for no reason. No point in getting strong enough to lift a bus if you can't catch it. I wanted explosive strength. We had parachutes for sprinting which was new to them, and used balls in all their fitness work.' Blair says that he ensured they had at least 150 ball touches during their fitness training.

But it is the introduction of grids that will be Blair's legacy. The small grids made out of cones or discarded tracksuits on the grass gave players limited time and space, helping to give them better peripheral vision, improve their reaction times and increase the speed of their reactions to movement.

Even Blair recognised that his grids were something special. 'I knew at the time that the grids were really helping the players and the fact that they were different to anything the players had ever seen before was great because it made them all the more challenging. I'd try to get the players and clubs doing them three times a week.'

Blair's fitness work with the players was overseen, as everything to do with the team was overseen, by Brian Lochore, the team manager. He chose two selectors to work with him in 1987 – John Hart and Alex Wyllie, both of whom were later promoted to assistant coaches, and stayed with the team throughout the tournament. The three men first met up to discuss a playing strategy for the All Blacks, in December 1986, and Lochore put forward the view that the All Blacks should adopt a fast-running, quick-passing version of the game, as played by Auckland (where John Hart was coach). He added that he believed they should select those players who were best able to play that sort of rugby.

A special trial was staged in Hamilton on 7 April at which the three men would look for the players who could best play the pattern of rugby they thought would win the World Cup. The final trial was on 9 May, two weeks before the opening game of the World Cup, in Whangarei when possibles v probables took to the field. The selectors were told to look for the men with the right personality, not just the best footballers. They felt it was important that back-up players had the character and personality to handle being virtually permanent reserves, and perhaps playing only once in the tournament. This was particularly relevant because the team would be in the unusual position of being virtually on tour in their own country with potential distractions all around them.

The cornerstone of the selection was the desire to adopt an Auckland style of play – a high-speed game based on superb physical conditioning, high level of ball skills, set-piece control, coupled with forward mobility, and strength and pace out wide where continuity would be created by players standing in tackles and offloading to supporting loose forwards.

'They were confident that the game plan, if executed correctly, would be the most effective way of winning the World Cup,' said David Kirk. 'Looking back, their planning and strategising was essential to New Zealand's success. They worked out what style was needed to win, picked players who could play that style and – boom – we won the World Cup. Much of the victory was down to their clear thinking in advance.'

'We encouraged players to think, be innovative and use their flair,' says Hart. 'Players were told to take opportunities; most other sides would be kicking for touch but we wanted the game played with the ball in hand. We had an attitude to attack and a commitment to defence.'

The ten key reasons why New Zealand won

1. The management team

Brian Lochore was a confident manager who clearly and consistently spelt out the way he wanted the team to play. There were no mixed messages, and no confusion about who was in charge. His relationships with Hart and Wyllie, his two assistants, were equally well managed. The coaches had enough power and influence to feel they were contributing while Lochore stayed in control.

'Lochore was very special,' said Blair. 'He didn't shout, he didn't scream and swear, he had a gentle manner. He was a gifted manager and his influence on the players was enormous.'

Kirk agrees with this assessment. 'He was a natural people manager. The players responded well to him and he kept two major coaches happy. We always felt that Hart's role during the World Cup itself was not as significant as Lochore's and no more so than Wyllie's. I think greatness starts with the administration and coaching of a team and we had that in 1987 with Lochore.'

2. Their physical fitness/preparation

'I have no doubt that the All Blacks succeeded in the World Cup because in physical fitness and ball skills they were far ahead of all opponents. They played each match at a sustained speed beyond the reach of any opposing side,' says John Hart.

3. The right captain for that team at that time

David Kirk did not fit the model of the traditional New Zealand rugby player but his ability to think, plan, be incisive and analytical unquestionably paid dividends for the team.

He was ahead of his time, with his ability to deal with the mental dimension of rugby as well as the physical. He says that, as early as 1984, he went to see the Australian Institute of Sport in Canberra to talk to a sports psychologist. 'I felt instinctively that matters of the mind were as important in sporting success as the more celebrated physical attributes of a player. I wanted to get all parts of captaincy right.'

Former All Black, Zinzan Brooke, applauds Kirk's captaincy in 1987. 'I remember the weight of expectation being immense when I captained. It's just like being the New Zealand Prime Minister for the day, because you carry the whole nation's hopes on your shoulders. Finding a captain who can cope with that pressure and remain in control is vital for a successful team.'

4. An 'aura'

A mystique about the team that makes them more than the sum of their parts, however good those 'parts' may be. It is that 'something' that gives you the psychological advantage, and makes other teams fearful of playing against you.

The All Blacks had this in spades: within the country and to the rest of the world. 'The All Black tradition is an expression of our culture, of our identity, of our ability to excel, to achieve great things,' says Kirk. 'The team exists in the abstract. It's more than its players. We come and go through the team like ghosts, for our seasons. Some of us are remembered, none of us are really missed.'

The players become legends, they are like superheroes. Brooke recalls the tales told to him, as a boy, about Peter Jones, a New Zealand flanker whose feet were supposed to be so big that it took a sugar sack to hold his boots. 'We all ran off and stuck our feet into sugar sacks to see how big Peter must have been,' says Brooke. He says that this image has always stayed with him. In his mind, and in the minds of many New Zealanders, All Blacks are just that bit bigger, faster, taller and stronger than anyone else in the world. 'You grow up thinking that they're something really special,' explains Brooke. 'That image is with you from an early age, and if you're a boy – you desperately want to be an All Black more than anything.'

With such history, such responsibility to the past and the future, has developed an astonishing aura and, in 1987, it had made New Zealand seem like an unbeatable force, even though they lost twice just before the tournament. There are ways of 'manufacturing' an aura, and appearing like a champion in waiting before you have won anything. Sportsmen try all sorts of tricks to separate themselves from the masses: the Olympian

Denise Lewis talked of travelling first-class when all her com-
petitors were travelling business class. The boxer Audley
Harrison spoke of surrounding himself with assistants in a bid to
look more important and out-psych his opponents. But, there is
no question, that when that which gives you your aura, and your
point of separation from the masses, arises organically out of the
culture and tradition of your side, it has greater impact and is
more enduring. Once you have an aura it becomes self-fulfilling –
you are difficult to beat because you have a reputation for being
difficult to beat, so people don't beat you and your reputation
grows. This is what happened to New Zealand rugby.

5. A big vision and clarity of vision

Lochore's vision for the team has already been mentioned. What
should be emphasised is what utter confidence and conviction it
takes for a coach to set out a big, clear vision in advance, and not
waver from it. It is relatively easy to pick up minor points along
the way – about refining defence or changing patterns of play. It's
much harder to take a step back, think 'outside the box' and
create a vision for the team that is bigger than the individual
matches in which they will play.

> The aim of the New Zealand team was not to win the World
> Cup but to be the best team in the world, to set new standards,
> to play better rugby than had ever been played. The aim every
> time was to play the perfect game. That was the vision [says
> Kirk]. I wouldn't call any of the aims of the earlier All Blacks
> teams I played in visionary. The aim in those days was not to
> lose to the opposition, a very different ambition to winning
> which was, in itself, a limited sort of ambition. Unless you have
> a vision bigger than victory, the team will remain in the box it
> has built for itself. If winning is enough, that's all that will be
> achieved. The team that concentrates on winning will
> inevitably start to lose. And the team will have to lose to start
> growing again. Only with a wider vision and the leadership to
> make it real will it be possible – even necessary – to change a
> winning team for its longer term health.

The distinction between aiming to be a great team that wins everything, and a winning team may be slight but it is, in reality, massive – a whole new philosophy grows out of such exalted aims. The All Blacks were successful because they didn't play to win, but played against the game itself – trying to better it, push back boundaries of what was considered possible. Ironically, this changed a little when the World Cup came along and shifted the emphasis from series victories to one-off, knockout games which had to be won at all costs, which may indicate why they haven't won a World Cup since 1987.

Certainly, in that first World Cup, the opposition became the means by which they brought their vision of rugby to the world. Winning wasn't the point but would certainly be a by-product of trying to play the perfect game. 'We aspired to a style that was unbeatable,' says Lochore.

6. A reason to win (i.e. a recent setback that motivates you . . . the cuttings on the dressing-room wall) creating real desire

New Zealand had a terrible year going into the 1987 World Cup, culminating in the defeat by France in Nantes. Paradoxically, this may have helped. 'Looking back, losing to France was the best thing to happen to us,' says Lochore. 'It gave us a low point to fight back from, and a memory to escape from. It gave us a new start and a new fighting spirit.' Indeed, 'remember Nantes' became the rallying cry of the New Zealand players during the World Cup.

'The game had been on a real downer,' says Brooke. 'A lot of the old hands had retired, the Aussies had beaten us in the Bledisloe Cup, and players were turning to rugby league. Even the America's Cup was more popular. Then in 1986 there was the rebel tour to South Africa, which caused a huge stir. A lot of people didn't want their kids to have anything to do with rugby. Hosting and winning that tournament was almost the game's salvation.' The players knew how much victory mattered, which gave them an added incentive that would simply not have been there if they'd had a simple year of victories going into the tournament.

7. Home advantage

Psychologists estimate that, across sports, home sides can have an advantage of up to 30 per cent over their visiting rivals. Indeed, recent studies in football have revealed that a home team can expect to score around 37.29 per cent more points than when they play away. The most recent study which focused exclusively on rugby union was reported in the *Journal of Sports Sciences*, May 2006, and evaluated home advantages both for national (Super 12) and international (Tri Nations) rugby union teams from South Africa, Australia and New Zealand, over the five-year period 2000–4. It was revealed that the overall home advantage in elite rugby union has a mean of +6.7 points, and that this changes little from year to year. Such a figure can easily be the difference between winning and losing, so there is no question that home advantage exists, but it is not as significant in rugby as it is in football, where fewer points separate winning and losing. Reasons for home advantage are debated extensively, but would include issues like crowd support, travel, familiarity with food, customs, pitch, environment, proximity to loved ones and referee bias towards the home side. In rugby studies of teams playing home and away legs, there is a significant advantage to playing at home (estimated, again, to be around 30 per cent improvement in the home leg).

8. Thinking players all over the field

The 1987 team had ten or more players who were the best players in their position in the world. Michael Jones brought a whole new dimension to rugby, with speed, power and explosiveness that were unmatched. John Kirwan was exceptional, leading players to comment: 'I had a rule of thumb when blindside running: if you can't think of anything to do, give it to John Kirwan as quickly as you can.' There was Grant Fox, a man with a ferocity of spirit and tremendous self-belief. He was a cold analyser who was vital to the mix of the team. In the forwards, there was John Drake at tight head prop, with Alan Whetton and Wayne Shelford bringing power to the pack, running through the tackle to make those extra few yards. These guys were the best players in the world at the time, the greats of their generation. They had rare physical gifts but they also dominated mentally.

'The players understood each other well and made very few mistakes. There were no unforced errors,' said Hart. Kirk adds, interestingly: 'They have that restlessness on the one hand and extraordinary relaxation on the other.' The players complemented each other because they were chosen to fit into the grand plan, so were relaxed in each other's company, yet paradoxically were so eager to win that they were never fully relaxed.

9. Non-playing members of the team were supportive (not energy-sappers)

It may seem odd to include this, but many of the players I talked to from 1987, insist that the players in the squad who did not make it on to the field were very different in the 1987 squad than they had been on previous tours, and having players who remained upbeat, confident and enthusiastic was a huge advantage for the team. 'There was no one there who didn't want us to win, who didn't believe that we could win. That made a massive difference. No little niggles, no complaints that undermined your confidence. If you have unsupportive characters in the squad, you might as well let the opposition players in on your sessions. It's vital that everyone in the squad believes the team can win.'

Andy Dalton, the man who was due to captain the side but withdrew through injury, was an important character in this respect, and Kirk is eager to point out how valuable he was to the squad – motivating players, and taking a lot of the burden off Kirk. Kirk called him a 'reluctant hero'.

10. They are confident and disciplined – on and off the pitch

One of the things that the New Zealand management insisted upon in 1987 was good conduct off the pitch as well as on it. 'External disciplines become internal standards,' declared Lochore, who assured players that training sessions would always start and finish on time, and that players should be ready for them and properly attired. He insisted that punctuality and dress standards were important in creating the right impression and showing respect for themselves, each other and the shirt.

The players were extremely confident on the pitch and off it, not expressing any doubts. They quietly and confidently got on with the task of producing their magic which they knew was better than that being produced by anyone else.

Becoming a winner in modern sport is challenging and increasingly complex. It's why teams work so hard, and train for so long to peak for a competition like the World Cup, which means that after every big event, there is a necessary deflation. This makes 'winning after winning' extremely difficult. New Zealand didn't win a World Cup again after this one in 1987; indeed Australia are the only team to have won two World Cups – eight years apart. Australia, whichever way you look at it, are the golden team of rugby World Cups; they are also the only side to have made it to the final in two successive tournaments (1999 and 2003). For them, the glory years started in 1991.

PART TWO: 1991

Glamour comes to rugby union

6

What did the first World Cup achieve?

There are two kinds of rugby players – those who play pianos and those who shift them.

The French assessment of the division of labour in a rugby team, as described by Pierre Danos, French piano player of the early 1970s

It was mild for the time of year; bright sunlight shone down through the windscreen and onto the passenger seat of my car, where a dozen size three rugby balls created a pile of quite reckless proportions. They were loosely held by the seat belt as I drove through west London on my way to Twickenham for the opening ceremony of the 1991 Rugby World Cup. Every time I braked or turned a corner, the balls would shift forward and threaten to tumble through the car. The fearful prospect of them doing so had reduced me to driving along at the slowest pace possible, trying valiantly not to brake. Anyone who has ever attempted to adopt such a driving manner in London will recognise that it is far from easy.

The 3rd of October 1991. I pulled into the Twickenham car park at last, and opened the boot of my car to unload the cones, shirts and New Zealand drills booklets that filled it. I had a whistle round my neck and 'Run With The Ball', sung by the England players, burst out from the radio. I was about to referee in the opening ceremony.

'The World Cup starts today,' shrieked the disc jockey. 'Come on Ingerland, Come on Ingerland.' Will Carling was on the front of all the newspapers, and details of his love life, his favourite car and his *Desert Island Discs* choices were on the pages inside. The tournament was in the sports sections, the gossip pages and on the nine o'clock news. There was no escaping it. This was the birth of 'sexy rugby' – there was a real buzz across the country about the players – men like Rory Underwood (he's in the RAF you know!), Jon Webb (he's a surgeon!), and Jerry Guscott, Rob Andrew and Will Carling whose images graced the glossy pages of every self-respecting magazine.

'And England are going to win it,' added the disc jockey, forging insight and knowledge about the game. His mounting excitement threatened to burst through the radio and set fire to the car. 'The first ever rugby World Cup. Amazing!' he enthused, as I gathered up the balls. 'Imagine that – the first ever rugby World Cup!'

What had happened to the 1987 tournament? Miraculously erased from people's memories? The 1991 tournament felt like the first World Cup to many in the northern hemisphere because it entered public consciousness in a way that the 1987 tournament never did. It had gone from being a secret from most of the world – tucked away in New Zealand and Australia and unfolding with a quiet simplicity, almost as if it were embarrassed by its very existence, to a major commercial extravaganza.

'Once the RFU accepted that the World Cups were here to stay, they took the view that we'd better prepare for them,' said Don Rutherford. 'They had no choice, really, if you want to compete you have to prepare – so England did. By 1991 they were a vastly improved side. They were Five Nations champions and there was a great feeling about the World Cup.'

The 1991 tournament was the biggest sporting event to take place in Britain since the football World Cup final of 1966. It was big news. Suddenly, television companies were interested, and the moment they were, rugby became a different sport. The BBC had been sole broadcaster of rugby over three decades, and its

1987 contract was worth £1 million, but – one World Cup later – the contract leapt to £7 million and was won by ITV. Twenty-four out of thirty-two matches were screened, making 100 hours of television time (there had been only twenty-eight hours of coverage from the 1987 tournament). The 1991 World Cup was set to make ten times as much as it had in 1987. In four years, commercially speaking, rugby had been transformed – it was seen as being on a different level by advertisers, TV companies and sponsors. It was a magnet for big deals and corporate backing. This all added up to wealth beyond rugby's dreams. Experts anticipated an audience of two billion in sixty-five countries.

As the money men flexed their muscles, so it became clear that some considerable muscle flexing would be required from the players too, if they were to achieve the professional standards that would be needed to justify the commercial backing. Although still amateur as individuals, the players were in the invidious position of participating in a sport that was not amateur in any way, shape or form. The sport was taking vast sums from commercial organisations and television companies. It was a professional sport. The only way the sport had of paying back the investment of millions was with fantastic performances on the pitch from the players and by offering the chance to meet the stars of the game afterwards. Suddenly, the demands on the players were infinitely greater – the time they needed to spend training would be vastly increased, and the impact on their working lives would be more profound.

In addition to this, they had new responsibilities to television companies and sponsors who'd invested ten times more than they'd ever invested before. Such commercial investment and such a hike in television coverage gave the players astonishingly high profiles and further increased their commitments to fans and the print media. Yet, these were men who were trying to hold down full-time jobs. Everyone in the sport except the players was earning money, and leading comfortable lives as a result of the sport, while the players struggled on, trying to work forty-hour weeks, play international rugby, and be the sole justifiers of all the money in the sport.

It is my view that the 1991 World Cup made professionalism inevitable. There were many stepping stones on the route to a fully professional game, but the World Cups, and the 1991 tournament in particular, marked the biggest step forward in the game's history. In fact, rugby became a professional sport in 1991. Rugby was professional in every way other than that it didn't pay its players. Is a sport amateur just because the players aren't paid? What is amateurism? My brother played tennis to a high level when he was younger. He won an amateur tournament, and could only be given a prize priced up to £39.99, because if he earned £40 or more he'd be, officially, a professional. Eh?

Rugby was labouring under a silliness and selfishness that is now hard to comprehend. If the sport as a whole had shunned commerce, slashed ticket prices and organised itself as a small amateur organisation run for and by the fans, then perhaps the players could have been constrained, too. But to have a form of amateurism which allowed the sport to be entirely professional in every way other than the fact that the players couldn't be paid, was simply crazy.

Jonathan Webb was a surgeon, struggling to combine work and rugby.

By 1991 I was a senior house officer. I was working for a guy who was fantastic. It was just me and him and he was terribly supportive. Southmead Hospital got locums to cover for me, and I took unpaid leave. I was away for six weeks and the hospital assumed that the RFU would reimburse me for lost wages. In fact, the RFU stipend equated to about a quarter of my salary. The common room committee [at Southmead Hospital] thought that was outrageous and had a whip-round for me.

A whip-round? For an international rugby player whose image was on the side of the buses sweeping through Twickenham, and who was a star of the multi-million-pound Nike advertising campaign? What an absurd and terribly undignified way in which to treat the players.

One other way in which the World Cup prompted the arrival of professionalism, was in ending the demonisation of the word 'professionalism'. The p-word was formerly hurled around like an insult – a filthy concept associated with greed, avarice and unsportsmanlike behaviour. It was a most unedifying thought – selling one's physical skills, prostituting one's God-given physical talents for a brown envelope containing £20 notes. Yuk. Very un-British. Amateurism was pure; its snow-white fingers stretched back in time to the great gentlemen of the sport who would never have dreamt of taking a penny from the game. In the faded but perfect sepia image of such men was this modern-day sport moulded. But things did change once the World Cups started. I noticed a very real shift in the understanding of the word 'professionalism' in the early 1990s. It had stopped meaning just the dirty, undignified pursuit of money, and had come to mean doing the right preparation, respecting yourself and all others who had worn the national shirt before you. It meant proper behaviour off the field and proper conduct on it.

Amateurs were drunk and aimless, self-indulgent and amusing sideshows to the real event – the professional players worked hard to be the best they could. The professionals were the real deal. What price for a ticket for the England versus Wales quarter-final dirge in Brisbane, compared to the fabulous, breath-taking, heart-stopping semi-final between France and Australia? Our lovely amateurish game was being exposed. Slowly, people began to realise that professionalism didn't have to mean the end of everything held so sacred, professionalism didn't have to mean copying football. Professional rugby could be amateur rugby, only better . . . higher standards, fairer distribution of the wealth in the game, the end of the shambolic committee structure that constrained the sport and the dawning of a bright new future for rugby. I genuinely think that's what professionalism began to represent to more and more people in the 1990s. Professionalism meant the creation of an environment in which players could make the most of themselves and be the best they could.

Sadly, back in 1991, the players could only dream of such an environment. They never got to experience such a thing, but remained nailed to the past by a romantic notion of amateurism held by the powerful elite in rugby. The committee men were becoming increasingly out of touch with the rest of the sport. Their silliness was being exposed but their power was not eroded, so the cat and mouse games started – with the players trying to earn themselves money from the game wherever they could, while the committee folk attempted to catch them out. The period between the first and the third World Cups, taking in the 1991 tournament, was known as 'shamateurism'. It was a sham. It was also a real shame.

The prospect of England players making money from the sport was possibly not at the top of Mike Weston's thoughts as he returned from Australia in 1987, and, still devastated by defeat in the quarter-final, was asked to offer his assessment of England's performance and to indicate why he thought things had gone so badly wrong.

> I submitted a report to the RFU on the World Cup and it high-
> lighted these things – first, it was a watershed for the game –
> several hundred million people watched it and it was a huge
> success. It lit a lot of fires in the game in a lot of countries
> worldwide. It was the start of something big. Second, it was
> clear that there were three distinct groups: the emerging
> nations, the four home unions and the three at the top who
> were much better than the rest . . . including New Zealand.

In their play, their training, and their attitude New Zealand had been more accomplished than any other team at the 1987 World Cup. The Rugby Football Union knew that in order to stop the humiliating defeats like those endured against Wales, they would have to change their approach to the game and become more like the All Blacks. They would do this in two ways – first by working with the national team to make them more like New Zealand – incorporating the fitness work and skills drills of Jim Blair as well as some of the tactical strategies of the World Cup winners. Second, by the realisation that much of New Zealand's success came from the fact that rugby is a huge sport there and all children want to play it. The old mantra used to be: 'Everyone in New Zealand either wants to be an All Black or marry an All Black.'

The RFU made a plan to set up a Youth Development Programme. I was part of that strategy. I began working as a Development Officer for the Rugby Football Union in 1991, stepping out of local newspaper journalism to try working with a governing body in an effort to 'do' something in my early twenties, rather than record the 'doings' of others. I was part of a team of development officers (there were around thirty when I started but this grew to over forty during my three years in the job). We were all appointed to develop and promote the game around the country, as a direct result of the shortcomings identified in the England rugby structure after the 1987 World Cup. We each had a county to look after. Mine was Berkshire.

Our brief was to develop the sport in schools and to encourage children of all ages to try the sport. We ran coaching courses, persuaded teachers to get involved, and linked schools with clubs to ensure there was a really strong playing base in the country.

It was in that role that I found myself at Twickenham for the Opening Ceremony, preparing to referee a youth rugby game. I would become the first woman to referee at Twickenham. Considering that, at the time, there were people at Twickenham who would happily have banned women from the ground, let alone allow them on the hallowed turf clutching a whistle, it was emphasised how hugely flattered I should be by the honour. 'Flattered' does not, if I'm honest, conjure up the emotions one feels when preparing to run out in front of tens of thousands of people wearing a shapeless rugby shirt, large baggy shorts and long thick socks. 'You look like a gay public schoolboy from the 1920s,' declared my friends when they saw my outfit. I'm sure there are worse things to look like, but it's hard to think of too many offhand. Still, however small an achievement in the grand scheme of things – it was nice to be the first woman to referee at Twickenham.

It's very easy to criticise the RFU, and in this book there are dozens of such criticisms, but they got some things right and the development programme of the 1990s was one such thing. It was regarded as the finest programme of its kind in the world. Technical Directors from other sports and other countries would come over to England to see what had been achieved by the RFU. We were forever being heralded as the greatest group of development officers out there. The fact that the sport was amateur but generating a lot of money was one of the reasons for it. If you have a sport where you can sell tens of thousands of seats, bring in a fortune through commerce and TV deals, but don't have to pay the players any of it, you have an extraordinary amount of money to invest in youth activities. As development officers, we had loads of equipment and promotional gear. We had tons of balls that we could leave in schools so that the teachers would carry on developing the sport. Anything we wanted, Twickenham would provide. Thousands and thousands of children play rugby today because of the scheme set up by David Shaw – a man whose commitment and tireless enthusiasm are not forgotten.

There was lots of fun to be had, as a development officer – I remember fighting to convince reluctant, stiletto-heeled teachers (and that was just the men!) what fun it would be to play New Image rugby on concrete in the pouring rain. 'C'mon,' I'd cry, joyfully, dressed in my fetching RFU tracksuit. 'Let's go and learn about rugby.' 'Must we?' they would whisper back, knowing that they were getting involved only because the school had been promised a free rugby ball for every teacher who took part.

The development officer's first job was to battle with the old image of the game – 'No, no, we don't drink aftershave any more. Those days are gone' – while selling rugby's new, wholesome image. 'Touch this ball, my son, and you'll turn into Will Carling.'

To be an effective RDO, you needed to understand the minds of men and children (arguably not too dissimilar) and realise that they can be easily confused. Paul Rendall, the former England prop, joined me for a promotion day to help coach the children during one 'rugby fun day' (that was a disaster – he was far too severe and I had to send him packing to the bar when I found him making ten-year-olds do press-ups every time they dropped the ball). Rendall and I sat before 200 children after the activities and asked if they had any questions. 'Do you still write them books?' asked one child. Rendall looked at her in confusion. I guess there's no more chance of him writing a book than there is of Ruth Rendell playing tight-head prop for England.

One of the key jobs of a development officer was to liaise between the burgeoning youth sections and the established men's teams. I remember having to convince one club that it should have a youth section in the first place. 'Think of the future of the club,' I insisted. They glowered back. 'Well, think of the money, then. You'll get a National Lottery grant.' They perked up a bit. 'When will these kids come?' asked a man known as Dodgy Bob. 'Every Sunday morning,' I replied. 'So, what time do we have to be out of the clubhouse, then? Only, we sometimes drink all night.' We settled on them getting out of the club by 10 a.m. There was mild dissent all round. To be fair, though, those who were still drinking at the bar when the children arrived helped to set things up for the mini rugby groups before staggering off home, so that was nice.

One of the more enjoyable parts of the RDO's job was organising big promotional events. Unfortunately, organisation is not my strong point. I found it hellish to coordinate writing to all the schools, hiring the giant rugby ball for two weeks (it's the size of a car, sits on a trailer and is pulled behind a Land Rover), working out a route to drive the ball through the narrow streets of Berkshire, and arrange radio interviews along the way. Suffice to say that the police were very decent about it when they had to help us lift a three-ton giant ball out of a ditch. We got to most of the schools, and a few unscheduled ones because I had messed up the itinerary. The radio interviews went well, but I did meet some hostility: a woman from Reading rang in. 'Will you tell me where that bloody woman's going next with her bloody ball – whatever radio station I tune in to, she's on there.'

Then there were big 'fun days' which the Rugby Football Union advised us to call 'road shows'. What a mistake that was! Hundreds of children would arrive in their best clothes expecting something like the Radio 1 road show and find me standing there with nothing but a trestle table and a couple of posters of men who hadn't played for England since the 1970s. Sometimes I'd have stickers. Wow! They couldn't have been less impressed. The Radio 1 road show had Kylie Minogue and I had yellow stickers saying 'I love rugby'.

Immediately prior to the 1991 World Cup, there was a 'Run the Ball' campaign whereby a rugby ball started at Rugby School and was passed around the British Isles and France – handled by schoolchildren across the country. The development officers were a major part of the organisation of this, and there were some fantastic ideas spinning around. Will Feebery, the officer for Hampshire and one of the stars of the development programme, suggested that it would be good to plant trees in the counties to (a) have a living reminder of the day the rugby World Cup came to town and (b) because it's always good to plant trees. Perfect idea! I was not yet working as a development officer when the trees were handed out to the counties, but three months after the World Cup, we had a meeting of the Berkshire Rugby Youth Committee.

'I'll have to do something about these trees,' said one of the members. 'They're filling up my garage. The missus is going crazy.'

'Me too,' said the others.

It turned out they'd taken delivery of the trees and no one knew what to do with them, so they stuck them in the garages of the Youth Committee representatives. I'm still not sure what happened to them.

Garry Smith was Chairman of the Berkshire Youth Committee when I was an RDO – a lovely man whom I liked and admired enormously. As my career at the RFU progressed, I came into contact with a lot of the committee men whom Will Carling would later describe as 'old farts'. I thought most of those operating at senior level were a desperate waste of time – labouring under dreadful misapprehensions about their own importance, they were rude and pointless. I am very glad that I met men like Garry Smith along the way – men who were decent, thoughtful, dedicated to the sport and great fun. Smith was a great asset to rugby. If men like him had sat on the leading RFU committees, the sport would have been a better place in the amateur days but, of course, he was too busy doing things and engaging with life to sit on endless weary committees.

Smith was a former military officer, working for the Ministry of Defence, and he had that distinctive military bearing which made people stop and listen to him . . . unless they were under ten. He was enormously helpful throughout my time with the county, and came to many of the events to help. At one 'road show', the children were running around and I needed to get them together. 'Leave it to me,' he yelled, and he shouted out to them in his best sergeant-major voice. Not one child stopped playing. He growled and shouted and was just about to put them into a line manually, when the children's teacher came along. She was about 5 ft 2 and eight stone. She clapped her hands delicately and all the children came running and formed a perfect line in front of her. I've never seen horror such as that etched on Garry Smith's face that day. Bloody children . . . no respect. What a great few years – working right at the heart of the sport, with such wonderful, engaging and delightful people.

The work I was doing in Berkshire and that others like me were doing across the country represented the RFU's commitment to the grass roots of rugby. At the top of the game, things were moving forward at great speed. Once Weston had presented his report and offered his advice, it was announced that he would remain as England team manager. The RFU issued a statement to this effect, and Weston considered what support team he would like. He decided that he wanted Martin Green as selector and Roger Uttley and Alan Davies as coaches, but the RFU would not support his choices because they had their own thoughts about who should be in the coaching team. Weston wasn't happy. So, just five weeks after his appointment was announced, he resigned on principle, and the search began for a replacement. Who would have the necessary skills to take England into this bright and glorious new era? The RFU officials thought and thought, then they came up with . . . Geoff Cooke. Sorry. Geoff who?

'He had no caps!' says Moore. 'We did all think "who?" when he was first appointed, but you only had to meet him or work with him to realise that he was exactly what England needed. In fact, as soon as he came in, things immediately felt better. He had charisma and organisational skills.'

Winterbottom agrees that things improved once Cooke started: 'He changed the whole psyche of the squad. He told us: "The All Blacks are the benchmark, so how are you going to beat them? You're not as skilful as they are and in two or three years' time you still won't be as skilful as they are. But you can be fitter than they are." That gave everybody a focus. Fitness was the way we were quickest to improve.'

'Individually, our fitness and skills improved quickly,' said Rory Underwood. 'But predominantly it was our team identity and ethos that changed. In 1987 we had good players but left a lot to be desired as a team.'

'The man was a revelation,' says Rutherford. 'He was on the same wavelength as us. He was a very good organiser, as was Roger Uttley. So many others would keep secrets to themselves, but if Cooke thought something was good for the team, or had any ideas – he'd happily share them. He just wanted England to be better.'

Cooke started with England in 1988, and would continue with the side until 1994, taking England to two Grand Slams, a World Cup final, and only thirteen defeats in forty-nine Tests.

He just seemed to know what he was doing, and didn't experiment as much [said Underwood]. We felt like we were the players for 1991 and he was working on getting us playing well together, instead of chopping and changing us all the time. We were given a wall chart that outlined the two-year plan which we had to follow if we were to take part in the 1991 World Cup, and it was a constant reminder of how much rugby was eating into our daily existence. The focus of the chart was England's game against New Zealand at Twickenham on 3 October, the opening game of the tournament, and it told us what levels of fitness should be achieved, what peaks we should be hitting, when we could relax training and when we should step it up. Everyone knew what was involved if we were going to do well in the World Cup, let alone win it. The training was hard for amateur players, with daily jobs to sustain, it was a massive commitment of time and effort.

Moore says, 'He [Cooke] took a team that was the laughing stock of everyone round Britain and the world, and helped to make it the team sport of the era where people expected England to win. When Cooke arrived, England were mentally in a mess, a tribute to the years of shocking selection, lack of confidence and failure.'

Under Cooke, England would play with an unchanged side through the Five Nations for the first time for thirty-one years. He was building, consolidating and trying to create a team. To make sure the players' fitness was right, he brought in Rex Hazeldine, a lecturer at Loughborough University's Department of PE and sports science. Through him, fitness checks were built into the rolling programme. 'I received a daunting memo in June just before one tour which said "your body fat has increased to 13.6 per cent and although it is still within the range of 12–15 per cent, you need to carefully watch your diet (high carb, low fat) and with the increased training over the next two months, this value will come down again",' said Underwood.

They were being coached, monitored, tested and advised. They received feedback and encouragement. They were treated like professionals.

Geoff had faith in his own ability, a rare commodity in the England set-up [recalls Will Carling, the man who would work closely with the England coach]. He lost his two first games in charge but refused to change tack. He also inherited many of the players who had under-performed with England in the mid-1980s ... It was only under his influence that they grew

into formidable rugby men. He believed in stability and organisation to build confidence, and he gave players time to
develop and the permission to fail. The trick is to make the best
of available resources and Geoff did that.

Cooke, at the time of his selection as England coach, was
working as a selector for the North (one of the divisional teams
operating in the late 1980s). Before the first World Cup, and several years before he became England coach, in his capacity as
selector, Cooke had gone to watch Durham v Lancashire in the
County Championships. While he was there, he saw Carling play
an absolute stormer of a game. Arguably, no player in the history
of the sport played a more important game for his county – it
would rocket Carling to the divisional game, then the international game and to become the youngest England captain in
history.

Cooke was so impressed with Carling on that occasion that he
selected him to play for the North division. North won the title
that year and Cooke recommended Carling to the England selectors as someone who could be taken to the 1987 World Cup.
Weston told Cooke that Carling needed to play club rugby to
have a chance of playing internationally. He advised Carling to
give Harlequins a try. So, for the rest of the year, Carling made the
250-mile round trip to west London. It meant he had to catch the
midday train from Durham, travel on the underground to pick
his mum's car up, drive across London to reach Harlequins by
7 p.m., train, grab a bite to eat and then do the whole process in
reverse, arriving back in Durham around 2 a.m. the following
morning. He did this three times a week. He never made it into
the 1987 World Cup squad, and says the reason he was given was
that he was too exhausted!

It's instructive to remember the pains that Carling went to in
order to make it as an international player. One tends to think of
him as having been gifted the England captaincy as some sort of
rite of passage after public school, university and army training –
one of those people in life who just glides through without so
much as a drop of sweat. Such people are myths. Scratch the

surface of any real achiever, however nonchalant they appear, and however much assistance and good fortune they have had on the way, and years of striving, heartache, determination and commitment bleed.

When Cooke was appointed England manager, he had his chance to play Carling – the man whose skills and personality he had become convinced were suited to top-flight rugby. Indeed, it is a measure of Cooke's respect for Carling that in his first match in charge – against France at the Parc des Princes in January 1988 – he gave Carling his debut. England lost 9–10 but it was the start of a beautiful partnership. England lost to Wales, then Scotland, then won three consecutive matches for the first time in eight years and the consensus was that Cooke was on the right track.

Ten months after that first match, Cooke made Carling the youngest captain in English rugby history. The centre was told that he was part of a long-term plan up to the 1991 World Cup. Cooke said that he would be there to support Carling. The new England captain described it as 'bizarre'.

The captaincy, while hugely flattering, made life difficult for Carling. He describes himself as being 'utterly terrified'. He was scared of what his teammates would think, then scared of whether he would actually be able to do the job. Nevertheless, with Cooke's advice, he developed a style of captaincy that suited him. He had a routine of ringing round the players regularly – trying to listen and find out about their lives to make sure he knew as much as possible about the people behind the players.

Some players offered him an astonishing amount of assistance. 'Without the help and advice of Rob Andrew,' says Carling, 'I wouldn't have lasted two minutes in the job.' It speaks volumes for the decency and sophistication of Andrew that he helped Carling come to terms with his new responsibilities, especially since Andrew himself must have been on the short list for the role and would have every right to feel aggrieved that the youngster had been given the title instead of him.

Carling's management style didn't always resonate with all the players. In the last Five Nations tournament before the 1991

World Cup, as England went for the Grand Slam with a match against France, he put handwritten notes under the doors of the players' rooms at the Petersham Hotel. 'Dean Richards probably still hasn't read his,' says Carling, years later.

But Carling was a hugely popular figure for the media and for those outside the sport. By the age of twenty-two, he had been in just about every magazine and newspaper in the world, and was driving round in a top of the range Mercedes. He had set up his own company called Insights, was invited to film premieres and mixed with the rich and famous. He appeared to be hugely confident, but he says he was always questioning himself, wondering whether he could do better. It had all happened so quickly. He had gone from divisional player to captain within a year, and he was still adjusting to the transformation. 'I have a clear memory of sitting on a train with Andrew and Kevin Simms and thinking, "I'm on a train with two England players, I hope someone sees me",' he said. Within a year, he was captain of his country.

Carling's first game as captain saw him lead England to a 28–19 victory over Australia at Twickenham (England's highest ever score against the Australians). Then, he led the team to victory over France in the Five Nations in England's first victory over them for seven years. England became favourites to win the 1989 Five Nations. 'To me, that day against France, when we won 11–0, was another of the little watersheds. We stuffed them up front, we shut them out, we never gave Blanco and their backs a chance. We scored a forwards' try when a steaming run from Richards put Andy Robinson over,' said Moore.

In the euphoria of that victory over the side that had finished in second place in the 1987 World Cup, England had no idea that they would reel off seven successive victories over France, ending when they lost the World Cup play-off against France in 1995.

A year before the 1991 World Cup, England were runaway favourites to win the 1990 Five Nations, even though they had to go to Paris and Murrayfield. 'There was a genuine relish and anticipation about being an English player,' says Winterbottom.

They thrashed Wales at Twickenham and swaggered up to

Murrayfield, to play a bit of rugby and collect the trophy. England were going to win the Grand Slam for the first time since 1980. Moore remembers them all smiling and signing autographs on the Friday and even on Saturday morning before the game. Some people were asking when the champagne would be delivered. They lost 13–7.

'It was horrific,' says Moore.

'We were devastated,' says Richard Hill, the scrum half.

Ultimately, though, that defeat worked against Scotland. For a couple of years, just the mention of Murrayfield 1990 was enough to stiffen sinews and resolve in the England players. The losses stay with a player far longer than the victories do. During Carling's tenure as captain, England never lost to Scotland again. As Jim Telfer, Scotland's coach, said: 'This could be one of the biggest mistakes ever made by a Scotland team. The England lads who played today will probably never forget the experience.' Carling used it as a rallying cry for years: 'England's history has been forged on the back of that result. Never forget that.'

England toured Argentina in 1990, and proved that the sport was still flushed with the spirit of amateurism as a players' court was convened after the Test, with Mark Linnett as the Judge. Bob Kimmins, whose wife had given birth during the tour, was ordered to drink three bottles of champagne, one of which went down in fifteen seconds.

One evening, Victor Ubogu and Chris Oti came back to the hotel saying they'd found a great bar that they thought the other players would love. 'Full of women – really friendly women,' they enthused. A squad outing was arranged for the next night, and it was blindingly obvious to all except Oti and Ubogu that it was a brothel. 'But they're so nice and friendly,' cried Ubogu as he was dragged out of the place. 'Yes, and expensive,' chorused the others.

One day on tour, Roger Uttley held a session and instructed the six dirt trackers (the second-string players) to run back from training to the hotel, so the six set off while the rest climbed aboard the bus. After a few minutes, the bus passed five of the runners, then it passed Skinner who was hailing a cab. When the bus arrived back at the hotel, the players got off and waited. Then, the cab that Skinner had got into pulled up, but it looked like there was no one in it. It inched up slowly, and the players realised that Skinner was lying on the floor. Luckily, the coaches didn't realise what was happening as the cab went round to the other side of the hotel so Skinner could get out unseen. The England flanker almost got away with the whole thing until he realised that he didn't have any money, so had to borrow some from Uttley.

While the players had their fun, the coaches – Cooke and Uttley – looked for the positive aspects from 1990, building on the fact that they had scored ninety points, more than any other team in the history of the championships. Their big aim, in trying to win the Grand Slam in 1991, was to get a win against Wales. England had not won at Cardiff Arms Park since 1963. It could not possibly be the case that England had a worse team than Wales on every occasion that they had played them since 1963; the reason they were losing must be to do with their psychological approach.

The thinking, planning and strategising seemed to be 100 per cent targeted on winning in Wales, and overcoming the 'Cardiff Arms Park voodoo'. Cooke organised the playing of the Welsh national anthem over the loudspeaker system at Kingsholm during the team's training sessions, to try and desensitise the players. It was still playing on the coach as they drove from Gloucester to Cardiff. They didn't stay in their usual place (the St Pierre Golf and Country Club near the Severn Bridge), but in the middle of Cardiff so they were subjected to all the bustle and aggression of Cardiff immediately. They even walked the 150 yards to the ground from the hotel so they became used to the crowds and the noise, the passion and the colour. Jerry Guscott recalls that the whole thing worked incredibly well, and that they became so desensitised to the Welsh national anthem that, by the time it came on as the teams were lined up on the pitch, he was heard to say: 'Christ, not again' . They won 25–6.

After the game, they refused to talk to the media or go to the press conference because of the RFU's continuing insistence that players couldn't make any money out of the sport despite the International Rugby Board having lifted a ban on certain forms of commercial activity in November 1990. The players wanted the BBC to pay the players for post-match interviews. The RFU said this would not be possible and the players saw red.

England's next game was against Scotland. They won 21–12. In Dublin they beat Ireland 16–7 and won their first Triple Crown since 1980. Then, to Twickenham to play France for the Grand Slam in what Moore describes as 'one of the most hyped matches ever'. England won 21–19. A Grand Slam at last.

It was all looking very good for the 1991 World Cup, and England were feeling like world-beaters . . . until, in the summer before the tournament, they visited Australia and Fiji on a seven-match tour, with a Test in each country, and lost four times. Cooke was worried. It was fine to be the best in Europe, but they clearly needed a different strategy if they were going to beat the super-powers. While the manager and his coaching team pondered what that strategy might be, the players opted for a different solu-tion, by setting up an impromptu band, and singing very loudly, and very badly, through the night. The hotel manager had heard enough of these drunken would-be rock stars, and roused Cooke who'd gone to bed hours earlier. Olver bawled 'Hello Wembley' in his best rock-star voice, as Cooke came striding across the lawns towards him. 'Fair play to you, Geoff,' shouted Nigel Redman. 'Still up with the boys at this time of night.'

It was all jolly good fun, but it was wearing a bit thin with the management who were working extremely hard to turn England's fortunes around. England lost 40–15 to Australia, con-ceding five tries. Cooke noted how the England backs played exceptionally well, but the forwards had rather let them down. Was there a strategy in this, somewhere? Should they play a backs-dominated game against Australia? A team meeting was held to discuss the findings from the tour, and it was agreed that, next time they faced Australia, this is exactly what they would do.

In Wales, little real improvement had taken place between the 1987 and 1991 World Cups. Indeed, it was a very difficult time for

Welsh rugby. The 1987 tournament had seen the end to a number of Welsh rugby union careers, and those who did not hang up their boots considered joining the newly moneyed rugby league clubs in the north of England. This saw a record number of top players move into the professional game in the late 1980s (sixteen first-class players, thirteen of them internationals, had moved to league by the time the 1991 World Cup came round). So Wales were left with a vastly depleted team. Added to this was the fact that there was a distinct lack of urgency at the WRU because Wales had done so 'well' at the first World Cup. England's disastrous showing had prompted massive changes, while Wales' 'success' had persuaded them that nothing needed changing.

> It all went wrong for Wales when they finished third in the 1987 World Cup because then everyone in Wales thought that everything was okay and didn't need to be invested in or worked on [said Paul Thorburn].
>
> In reality, they had only just come third in 1987 – they scraped past Ireland 13–6, beat Tonga 29–16 and overcame Canada 40–9 to reach the quarter-finals. They beat a lacklustre England who played very badly.
>
> In the third-place play-off they met a disgruntled Australia who had seriously expected to be in the final, and they had a one-man advantage for most of the match after David Codey was sent off for stamping, but won by just one point.

After the 1987 World Cup, Wales won the triple crown in the 1987/88 season, further convincing the Welsh authorities that the team was in good order, indeed flourishing on the European stage. Like England, they came unstuck when they attempted to leave Europe. They went on a suicidal two-Test tour to New Zealand. It was ill-conceived, and did immeasurable damage to the Welsh game. Two fifty-point defeats were hard enough to swallow but to lose three provincial matches was a disaster. The tour left Welsh rugby in tatters and caused the Welsh rugby union general committee to get rid of coaches Tony Gray and Derek Quinnell. John Ryan, the former Newport and Cardiff coach was recognised as the best club coach in the business, so was appointed, but not even he could halt the decline in international results. As he attempted a change of style, advocating a more set-piece-orientated approach, so the defeats continued. Players came and went as he tried to find a winning combination. After a 28–6 opening triumph over Western Samoa in 1988, his men lost their next four games, including a 15–9 home defeat to Romania. A 12–9 home win against England in the 1989 Five Nations series brought Ryan a brief reprieve, but it was the second and last win of his nine-match reign as coach and, in the next three games, Wales went down 34–9 to the All Blacks, 29–19 to France and a record 34–6 to England at Twickenham. The latter was Wales' heaviest defeat by England and their worst showing in the Five Nations championships. Ryan quickly decided enough was enough, and stepped down to allow a new man to build up to the 1991 World Cup. Ron Waldron came in and did his best but the truth is that Wales were in disarray, with three national coaches having passed through the team in the preceeding two years. In July Ron Waldron was replaced by Alan Davies only weeks before the 1991 World Cup. No one seemed to have a clue what was going on. Their preparation could not have been more different to that being enjoyed by England. It points, perhaps, to an interesting trait – this 'if it ain't broke, don't fix it' feeling that runs through British society is terribly corrosive because it means things have to keep going wrong before you have any chance of going forwards. England's disaster in 1987 prompted wholesale changes and a fresh new look for 1991. Success in 1987 meant that no sweeping changes were made to the Wales team.

Since Ireland's return from the 1987 World Cup, they had struggled to find any sort of form. They conceded thirty-five points at Twickenham in 1988, and another twenty-three in 1990. It looked as if they would drop off the bottom of the European table. A real gap had opened up between them and England. Then, in 1991, although they still didn't win a game, there were sure signs of a resurgence. They drew against Wales and lost their other matches by the slightest of margins. They also scored ten tries and sported an outstanding back line, including a 21-year-old wing called Simon Geoghegan who scored in three of the four matches.

The problem remained, though, that – as close as they came – Ireland still didn't win anything. They hadn't developed a winning habit. They were also unpredictable – their play swinging from really quite decent to nowhere near good enough.

Scotland had been through a more cheery time since the 1987 tournament, largely orchestrated by Ian McGeechan who became coach of Scotland in 1988, at the same time as Cooke in England. Along with forwards coach Jim Telfer, he led the revival of Scottish rugby that culminated in the Grand Slam of 1990. He also coached the Lions on their highly successful tour to Australia in 1989.

Scotland also managed some near success outside the Five Nations, when they followed up their Grand Slam with a tour to New Zealand and came close to beating the All Blacks in the second Test. For the first time on a major tour, Scotland did not lose a non-international match.

But it was not all plain sailing, and there were a few unsettling results for the Scots, including a 24–18 defeat by Canada, and an 18–12 defeat by Romania. The defeat to Romania was a particularly difficult one for Scotland, given that Romania was going through extraordinary difficulties at the time and was in the clutches of a bloody revolution.

7

The second tournament arrives

An enslaved nation could never play free-flowing, adventurous rugby. Forty-five years of communism rule mutilated the soul of Romanian rugby.

A Romanian journalist when asked why the fly-half in the Romania team kicked all the time

The period between the 1987 and 1991 World Cups was one of great change in most of the world's rugby-playing countries, but nowhere more so than in Romania, where events far away from the rugby pitch were having a huge impact on society and, ultimately, on the sport.

Romania is a country with a long history in rugby, and is one of the three teams that competed in the 1924 Olympic Games in Paris (France and USA were the other two). For the period between the World Cups, it was in the grips of a bloody revolution. The 1989 toppling of the Ceauçescu regime left the country in a state of virtual bankruptcy. All areas of life in the country suffered. The feeding and housing of a desperate people was a priority. Rugby was clearly a matter of little concern in this context, and it suffered in many ways, not least because so many leading players were killed in the uprisings. One such player was Florica Murariu, a flanker and former captain of Romania and a man who had been present at some of Romania's greatest victories. He was shot a year after he had captained Romania to a famous 15–9 victory over Wales in Cardiff – killed by a young soldier who fired indiscriminately in a panic at a roadblock and hit the rugby player, also an army officer, killing him outright.

Considering what the country was going through, it is astonishing that Romania qualified for the 1991 World Cup, astonishing, even, that they remembered a World Cup was taking place.

'It was important, though,' says Raduta Laurentiu, a Romanian journalist, 'to try and make things normal again after what everyone had been through. Yes, it was a time of great hardship, but to cut sports out of the picture, and to isolate ourselves from the wider sporting world would have made life more difficult still. I think sport can play a role in reunification of a society after great trauma.'

Romania's coach in 1991 was Ross Cooper, a New Zealander, who had begun to coach the side in 1990, just a year after the revolution. Cooper had originally acted as Technical Adviser to the Romanians during their U-19s trip to New Zealand and had been astonished at how outdated the training methods of the Romanians were. 'They had just one ball with them and no other equipment,' he said. 'They worked hard, but they had nothing.'

Cooper realised how little they must have when he saw the reaction of the Romanian players in New Zealand. They had admired the lush green grass, and marvelled at the access to basics like bread and milk without queueing, and displayed an extraordinary reaction when Cooper tried to collect their passports to keep them all together in the hotel. Christian Stan, the hooker, thought his passport was being taken off him because he had not played well. He started shouting that it was an infringement of his democratic rights, so they let him keep hold of it. Whenever the players heard police, ambulance or fire sirens, they would become unnerved because it brought back memories of the revolution.

The manager of the Romania team approached Cooper and asked him to work with the team. 'The players were very different from other players I'd worked with,' said Cooper. 'They'd come from so little, they were grateful for everything. Throughout the tour, they received the daily allowance of approximately $30 approved by the IRB and I never saw one player spend so much as a dollar. They saved every cent ever paid to them and took it home. I knew that I could work with players who had such self-discipline, and I found myself wanting to help them.'

Cooper went to Romania, and what greeted him was amazing. He recalls the first World Cup school he attended, based at Constantia, on the Black Sea. His hotel bathroom had no shower and there was no plug in the bath. When he mentioned this to the hotel management they shrugged and advised him to wedge his heel into the plug hole. He asked the players and they, too, merely pointed to their heels and said that they all bathed by jamming their heels to prevent the water leaking away. Cooper found he had to retire early because there were no light bulbs in his room, and when he woke up, it was to a breakfast that consisted of green salami and a weak cheese that he never managed to identify.

On the training pitch, Cooper started by working with the forwards – upping their intensity and commitment. When he moved on to the backs, he found 'all their flair had been suppressed'. The process of coaching the team was laborious, with Petre Ianusievici having to translate all Cooper's skill drills from English into Romanian, with all appropriate diagrams, before they could start. Ianusievici attempted to photocopy them for all squad members, but there was not enough paper and when he went to buy some, he found there was no more left in Constantia.

Cooper managed, somehow, to communicate the coaching drills, and the team worked hard in the months leading up to the tournament, then, at the end of September 1991, they prepared for departure. But, just as they were about to leave, there was an uprising by the country's disenfranchised miners who were marching on Bucharest to present their case. With a military escort, and in scenes reminiscent of Fiji in 1987, the team made it to the airport and flew out of the country bound for the 1991

World Cup about twelve hours before the miners reached the city.

The Romanian players arrived in London before flying out to France where they would be based. There they joined fellow Pool 4 teams: France, Canada and Fiji.

After the dramas of the 1987 World Cup, things were a little smoother for Fiji in 1991. Indeed their biggest problem was how they would cope with the cold weather in France for the duration of the tournament. They prepared themselves by conducting a short tour of New Zealand's south island before leaving for France.

Canada had worked hard since 1987 to provide players with regular access to first-class opposition in preparation for the 1991 tournament. They had a new coach after the first World Cup, with Ian Birtwell coming in for Gary Johnston in the autumn of 1989, and the sport in the country appeared to be thriving, with over 12,000 players on Canada's books across all the provinces, and with an annual budget of more than Canadian $900,000 managed by the CRU's professional staff in Ottawa. In 1991, rugby came under the federal government's Sport Canada ministry and thus benefited from annual funding of about $250,000. Commercial sponsors added another $100,000.

In Pool 3 was Argentina, a country struggling to cope in the modern game because of their refusal to make any sort of concessions towards professionalism. They remained very strictly amateur while many governing bodies allowed players to make some money on the fringes of their involvement in the game. Argentina's stance meant there was an exodus of players to European clubs, and as soon as players left, they were excluded from the national squad. Effectively, Argentina were banning many of their best players from running out for the national team.

Another country passionate about rugby – Zimbabwe – qualified by right in 1991 after being offered a place in 1987, and was in Pool 2 with Japan, Ireland and Scotland.

Rugby in Zimbabwe has a long history – it began in the late nineteenth century when the country was known as Rhodesia. The first match was played in 1890 on the dry-sand bed of the

River Shashi on Rhodesia's border with Botswana. Rugby in Zimbabwe is hard – the vast distances between cities and the sparse population together with lack of organised transport create terrible problems in coordinating a rugby team. At the turn of the century it was worse – a rail link from the south of the country did not reach Harare until 1901, so players had to travel for three weeks to cover the 600-mile distance for a game in the capital.

Zimbabwe had been working hard to reassert itself as a major player since the country gained independence in 1980, when it also lost so much assistance from South Africa. In its day, Rhodesia was one of the most feared teams in the Currie Cup but after 1980, the standard plummeted.

Zimbabwe knew that developing black youngsters was vital for the future of the game (in 1980, the game was played in about 170 schools across the country and approximately 85 per cent of the 10,000 participants were black youngsters), so they launched an ambitious development programme after the first World Cup. Former Moseley regular Colin Osborne was technical director for the 1987 development initiative and the man behind a real regeneration in the sport. Before long, rugby became the fastest-growing sport in the country. Then, of course, they needed more people to coach the youngsters.

A shortage of qualified rugby coaches is the main problem confronting Zimbabwe rugby [said David Shepherd, chair of Mashonaland Union]. The success of the game in schools has taken us somewhat by surprise. In 1987 they started to develop the game in high-density areas for black people, and became victims of their own success, with rugby developing a very high profile and the sport starting to provide black people with a well-organised and disciplined set-up. They introduced mini rugby and pushed the game at senior school level. There was a sudden surge in popularity. We need to capitalise on that now.

Joining them in the group was Japan who were utterly delighted to qualify for the 1991 tournament. Television screens were erected in railway stations and other public places across Japan. In 1991, there were 3000 clubs (including schools) playing rugby, and more than 80,000 players. Many more were eager to play the game, but there were insufficient available playing fields.

In Pool 1, with England, were New Zealand, Italy and USA. Rugby in the United States exists without government funding or significant gate receipts. The budget for 1990 was US$382,000, of which sponsorship provided US$290,000. It is thought that there were around 260,000 people involved in the sport in USA, but the fact that they were spread around 1311 clubs covering the vast country, indicates how difficult it was for them to get the team together for training and development sessions. Despite the size of the country, and the fact that their women's side was the best in the world, the game had not gripped the heart, mind or soul of the average American male, and the team remained very much outsiders in rugby – one of the sport's 'minnows' if that term can be applied to a country as vastly populated and commercially resplendent as the United States of America.

There is no doubt that, in 1991, the key contenders were the British and Irish sides and France, the joint hosts of the tournament, and Australia and New Zealand. Much had changed since 1987 – but not that much.

For New Zealand, the inaugural World Cup had been a resounding success on so many levels – rugby had been given a kick start in the country after the dismal period leading up to 1987, when the Cavaliers' trip to South Africa cast such a shadow over the game. New Zealand had proven themselves champions by such a considerable margin in 1987 (no team could get within ten points of them) that they became the last word in how to win at rugby – their lessons, thoughts, plans and playing styles were copied around the world. The pendulum of success, though, has a nasty habit of clocking all great teams on its backswing – pressuring them to repeat the triumph and discouraging change and forward momentum.

Winning after winning is a difficult thing to do, but it did seem as though the New Zealand team of the late 1980s would manage it. After their defeat at the hands of France in 1986, in Nantes, before the first World Cup, they did not lose again through the World Cup, and for the following three years – a staggering fifty matches unbeaten until Australia beat them in 1990. They had performed with astonishing consistency, but even before their defeat by Australia, doubts were being expressed about the team's ability.

It was almost as if by winning they were avoiding the real truth of the fact that they were no longer the force they once were. Again, that horrible trait of 'if it ain't broke, don't fix it' was raising its ugly head and, though the All Blacks were in decline, while they kept winning, nothing would be done.

Bob Stuart, a former Test captain, watched the All Blacks' 1989 clash with the Barbarians at Twickenham and declared that there were flaws developing in the All Blacks' system. The succession of victories, it seemed, was papering over the cracks.

By the time of the defeat to Australia in 1990, opposition sides had worked out how to beat New Zealand, and changes were needed. But, it seemed, there was a reluctance from the management to make the wholesale changes that were deemed necessary. New talent needed to be brought in across the pitch, but the only change that was made was to drop Wayne Shelford, the captain, much to the horror and dismay of the New Zealand public who adored their gritty and uncompromising leader.

Added to all this, was the simple fact of the enormous friction that existed between Alex Wyllie and John Hart who had been jointly selected to coach the New Zealand team without Lochore, the man who had been in charge in 1987. 'It was madness, utter madness,' said Bob Dwyer, the Australia coach, with a small chuckle. 'Employing two people who did not get on, and telling them to coach the New Zealand team jointly was an insane thing to do . . . It made my job a lot easier though.' Wyllie had been coach for most of the fifty victories (forty-six of them), but suddenly he found himself with a co-coach, entirely against his will.

There were many incidents when the two men found themselves at loggerheads with one another. One such incident concerned Mike Brewer who was told that because he wouldn't remove the strapping from under his foot to undertake a particular fitness test, he would not be able to participate in the World Cup. 'He was a vital member of the squad and should have made the trip,' said Wyllie. As New Zealand was playing the opening fixture of the World Cup against England, Brewer was captaining Otago in an NPC championship match in Carisbrook. 'That was the moment when I realised just how absurd all this had become,' said Wyllie. Wyllie and Hart's lack of strong confident leadership because of the enduring power struggle between them for the duration of the tournament contrasted massively with the situation in Australia, where Dwyer had exerted real control and had formed his players into the best team they could possibly be.

Bob Dwyer became coach of Australia when the team returned from the 1987 World Cup in fourth place. Their lowly finishing position had produced bitterness and controversy in Australia, so Alan Jones, the voluble, demanding coach, was sacked in favour of Dwyer (the man whom Jones had replaced four years earlier), and pressure was on him to succeed in the 1991 tournament. Dwyer was undoubtedly helped by the fact that the Australian Institute of Sport had begun admitting rugby players soon after the 1987 World Cup, and acted as a substantial support and back-up service to him and his coaching team – assisting with talent identification and the development of gifted players, as well as giving the coaches access to a raft of experts. Nutritionists, bio-mechanics, psychologists and physiologists were suddenly on hand. With such a resource at their disposal, a new coach and a group of talented players, including the 'Holy Trinity' of Nick Farr-Jones at scrum-half, David Campese on the wing and Michael Lynagh, the goal-kicking machine, at fly-half, Australia were expecting to do well in 1991.

In fact so competitive were they, that it is easy to forget that there were only 36,500 senior players in Australia at the time, in a competitive structure focused chiefly on the Sydney and Brisbane club championships, and the growing Canberra premiership, and that rugby league was a real threat.

Brian Smith says:

In 1991, I'd just finished a three-year degree at Oxford and had to wait six months for the World Cup. I had no money, I sold my car. I needed a job, needed some cash. I was offered a rugby league contract back in Australia and I took that opportunity. Rugby league was the game in Australia and the Winfield Cup was the ultimate test ... The likes of Brett Papworth, Matt Burke, Scott Gourley and myself all played rugby league professionally. It was the way things were back then; people either went to rugby league or they got a proper job.

'We never let that affect us too much,' says Dwyer. 'I worked hard with the players I had, and made them the best I could; if guys left for league, they left for league. I couldn't control that.'

8

The pool games

What was wrong with rugby in the post-war period when we
had far more resources and players than any other country and
far, far less success?

Brian Moore

The coach wound its way from the England team's rural
Hampshire base – through narrow lanes, along tree-lined
streets and out towards the motorway. People stopped, stared
and cheered as the coach passed – waving at the players inside.
On the coach, no one spoke. Through the heavy traffic it went,
heading for Twickenham stadium as police outriders guided it
in through the throngs of fans who had gathered by the roadside
to lend their support. Still no word on the coach – just silence.
The journey from the hotel to the ground for the opening game
of the 1991 World Cup was conducted without the England
players uttering a word. They stared at the floor, looked aim-
lessly out of the window but didn't speak. 'It was odd,' says
Jason Leonard. 'There's usually a lot of noise on the way to
matches. This was different.' The players recall the silence as a
heavy presence, sitting among them. Why? Were they mentally
rehearsing? Getting themselves in the right psychological state
for the match ahead? Will Carling thinks not. 'We were turning
the New Zealand team into monsters from another planet in our

heads,' says the England captain. The heavy silence was the result of nerves.

The first game of the 1991 World Cup was huge for England – against the reigning world champions, and to be played at Twickenham where they hadn't lost since 1988. Every player knew how important a victory was, and how good their opponents were because, for the previous four years, their ears had been filled with talk of the great New Zealand team and how they must try to emulate them in all possible ways. Now they faced a crucial game against them. If they lost, they would face a likely quarter-final against France who were sure to top Pool four (also containing Canada, Romania and Fiji). If they won, they would face the runner-up in that pool – a vastly easier draw. But, after years of idolising the All Blacks from afar, how were they supposed to be in the right psychological state to beat them?

'The silence was worrying. It's never quiet on the bus to matches,' says Underwood. 'I suppose we were all feeling the pressure. We all knew this was a big game and were quite nervous about it, and nervous about what New Zealand would throw at us. Looking back, it wasn't a good sign at all.'

The extraordinary respect afforded New Zealand, and the premature assumptions about their greatness, cost England the first game of the 1991 World Cup before they ran on to the pitch. They lost the match 18–12, opening the tournament less than gloriously. It was a match littered with twenty-seven penalties. England's anxiety showed throughout. Passes were mis-timed, moves went unfinished and possession was lost. Wyllie, New Zealand's coach, described it as being a classic 'game that opens a tour' – just all about his team getting a win under the belt. He seemed happy to have the victory, but it was clear that New Zealand were not the impressive force that everyone had expected to see.

For England, the previous four years had been spent chasing the New Zealand dream and mentally building the All Blacks into an unbeatable force. England tried to be like them, play like them, train like them and win like them. And all without any contact with them. England had not played New Zealand since before the 1987 World Cup. Insane? Absolutely. The lack of contact combined with the constant reference to New Zealand skills drills and the brilliance of the All Blacks had led to the deification of New Zealand rugby. The players had been turned into a combined mystical, mythical force – a flash of black lightning, a superteam to be looked up to and respected. For many of the players in the England team, the opening game of the 1991 World Cup was the first time they had ever played against the All Blacks. 'We treated them like gods,' recalled Carling. 'We had their greatness rammed into us over and over again, and that they were an awesome winning machine. We had countless videos of their training to illustrate tackling, mauling, rucking and commitment over a long period of time, and it did condition us to thinking that we were going to come up against this mighty machine which was unbeatable.'

I agree entirely with the former captain's assessment.

When I began working with the RFU in the early 1990s, the first document I was given was the New Zealand *Skills Drills* book. It was considered the ultimate in modern rugby thinking. So, we went on our merry way – teaching the drills and practices to junior schoolchildren and delighting in the fact that we were just like the New Zealanders. There was a certain prestige even in copying them. Coaches would proudly announce that these drills came straight from New Zealand. They even had names like 'Auckland grids'. In effect, we were force-feeding children with the idea that New Zealand was an utterly superior side. Psychologically – it was a ridiculous thing to do. Why not nick the best bits of the drills package, rename them – the Guscott Grid, the Carling Catching Game and mix them with the best thinking from this country? Why copy everything that New Zealand did so inanely as if English coaches had no ideas of their own? Was it any wonder that England never caught up, let alone overtook, if they were forever fighting to sit in the New Zealand slipstream?

It was as if English coaches were producing cover records of every New Zealand hit. In music, some cover records are perfectly acceptable versions of the original, but rarely are they as good. The worst cover records are those which are just direct copies of the original – with none of the artiste's personality on show. That's not producing a cover version of a record – that's karaoke. So much of the coaching that was going on in England at the time was karaoke coaching, and by doing it, England were giving the southern hemisphere sides a twenty-point advantage.

> Something which people don't always understand about rugby [says Martin Johnson]. It's not that you're going out there thinking 'we can't win against this team' – it's more subtle than that. It's that you associate the southern hemisphere countries with difficult games which puts you at a disadvantage because you don't really expect to win them. I watched the old rerun of past England v New Zealand games the other day and kept thinking that England were much better than I remembered them being. I watched that match and thought – I wish they'd have realised back then how good they were. If they'd realised that – they might have won.

For England, losing to New Zealand was deeply disappointing. Their defeat subjected them to a second-place finish at best, and New Zealand hadn't even been the overwhelming power of the players' darkest nightmares. England left Twickenham and headed back to their hotel – Tylney Hall Hotel in a beautiful location outside Basingstoke. 'In some ways it was just a relief to get that opening game out of the way,' said Moore. 'We lost it, but at least it was over and we could concentrate on planning for the French.' Back at the hotel, Jon Webb continued the bad luck by playing golf and smashing a ball through the window of a car in the car park.

England and New Zealand were in Pool 1 with USA and Italy. After their opening victory over England, the All Blacks went on to beat USA 46–6 in Gloucestershire but, again, it was not the demolition that so many people had confidently predicted. They beat Italy to be the clear winners in the group but Dwyer,

Australia's coach, admits that he smiled to himself on more than one occasion as the pool stages unfolded and he became increasingly confident that his players 'could take the New Zealanders with ease'. England finished in second place, and prepared to play France in the quarter-final.

North of the border were the Pool 2 teams – Scotland, Japan, Ireland and Zimbabwe. Everyone expected Scotland and Ireland to qualify without any problem, but the two minnows in the group were not to be discounted. Japan had beaten Scotland 28–24 in Tokyo two years previously and Zimbabwe had such a strong history that no one wanted to completely overlook them.

In the end, though, neither Japan nor Zimbabwe could halt the progress of Scotland and Ireland, as Scotland beat Japan 47–9, and defeated Zimbabwe 51–12 and Ireland beat Japan 32–16 despite some lovely running, good handling and three tries from the Japanese, then they beat Zimbabwe 55–11.

Scotland finished top of the pool after beating Ireland, and in doing so won a place in the quarter-final. Ireland faced a quarter-final against Australia in Dublin.

Pool 4 was played in France, between France, Romania, Fiji and Canada, with the hosts making a positive start with a 30–3 victory over Romania in Béziers. Despite the victory, though, it was an incredibly error-strewn game, and did little to convince that France were a serious contender for the Webb-Ellis trophy. Looking equally unconvincing were Fiji, who so many had hoped would regain their form in this World Cup after their joyful performances in 1987. They lost 13–3 to Canada, with neither team playing well. 'Not a great game,' said Rees, afterwards. 'And it wasn't made any easier by the fact that we weren't supposed to be drinking, so didn't have a beer which was probably the first time ever. Dismal stuff!'

Serge Blanco did his bit for the image of his country by smoking before every game, and appearing in a tracksuit and trainers instead of adopting the smart French outfit worn by the other players.

France finished comfortable winners of the group, with Canada qualifying in second place after a 13–3 victory over Fiji and a 19–11 win over Romania. Romania beat Fiji 17–15 and France beat Canada 19–13. So far there had been few surprises in the tournament.

But that was before the matches in Pool 3 . . .

9

Western what? The story of Western Samoa

We all stood in the lovely setting of Cardiff Castle, in our Western Samoa tracksuits, looking miserable. It was the day before the match against Wales and we started to tell each other who was annoying and who was a pain. We had a real honesty session – all of us getting angry. We got everything off our chests, and it cleared the air.

Pat Lam on how Western Samoa prepared for their giant-killing game against Wales

When all other memories have faded, the jokes still remain – as fresh and as cutting today as when they were first told, over fifteen years ago. 'What's the difference between Cinderella and the Welsh rugby team?' asked a million or more bright-eyed rugby fans. 'Cinderella eventually got to the ball!' Boom, boom.

As the joke implies, there was one particular match in 1991 when Welsh rugby players didn't get to the ball very often. Why? Because they were tackled, thumped, boshed and bashed out of the game by the men of a tiny island country that makes its money by exporting coconut products. A country that has an entire population about half the size of Cardiff. Yes, readers of a sensitive or Welsh disposition may wish to avert their gaze at this point – for this is the ground-breaking moment when Western

Samoa, playing in their first World Cup match ever, beat Wales – the team that had finished third in 1987. Who other than diehard rugby fans had even heard of Western Samoa before they crunch-tackled their way into rugby folklore? Where was Western Samoa? West of Samoa? What was it? Where had these big, fast players come from, and where did they learn to tackle like that?

'Suddenly people started asking questions,' said Bryan Williams, Western Samoa's coach and a former All Black (the first New Zealand player to coach the Samoans). 'Western what? Samoa? What's that? they asked. Well, it's a country, I told them. A country where they love rugby and play it very well.'

Indeed, so well that they beat one of the established rugby nations and effectively ended Wales' run in the World Cup.

Though the scoreline was close – the match finishing 16–13 in favour of the gentlemen from the South Seas – the impact of the result reverberated around the rugby world. The tiny island nation had effectively denied Wales a place in the quarter-finals. 'It's a good job they weren't playing the whole of Samoa . . .' ran the jokes.

Rugby's first giant-killing had taken place, and few people could believe it – especially the Welsh fans in the crowd who'd indulged in a little dressing up for the game – blackening their faces and coming as Western Samoans. There was a feeling of utter shock everywhere. Somehow, when the intellectual discussions had taken place about the need to expand the rugby world, and the incredible opportunity that the World Cup would provide to bring on the smaller nations, no one stopped to consider the awful truth that, as the smaller nations improved, they would start beating the more established nations. No one considered, either, how embarrassing that might be, or how many jokes might begin to circulate.

It was all quite surreal [said Pat Lam, who was in the team that beat Wales, and would go on to captain the Samoans in the next two World Cups]. There had been disappointment at home in 1987 that we weren't invited to play so, when we qual-ified for 1991, there was a lot of excitement in Samoa. We travelled over to Britain as cheaply as possible. We heard the stories of New Zealand players being flown from one side of their country to the other in a jet black plane that had 'All Blacks' written on the side, and we were going from one side of Samoa to the other in a small grocer's truck, but none of that mattered. It was just very exciting – to be playing in the World Cup for the first time.

When we got to Britain, no one knew who we were. They were all saying 'What's Western Samoa?' Before we played Wales, we'd walk around the place in our tracksuits and people would come up, peer at the team's logo and ask 'What country's that?'

Then the Welsh coach announced that this was the most important match in Wales' 110-year history, and the newspapers started to take us more seriously. I still don't think they thought we'd win though. Then, when we beat Wales, things changed overnight. Suddenly, everyone had heard of Western Samoa. We couldn't walk around anywhere in our tracksuits or we'd have people rushing up and asking for autographs, and wanting to talk to us about how we beat Wales. It got to the stage where we couldn't walk down the road. It was incredible.

Not quite as incredible, it turned out, as the scenes back in Western Samoa where 20,000 people had packed into the main stadium in Apia – the country's capital city – at 2 a.m., to watch the match. Brian Lima, one of Samoa's star players, played in the victory over Wales, and has played in every World Cup game for Samoa since. 'It was crazy at home,' he says. 'Rugby is the number one sport in Samoa, and they had no satellite televisions back then, so loads of people headed for the ground in Apia and watched it there instead. Many of them had been at the ground all day – arriving in the scorching midday heat to get the best seats, they had prepared food to take with them and share with the others.'

The players were shown the footage of the scenes in Apia in their hotel room as their coach congratulated them after the match.

Players were crying when they saw it [says Lam]. All these people in the boiling heat to watch us. There were lots of tears shed. The room in the hotel was wallpapered with faxes. We were so proud of what we'd done. We wanted children to start saying that they wanted to play for Samoa. When I was growing up, it was all about playing for New Zealand – that was everyone's dream. I think people felt pride in Samoa and realised that the men from Samoa were playing some of the best rugby in the world. We definitely changed things a little in that World Cup.

It wasn't until they returned home that they realised just how much things had changed. They never won another match in the 1991 World Cup but it was as if they'd won the tournament. When they arrived back at 6 a.m., in the dark, they were greeted by the Prime Minister.

'People lined the streets and were hanging out of the trees to watch us,' says Lima. 'There were street parties and celebrations. They were just so thrilled at how we had done.'

Lam agrees. 'Along the 33-kilometre route from the airport to town, there were floats waiting for us, and they wanted one player to get on each float. It was like a national holiday. We had a big march from the hotel to the government buildings for a massive party. For months afterwards, rugby was being played everywhere you looked – it was a big thing for Samoa, in fact a big thing for the Pacific Islands.'

Like Fiji, Samoa is a group of islands in the Pacific Ocean. The country gained independence from New Zealand in 1962. It has a population of 185,000, and was known as Western Samoa until July 1997, when the constitution was amended to change the country's name from Western Samoa to Samoa. Agriculture employs two-thirds of the labour force, and provides 90 per cent of exports. The staple products of Samoa are coconut cream, coconut oil, noni (juice of the nonu fruit, as coconuts are known in Samoa) and copra (dried coconut meat). They also do a roaring trade in cocoa (for chocolate), and bananas. Samoa is a very religious country, and the culture has a heavy focus on mutual respect. Currently 98 per cent of the population identify them-selves as Christian. Going to church is a strongly held value for Samoans, and usually, the only members of the population who do not attend a church on Sunday are preparing the Sunday meal.

Village life is organised and controlled by chiefs. Interestingly, Lima was a chief when he lived in Samoa. 'It's a traditional thing,' he says. 'Every village has chiefs, and there are two or three higher chiefs who make the decisions. For example, if you steal something, the chief will decide what will happen to you. It is he who makes a decision about whether the police will be called, or whether there should be a court convened. Being a high-level chief is an honour for the work you have done for your family and the community. Samoa is all about the community. Everyone knows everyone else in the village very well.'

Rugby is an extension of this way of life. The Samoan team is known as Manu Samoa – named after a famous Samoan chief of ten generations ago. The team has its version of the haka, called the *siva tau*, which is performed before every game. Rugby is the country's number one sport, and around one in eleven Samoans plays rugby regularly.

'That's why there was such a great reaction to the win against Wales,' says Lam. 'Because the people of Samoa really care about their rugby.'

It seems that several reasons can be offered for Samoa's vic-tory in 1991 – they were fit, eager, confident and there were low expectations of them. A plan had been mapped out by Alan Grey, chairman of the Western Samoan Rugby Football Union, before they left for the competition. Then, there was the little-known fact that they paid a visit to Cardiff Castle the day before the game for an honesty session which resulted in them 'bonding like we've never bonded before'.

'That session at Cardiff Castle was amazing,' says Lima.

'In my opinion,' says Lam. 'That's what did it – it gave us such an edge going into the match against Wales that we had to win.'

The second reason is the simple matter of their close proxim-ity to, and great relationship with New Zealand. 'Lots of us in the

Samoan side went through the New Zealand system,' says Lam.
'I went to school in New Zealand – I was grounded in the All
Black way of playing. Guys like Frank Bunce and Steve Bachop
would go on to have great All Black careers – they were in the
Samoa team in 1991. The team was a mixture of local guys and
New Zealand guys – but even the guys born and raised in Samoa
were hugely influenced by the New Zealand way of playing.'

In fact, there were sixteen New Zealand-based players in the
Western Samoan squad in 1991. Lam was very much a product of
the New Zealand rugby system, as a first XV player at
Auckland's St Peter's College and captain of the national sec-
ondary schools' side in Japan in 1987, the year of the first World
Cup. He went on to captain the New Zealand colts in 1989, and
played for New Zealand at sevens before committing himself to
Western Samoa.

'The guys were confident, coming over to the World Cup
because they had worked hard,' says Williams. 'They were
unsure what to expect, and when they arrived, the noise and traffic really bothered some of them. There were times, for example,
when they couldn't hear line-out calls because of the noise the
crowd was making, but they were always confident. They
believed they were good enough.'

So Samoa arrived at the World Cup in a position of great
strength – no pressure, lots of talent, low expectations and an
eagerness to shine.

The trouble was – being underestimated, ignored and largely
patronised was taking its toll on the players.

> They were getting fed up [recalls Lam]. They wanted to get out
> there and play and prove they could do it, but they had to wait
> for their first game [the tournament started on 3 October and
> Samoa's first game wasn't until 6 October]. We watched the
> other two sides in the group play, and we wanted to get out
> there and start ourselves. Everyone was feeling on edge – there
> was a lot of friction in the group and players were fed up and
> angry and niggling at one another.
>
> There was an edginess creeping in to training sessions [says

Lam], the guys were getting frustrated. It was as if they were about to burst. Then we were at the bar having lunch the day before the Wales game and the tension seemed to really mount. It was awful. Frank Bunce said 'right . . . we need to have an honesty session. We need to sort this out.'

Steve Bachop suggested Cardiff Castle – so off we all trooped. We all stood in the lovely grounds, in our Western Samoa tracksuits, looking miserable. It was the day before the match against Wales and we started to tell each other who was annoying and who was a pain. We had a real honesty session – all of us getting angry. We got everything off our chests, and it cleared the air. Guys that had bugged me got told. I felt lighter, unburdened by the time we left and, as we walked away, I thought 'we're going to win'. It suddenly felt all right. Suddenly it seemed like we couldn't lose.

They duly beat Wales and, after the match, Lam walked into the changing room.

It was all hugs and tears; we had our team prayer and we started singing our traditional Samoan songs and hymns. We partied all through the night. It was strange suddenly to find ourselves headline news. We had the same sponsors as the All Blacks, but they had given us far less kit than them; that all changed when we won and loads of gear started arriving.

The funniest was in the hotel, where we could have whatever we wanted to eat, whenever we wanted it – just because we'd won.

For Wales, the shock defeat meant that to qualify they now had to beat Australia and Argentina. Failure to do so saw them leaving the tournament after the pool stage.

While Wales were in some despair, in the Australia camp frustration was growing. Bob Dwyer, the man who had organised the campaign like a military operation, preparing for every eventuality and making sure every player, every move and every play was planned to within an inch of its life, was becoming frustrated

by the rather amateurish organisation of the tournament. The
Australians were based in Pontypool for their first game, and ran
out to see the scoreboard read 'Pontypool v visitors'. Their first
game was against Argentina, and they scored first, but saw that
the scoreboard read 3–0. Dwyer's anger was compounded by the
news that his wife had tried to get a bus to the ground from the
car drop-off point, and found herself having to walk for nearly an
hour in the rain to get to the stadium when the advertised bus
failed to materialise. 'Is this a World Cup or not?' he asked in
frustration. Australia beat Argentina 32–19, then went on to beat
Samoa 9–3 and Wales 38–3. Wales beat Argentina 16–7, but as it
was their only victory in the pool they finished in third place.
Western Samoa beat Argentina 35–12 to qualify for the quarter-
final.

10

The tournament hots up

Jeff Probyn kept pulling me down in the scrums by grabbing my shirt, so before the final I cut the left sleeve off my jersey so he couldn't do it. Ha! I thought – I've been clever. I found out afterwards that David Sole of Scotland and Steve McDowell of New Zealand had been doing it for years – every time they played Probyn they got the scissors out.

Tony Daly, Australia's prop and the only man to score
a try in the 1991 World Cup final

To the untrained eye, it may have looked like a piss-up, but no, when the England team marked their qualification for the 1991 World Cup quarter-finals with a weekend in Jersey it was 'team building'.

Actually, it was,' says Jason Leonard. 'Playing the World Cup had been strange because you're on tour, but not away from home, which means there are different pressures to when you play on the other side of the world. There was a feeling that it was good to get away for a few days.'

Wives and girlfriends joined the players in Jersey, where they played golf and relaxed, away from the public eye . . . and had a couple of sherbets.

One night, Winterbottom, Mike Teague, Dooley and Moore went out, returning at around midnight, smiling, laughing and falling over a lot. Moore decided to round off the evening's events by taking full

advantage of the RFU's tab to organise an impromptu wine tast-
ing of the most expensive wines and champagnes that the hotel
could lay their hands on. The food and drink bill that night came
to £4000 and most of the squad had already eaten out. By the
time the evening was up, Winterbottom had declared his love
for Teague's wife . . . several times. He announced his plans to
marry her, move to South Africa and have five children with her.
His teammates were amused when he didn't appear at breakfast
the next morning, more amused still when he failed to appear
for the rest of the day, and quite hysterically amused when they
discovered that Dewi Morris had had his video recorder with
him the previous night, and had recorded Mr Winterbottom's
declarations of love for posterity. 'France did not stand a chance,'
remarked Moore. 'The bonds between the players, as we arrived
back, could not have been tighter.'

The quarter-finals were held in France, Scotland and Ireland, with
the semi-finals at Lansdowne Road and Murrayfield, the third-
place play-off at Cardiff Arms Park and the final at Twickenham.
It meant there would be nineteen venues as opposed to the eleven
used in 1987, despite the advice that it should be fewer rather
than more venues.

Of the four games played, England's match against France in
Paris was considered the toughest, and certainly the most difficult to predict. The match would be Serge Blanco's final game
if France got knocked out, so his teammates were clearly hoping
to avoid making his ninety-third appearance for his country his
last. But England were equally eager to avoid defeat. They had
not lost to France for three years, and had no desire to break
their winning streak in the World Cup quarter-final.

The tension mounted at the beginning of the match when the
England players stood in the tunnel to run out and the French players were led in beside them. The officials wanted the two teams to
run out together – side by side, instead of one team at a time.

We started eyeballing each other, seeking out our opposite
numbers for the big stare in a moody and mean silence. Once

eyes locked, no one would look away. After about forty seconds, forty seconds which seemed like an hour, full of muttering and unshaven glowering, we ran out. That charged moment sent the atmosphere of the game into orbit [said Moore]. Some of the French were in tears when the anthem was played. It was the most ferocious, harsh, brutal match that I have played in.

France were rampant – running with ferocious intensity. 'I've never seen a French team as committed,' said Carling. The referee asked the captains to calm the players down at one stage.

Then came the moment when England's captain realised his team had won. 'I was no more than a yard from Blanco,' said Carling. 'I studied his eyes and saw that he had gone. That was the point when I knew that we had them.'

England won 19–10, but the tension remained, and boiled over in the tunnel when Daniel Dubroca, the France coach, allegedly called David Bishop, the referee, 'a cheat' before assaulting him. Dubroca denied both claims, and resigned soon afterwards. No action was taken by the World Cup committee. They concluded that Dubroca's English wasn't good enough for him to have seriously insulted the referee and the matter was dropped. England were through to the World Cup semi-final for the first time. 'There was a tremendous sense of dedication and purpose in the team, said Winterbottom. 'We were European Champions playing in the World Cup in Europe. We were in the semi-final. It was wonderful. After that France game, I celebrated for two whole days.'

In Dublin, things were no less fraught, as Australia and Ireland fought for a semi-final spot. Australia were expected to win the match easily, with Irish newspapers and rugby fans urging 'Don't be too hard on our boys, please don't win by more than forty points' – poor old Ireland, they didn't stand a chance. In the event, things looked like they might be very different . . .

Campese set Dublin alight early in the game with the first of two tries in the seventeenth minute. His second try meant

Australia led 15–9, and seemed to have the whole thing sewn up.
Then Gordon Hamilton went over to score what he surely thought
was the winning try. When Ralph Keyes converted, Ireland
were in the lead – 18–15 – with five minutes remaining. Victory?
Not quite. A move rehearsed in the days before the match saw
Campese run into midfield and pass out of the tackle for Lynagh
to score the match-winning try.

'We were lulled into a false sense of security,' recalled a shell-
shocked Bob Dwyer. 'We thought it would be an easy victory. Of
course we nearly paid for that thinking.' Australia's forwards
just couldn't seem to exert themselves on the game, and it was
only the sensible thinking of Lynagh – stand-in captain for the
match because Farr-Jones was injured – that saved Australia.
Heeding his coach's words that he should not panic, should stay
focused on the task and ignore the scoreboard, he was precise
and simple in the instructions he issued. He pulled his team
through. 'We are unashamedly a patriotic group,' said Dwyer.
'The boys felt great national pride after they had saved that
game.'

> The best moment of the whole World Cup, for me, was at
> Lansdowne Road, against Ireland in the quarter-final [said
> Lynagh]. I was acting captain. I had to come up with a plan or
> we would be on the plane back home to Australia the next
> morning wrapped in failure. I just said 'if you get the ball, hold
> on to it'. I intentionally wanted to avoid, at all costs, any nega-
> tive talk, like 'Don't panic'. I wanted to give the players things
> to do rather that tell them what not to do. I kept saying to
> myself 'do not use the word "don't".' I wanted to keep the
> instruction as simple as possible.

Lynagh called a specific move through Campese. 'We had
identified a weakness in the Irish defence by studying them on
video, and came up with a ploy to exploit it,' he said.

For Ireland, it was desperately disappointing not to win after
coming so close. They were fewer than four minutes away from a
place in the World Cup semi-finals after an incredible game.

Phil Matthews, the captain, said, 'I remember that it was Jim Staples' birthday on the day of the match and he'd been woken at 8 a.m. by a young girl wishing him Happy Birthday. The whole day had such a good feel to it. I remember there was a real confidence in the squad, and every player was up for the game. Even when Campo got going and scored his two tries, I still didn't give up hope.'

Over in Murrayfield, the question was – could Western Samoa go all the way? Ian McGeechan, Scotland's coach, said: 'We've done our homework on them.' He was aware of the huge tackles that the Samoans prided themselves on, and was well aware of what his team would need to do to beat them. As for the Samoan players, they struggled to cope with the magnitude of the event, and the huge crowds that confronted them in Edinburgh. They were used to playing in front of 20–30,000 people, then all of a sudden they were playing in front of 56,000. They couldn't hear the line-out calls, they were confused, baffled and bewildered.

'The guys stood in the line-out and jumped when they saw the ball. They didn't know where it was going because they really couldn't hear anything,' Lima said. Scotland won comfortably, 28–6. But there's no question that just being there was a small victory for Western Samoa who ran a popular lap of honour and did another performance of *Manu Samoa* before quitting the tournament to which they had brought such grace and character.

'The whole thing was amazing from start to finish,' said Lam. 'It is impossible to calculate the impact of the whole thing on Samoa.'

The Principal Stats Officer at the Samoa Tourism Authority has tried! She says that enquiries rose by around 30 per cent straight after the World Cup which can be directly related to the tournament, and press enquiries and requests for information about the country from the media were five times what they would normally be. Further, there was an 'appreciable' lift in the numbers travelling to Samoa in 1992 and 1993.

The other minnow side that had qualified for the quarter-final stage was Canada who faced New Zealand in Lille.

We were so pleased to qualify, of course [said Gareth Rees]. We'd come to the tournament to really show what we could do. Before we left, our coach said to us that there was nothing we could do about the fact that we hadn't been playing since we were five years old. We might not be as skilful as the other sides, but we could be fitter and tougher. The coach said 'If I put the Canadian pack and the Welsh pack in this room and shut the door – I would expect the Canadians to be the last men standing.' That was our attitude going into the tournament, but we'd been on the road so long that by the time the quarter-finals came round, the guys were completely exhausted. We'd had lots of gripes during the pool stages that had made bits of the tournament quite unpleasant and the whole thing quite wearing.

The Canadians felt they were being asked to sleep in beds that were too small, eat unpleasant food and stay in cheap hotels. They were sure that everyone was messing them around because they were Canadian and not one of the big sides. The players were taken on a trip to Vimy Ridge – a monument to Canadian soldiers from the First World War – to try and motivate them and re-energise them about the tournament.

There are not too many great Canadian moments to celebrate – we're still talking about the day that Canada scored a goal in hockey against Russia and how great that was [said Rees]. So we were a bit sceptical about the trip, but when we got there, it was incredible – we saw the battlefields, memorials to Canadians, tunnels where they fought and conditions where they lived . . . It put everything in perspective. Maybe the bed where the second row's feet were sticking out at the end wasn't the worst thing! It was a moment when you look around and realise that anything can be done. If these men could do it in the First World War, so could we in a rugby match. 'This is something special,' we thought. If we start to believe we can do it – that's a pretty big first step.

The All Blacks won the match 29–13, but Canada played well. Full back Mark Wyatt was captain of Canada that day – and got on to the scoreboard when he slotted over a penalty. Al Charron, the no. 8, drove over for his first international try. Scrum-half Chris Tynan also crossed to score, and fly-half Gareth Rees kicked a conversion. The Kiwis had superior attacking powers, though, and scored five tries. Charron said: 'We came of age as a rugby country in 1991. We felt we had something to prove and we did that.'

Rees was pleased with another judgement of the performance: 'Some of the All Blacks have subsequently told me that we took lumps out of New Zealand and made their job much harder in the next match [the semi-final against Australia].'

The vanquished returned home, leaving the semi-finalists to continue. First, it was England and Scotland at Murrayfield, followed by Australia v New Zealand in Dublin.

The England players settled into their Scotland base quickly. On the first night, Guscott lost a game of spoof in an Indian restaurant (not the best location for losing a game of spoof), and he had to eat the plate of chili pickles. Then, the next day, a group decided to organise a shooting party in the Highlands. In the group was Teague, Richards, Olver and Morris. The most experienced at this activity was Olver who kept telling the other members of the group about the number of shoots he had been on. But very late in the day up popped a couple of pheasants and Teague was struck in the head by a shot from Olver. It was just a flesh wound but the group decided to keep the affair quiet in case Geoff Cooke decided to ban any kind of recreational activity. It meant that Teague had to sit in team meetings with his hand covering the mark on his head.

From this explosive start, came the match that was rather tame by comparison, with neither side managing to move ahead. England ground their way to a 9–6 victory after Gavin Hastings missed a kick in front of the posts.

It was an astonishingly disappointing match for Hastings, who has been such a long time servant of the game. He collapsed to his knees after the miss, burying his head in his hands.

Members of the England team found him at Boroughmuir rugby club the night after the match – completely inconsolable. He felt like he'd let the whole of Scotland down.

England had won, and were through to the final, but their approach to the game had not been popular. 'I believe the game is played to run the ball – to move it, not just kick and chase it,' said John Hart. 'If any team can win the ball, as England did, and not move it past first five-eighth [fly-half], I wonder why we are playing rugby.'

Dwyer wasn't impressed either: 'I am a little disappointed in England's philosophy,' he commented. 'They just restrict their game, but it's up to them. They have more capability than they show, and it seems a shame not to utilise that potential.' And Ian McGeechan, the Scotland coach: 'England wanted to strangle the game, we wanted to keep it alive.'

But away from all the rhetoric, the fact remained that England were in the World Cup final and rugby fever was beginning to spread through the country.

The southern hemisphere clash to see who would face England at Twickenham was played in Dublin between Australia and New Zealand. After ninety-two encounters, the near neighbours were playing each other in a World Cup match for the first time, and on a neutral ground for the first time. New Zealand had triumphed in the vast majority of the team's previous encounters – winning sixty-four, and losing twenty-four, but Australia had won two of the last three matches and had done a considerable amount of work with their forwards following the narrow victory over Ireland. They declared themselves ready for anything that the New Zealanders could throw at them. The All Blacks, it turned out, had little to hurl in their direction, and the Australian forwards had a storming opening thirty minutes. They went on to win 16–6, and thus peel New Zealand's all-black fingers from the Webb-Ellis trophy.

Dwyer rushed into the Australia changing room, shouting 'You were wonderful – there was only one team in it.' He didn't see Wyllie, the All Blacks coach, standing there. 'Sorry,' he said, but Grizz was magnanimous in defeat. 'Yes, you're right – there was only one team in it,' said the New Zealander.

The reason that there was only one team in it was that the 1991 semi-final between New Zealand and Australia was one of the great tactical calamities of All Black history, and confirmation that they should have made fundamental changes to their side before reaching 1991. But when you're marching through fifty matches without defeat, I guess changing the way the team operates is not top of the to-do list. Zinzan Brooke has a very clear idea of why the All Blacks lost. 'Let's be honest,' he opines. 'We got our heads stuck up our arses. We picked the wrong players and they did the wrong things.'

Having lost the semi-finals, New Zealand and Scotland were forced to face each other in the third-place play-off. A crowd of 40,000 people turned up to watch. There was no dignity to be gained from coming third, so the fight lacked commitment. New Zealand won 13–6, with Walter Little scoring the game's only try. John Jeffrey and Finlay Calder retired after the game, and Hastings continued to blame himself – such is the curse of the kicker in rugby union.

The Australians packed up and left Ireland for London. They bumped into the New Zealand team at Dublin airport. 'Whatever you do – don't let England beat you,' urged the kiwis. When Australia arrived at their base in the capital, they had received hundreds of supportive letters. Former Australia centre, Tim Horan, recalls faxes arriving for them constantly. 'The messages were quite extraordinary: offers of free accommodation at five-star hotels, free evenings at massage parlours, free beach holidays – anything and everything,' recalls Horan. 'One evening, Marty Roebuck was flipping through the new faxes when he came across a belter. A girl from Adelaide had faxed in: "To whoever scores the first try in the final, I will offer you fantastic free sex."' Below she put her phone number.

The humour was not lost on the Australians during the match when the two props, Ewen McKenzie and Tony Daly, crashed over to score together. 'The first try!' says Horan. 'Rumour has it that five seconds later, the Adelaide lady disconnected her phone.'

England moved to Richmond from Hampshire, and stayed in the Petersham Hotel before the final, discussing behind the scenes what tactical approach they should adopt. In the tournament thus far they had been criticised for relying on the power of their forwards, and on kicking, but it had been effective. They had controlled the game. What did it matter that other players and coaches had criticised them? They were in the final. But Uttley, Cooke and Carling were considering changing the team's strategy. They had promised themselves, after defeat by Australia in the summer, that they would play a backs-dominated game next time they met – in order to get possession. They thought back to that tour on which they'd been continually denied ball. They had to assume that it would be the same this time, so they decided that they should plan for a wider game. Carling says all the players were in agreement with this decision. Moore says that many of the forwards said it was inadvisable to change the way they were playing.

The week leading up to World Cup final at Twickenham was huge. Rugby was on the radio, television, newspapers and magazines. The players recall coming down for breakfast on the day of the final and feeling as if the whole world was watching them. In the foyer it was bedlam, with reporters, cameras and supporters jostling for position. People battled to see what the players were having for breakfast. Nothing like this had ever happened in rugby union before.

The teams were presented to the Princess Royal, patron of Scotland, before the match. They all shook hands courteously except for Moore who couldn't resist a little dig. 'Sorry about last week, Ma'am,' he said. The Scotland players had travelled down for the match, and watched from the stands dressed in kilts and Australian hats and scarves. 'Perhaps the Scots despise the England team because we have figured out how to beat them consistently,' suggested Moore.

Finally the match kicked off, and England were in control. They had easily enough possession to win but made mistakes, sometimes under pressure, sometimes not, losing it as fast as they were gaining it. Meanwhile, the England pack – weighing in at 818 kilos, was keeping the 853-kilo Australian pack under control. The combined weights were the heaviest entered in a Test match. From this heaving platform, England were having by far the better time of it in the forwards. But they kept the ball alive and threw it around, while the forwards screamed that they needed to play a tighter game and make use of the advantage they were winning.

Dooley dominated Eales in the line-out. England's scrummaging was tight and low. One of the most powerful images of the first half was of Simon Poidevin, being brought down in a heavy tackle by Mickey Skinner. The tackle 'shook the bones of the people watching in the grandstand', according to Dwyer. After the match, Poidevin was asked how he enjoyed the tackle. 'I didn't lose possession, did I?'

In the second half, the match was terrifyingly close – with England getting the best of first-phase possession, particularly from line-outs. But the midfield failed to provide the space England needed to go over the line. The Australian back line had an outstanding, well-organised defence. The England solution to this was to launch themselves at Australia with ball in hand. The crowd was delighted and the Australians were surprised. But because England still failed to breach the Australian defence, they didn't get anywhere. Further, their strategy was playing into Australian hands, but the more expansive game helped Australia compensate for their lack of first-phase possession by providing them with it in second phase thanks to the pressure of the Australian defence forcing England to turn the ball over.

England won plenty of loose ball. The terror of not winning possession never materialised – here they were with plenty of possession but they were just hurling it away. They lost 12–6 on a day when many forwards believed they should have become world champions. They were running the ball against a well-organised Australia defence. Every time they kicked – they triumphed. When they passed it, they lost it.

'So why the f**k didn't we stop passing it?' asks Leonard.

'Why, oh why, oh why, didn't we think about what was going on, and change tactics? Marty Roebuck was dropping the ball when the kicks were aimed at him, but we stopped kicking it and started spinning it. We knew Campese's only weakness was under a high ball, but instead of lobbing high balls at him, we took him on. Why would we ever do that?'

The views expressed here about the World Cup final are not new. The players have been expressing their frustration that they didn't change tactics for over a decade. But Carling, one of the triumvirate of men who made the decision to play a wide, passing game in 1991, says it is naive and unfair to say that England lost because of their tactics. He sits back in his large armchair and urges people to think about the situation. He says that Australia did not win that World Cup final because of English tactics, they won because of Australian tactics. Put simply – Australia were the most complete side in the World Cup, and that's why they won. In three seasons of continuous rugby of twenty-five Tests, Australia lost four matches. They were a good side – pure and simple.

'Look at the stats,' he says. 'We won loads of possession but some of it was second, third and fourth phase. We wouldn't have won any of that if we'd kicked.' He says it's misleading to say that if England had kept the ball they won, they would have won the game – because if they'd played a tighter game, they would-n't have secured the same possession. Also, it is important to bear in mind how good the Australian defence was. The Australian try-line was crossed only three times in the whole tournament (twice by Argentina in their first game).

'It was never a case of the forwards wanting to play one way, and backs another way. If the forwards had wanted to play differently, they would have. A captain can't suddenly take a unilateral decision to completely change a game in the middle of it. You've got fifteen players making decisions.'

Dwyer agrees with Carling. He said he was expecting England to attack through the midfield, as they had done with limited success in Sydney. 'They made a few holes in the defence then and we thought they were bound to try it again. We were so sure of this that we spent time examining our deficiencies in that area,' he said. Australia also paid a lot of attention to scrummaging, and Tony Daly, the loose-head prop who was the only man to score in the final, cut the left sleeve off his jersey because Probyn made a practice of pulling on his shirt. 'We thought we knew how they'd play it, but we were wrong,' says Dwyer. 'They played an open game and they lost – that doesn't mean if they'd closed it down they would have won. If they'd played a tighter game, we'd have defended accordingly.'

Around the England dressing-room after the match, players were slumped on the benches in a mixture of sheer fatigue and dismay. Heads were held in hands as players stared inconsolably into space. Australia, too, were exhausted, and whatever small consolation it may be to the England players, there's no question that they managed to completely wear out their opponents. 'Against the All Blacks we felt we could have gone on another forty minutes. England ran at us so many times, we had to make so many tackles that it was a far more tiring game. I just lay in the bath for thirty minutes afterwards. I was so absolutely exhausted,' said Farr-Jones.

'They were there for the taking,' mused Paul Ackford. 'As each minute of the second half ticked by, the Australian forwards grew ever more tired. By the end of the match they were surviving on willpower alone.'

But Ackford says that it was not a ridiculous idea to go for a fast, running game, just a ridiculous idea to introduce it in the final for the first time.

England's mistake, in 1991, wasn't that we played a different way in the final but, rather, that we didn't play that way all the way through the tournament.

The final sessions, in the week leading up to the match, were slick and remained true to our pledge. This running rugby lark wasn't that difficult. Quite good fun, in fact. Rory, Jerry and Will looked in fine fettle and the handling was particularly sharp. So much for the theory. When it came to the big day, we found we could not transfer the excellence of the unopposed training sessions to the intensity of the live match. Passes were dropped, opportunities went begging. But that wasn't the whole story. Around half-time, when we started to get on top of the big Aussie forwards, we should have thrown the running rugby option out of the window. We didn't, and the rest is history.

11

The day that England changed their tactics

The strangled cry he gave as I sauntered off to rejoin play was immensely satisfying.

Will Carling recalls a special moment with David Campese when he stepped on the Australian wing's 'bollocks'

How did Australia do it? They did not have home advantage nor did they have an easy ride through the tournament – facing New Zealand and England in quick succession. But one thing they did have was a coach with boundless self-belief, and utter conviction that the team would win. He had it in the final, the semi-final, the quarter-final and in the pool games. He even had it a year before the tournament started . . .

It was a warm afternoon in November 1990 when Bob Dwyer reached for the phone and began dialling the number he had been given for the hotel where the Australian captain was staying. 'Nick,' he said. 'Where are you?'

Nick Farr-Jones explained that he was in Adelaide, competing in a celebrity car race. 'Why?' he asked Dwyer.

'No reason,' said the Australia coach. 'Just calling to say that today is November 2nd. It's exactly twelve months before the

World Cup final. I want you to have a glass of champagne tonight, and toast our victory in twelve months' time.'

Farr-Jones smiled and promised to do just that. 'And I did,' recalls Farr-Jones, with a smile.

Dwyer did, too. After phoning every player likely to make the squad for the 1991 World Cup, he gathered a core of Australia's leading players around him that evening, and they raised their glasses. 'In twelve months' time,' he intoned. 'We will be toasting our victory in the 1991 Rugby World Cup.'

Across Australia, men lifted glasses of champagne to their lips and projected forwards twelve months to the moment they would be victorious at Twickenham.

How about that for a story illustrating how to create a winning team? Telling players a year before the World Cup kicks off, you know that they will win it. Belief is the cornerstone of success. Only great players win World Cups, but there are great players who do not win World Cups, and in assessing the qualities that a World Cup winning team needs – belief is right up there, at the top of the pile. Arguably, it is impossible to win anything of value without it.

One may ponder why the Australians appear to have a more natural inclination towards confidence and self-belief than the British do. Is it to do with its being a younger nation? A nation struggling to make its mark on the world, like a younger sibling fighting to succeed in his own right, away from the suffocating shadow of an older brother's achievements.

In 1987, the Australian team had confidence, too. In some respects the manager's confidence 'backfired' because he had booked the players' flights to New Zealand assuming they would be in the final, then had to cancel them when Australia were knocked out by France at the semi-final stage. And yet how much of a 'backfire' was it? It would seem that the risks associated with being hugely confident are not really risks at all compared with those of not being confident. A risk of embarrassment at the most.

The first World Cup get-together of the year for the Australia team was in January 1991, at the University of Queensland in Brisbane, where the squad of forty-five players was reduced to thirty-six. Prior to this, the forty-five elite players had been working on a detailed, scientific programme for two years, having started it in 1989. 'More than anything else,' insists Bob Dwyer, 'getting the players involved in such a detailed programme so early on made the difference between ourselves and the rest of the world when it came to the World Cup.'

Dwyer was determined, from the moment he took over the coaching of Australia from Alan Jones in 1988, that the players should be properly prepared. 'The programme was well-researched, and covered strength, fitness, diet and psychology. I knew I was asking a lot of the players and for them to follow the programme seriously would require them to undergo a cultural transformation, but I also knew how important it was that the players were properly fit for the World Cup.'

The programme was highly structured and was specific for each player, depending on size, physique, strength, stamina and metabolism.

Dwyer became fixated on making sure his players were fit when he studied Australian players of the past in order to work out why some were more successful than others.

He established that in the 1960s there had been a resurgence in the sport, with players like Ken Catchpole and Rob Heming coming through. Dwyer established that the upturn in standards in the Australia game was a direct result of the Australian Rugby Union improving the way the team was prepared by appointing a National Director of coaching. In a cruel twist of irony, the appointment was made as a direct result of the Australians seeing how effective the Welsh National Director of Coaching, Ray Williams, was. By 1991, Williams was World Cup Tournament Director, and must have been ruing the effect he'd had on the Australia team!

So, back in 1988, the newly appointed coach of Australia had established the importance of proper preparation, and was considering what he should do to ensure that his players were as fit as possible. Meanwhile, the Australian Institute of Sport was adding rugby to its list of sports to be covered by its programme, and was appointing rugby coaches to the staff there. David Clark and Brian

O'Shea were selected to head up the rugby programme. They would be able to draw on the institute's specialists – physiologists, bio-mechanics and nutritionists – as they established the best route forward for rugby in Australia. Dr Frank Pyke was selected to run the scheme.

At the start of each year, a player would have a programme mapped out for the first third of the year. This third would be further broken down into four-week blocks – for example, in the first four weeks of the year, players would be told to run or swim every day, do strength exercises four times a week, work out in the gym five times a week and eat certain foods in certain quantities according to specially selected menus. Then, in weeks 5–8, the programme would be modified slightly, and in weeks 9–12, modified and inten-sified further. In addition to these practical tasks, the players were lectured on fitness, nutrition and psychology throughout the year.

'The players were promised that if they followed the training programme, they would get appreciably fitter and there was no question that they would become better at playing rugby. It would make them fitter, tougher and smarter,' said Ben Whitaker from the AIS.

The impact of the training programme on the team was dra-matic.

In some cases, the preparation programme changed the player's whole approach to the game, and his understanding of how best to prepare for a game [said Bob Dwyer]. It changed his understanding of his body as a mechanical apparatus and his understanding of his own physiology. Education itself is a motivational tool – the more a player knows about his body, the better he trains, the fitter and more powerful he becomes, which in turn encourages him to want to know more. On the field there were real physical benefits, but the players' mental attitudes were changed, too – they were more confident because of the training they had done. In short, they had developed the mental attitude of an elite athlete who knows that it is the extra 1 per cent in performance that separates the best from the second-best.

It is worth reflecting at this point on the fact that while in many countries around the world the obsession was in copying everything that the New Zealand team had done in the 1980s to become world champions; in Australia they were going their own way entirely, and taking rugby on to a new level.

For example, in 1990, the physiology team at the AIS analysed the running styles of the players, looking at the movement of the lower back and pelvic girdle under acceleration. They also looked at pronation of the feet and the subsequent effect of the lower leg position and influence of stomach muscles on the positioning of the pelvis. This was done because Dwyer wanted to make sure the strength training they were doing wasn't causing imbalances that would result in later injuries.

Then, at the beginning of 1991, with the squad whittled down to thirty-six, at the University of Queensland, tests were conducted to assess players' fitness levels, their cardiovascular and anaerobic fitness, as well as their strength, vertical and horizontal power and body fat levels.

On the basis of these results a training programme was developed for the next few weeks. The process was repeated in February 1991, at a camp in Sydney. It was also in February that Dwyer sat down and sorted out issues relating to the wives and girlfriends, and when they would be flown to Test venues. He looked at whether there would be team dinners, flights, hotels and all those things that Clive Woodward would later memorably call 'critical non-essentials' – those things that are not directly related to the playing of the game on the field, but are important to get right in order that the players can relax and concentrate on rugby.

'What motivation really means is providing an atmosphere in which a person can realise his or her potential,' he said. 'By providing this atmosphere, you will do far more to motivate a rugby player long term than trying to generate a mood of fierce determination in the team before a match.'

In common with the New Zealand team in 1987, Dwyer also insisted on his players behaving in a civilised and respectful manner at all times. 'The idea I have tried to foster in Australian players is that while being chosen to play rugby for Australia is certainly a great honour, it also imposes on them a tremendous responsibility – first to other players who tried to make the team but didn't, and, second, to Australian rugby followers at large. It is harmful, in my view, for players to see themselves as inherently special. Instead, I feel they should feel a need to deserve the success they strive for.'

The net result of all this was that the Wallabies who won the 1991 World Cup final were smiling, charming, hard-working and respectful. A delight to work with. Worthy champions.

When it came to selecting the players who would take the field in green and gold for the 1991 tournament, Dwyer said: 'Speed and power are the keys to the modern game' – i.e. the optimum combination of weight and acceleration which makes a player effective. Before the tournament started, they uncovered two players who fitted this description impeccably: Willie Ofahengaue – a player with both size and acceleration; and John Eales – a man who would become a hugely influential rugby player.

Dwyer was eager to have a world-class player in each position, so set about establishing where the gaps were. The second row was immediately thought to be a weak area, until some chap called Eales was discovered. Full back was a problem, too, so Dwyer looked around for the right sort of player to slot into the team.

The first Test that Australia played in World Cup year was against Wales. They won 63–6, and played well. Then they played England, the reigning Five Nations champions, and beat them with raw precision and an exacting style. The difference between England and Australia was shown brutally, as the Aussies won 40–15. Next Australia faced the All Blacks in a real test of how far they had come in the four years since the last tournament, and in the three years since Dwyer's arrival. They won 21–12. The result sent shock waves through the New Zealand rugby establishment, and delight through the Australia team.

The Australian forwards, in particular, were dominant against New Zealand. The rest of the world started to wake up to what

Dwyer had known for years – Australia really did have a chance of winning the World Cup. They had beaten Wales, England and New Zealand in fairly quick succession. Public excitement was building. A group calling themselves the Wallabies' Supporters' Group began holding a lunch before each international. Dwyer is sure that this growing feeling of support in the nation had the effect of lifting the players further.

Then came the main event – Australia were beaten in the return match against New Zealand. It was a far from over-whelming defeat, since Australia lost 6–3, but their discipline was extremely poor and it sent them scurrying back to the drawing board to assess where things had gone wrong. That back-to-the-drawing-board moment, as we have learned through the studying of New Zealand in 1987, can be the making of a team.

'With hindsight it can be argued that the loss of this Test to New Zealand was a blessing for us in the long term. If we had not lost to the New Zealanders then we might have lost to them in the semi-final of the World Cup. We were compelled by defeat to refocus our attention.'

While Dwyer and his coaching team were focusing on getting the Australia players absolutely right for the World Cup, the men who had previously been employed to watch all players in Australia, and make sure that any talented ones were considered by Dwyer, turned their attention to the opposition. Dick Marks, David Clark and Brian O'Shea were assigned to watch videos to provide comprehensive breakdowns about key players in the opposition sides across the world. Dwyer then had information that he could use to inform tactics.

Despite all the work that Dwyer did in preparing Australia for the 1991 World Cup, he insists that one should never overesti-mate the impact of a coach on a team. It is his estimate that a coach's contribution languishes around the 7 per cent mark. However, it is important to remember how difficult it is, at inter-national level, to make a 7 per cent difference to a team. In that respect, it would have to be said that having the right coach on board is crucial. There's no question that a coach can be the difference between winning and losing. I suspect that the old maxim is true – 'a coach can't win without good athletes, but he can lose with them'.

It would also be true to say that a coach can't make bad athletes good, but he can fail to organise, motivate and inspire good ones sufficiently, so they don't maximise their potential.

Dwyer hated the macho posturing on the pitch, and hated hearing players mutter inane comments like 'Come on, guys, we've got to score, we've got to score.' He wanted them to work out what they were going to do to score, then do it.

He extended this theory to assessments of coaches, frequently suggesting that the measure of a coach's success should not be whether the team wins or loses but whether it is better at the end of the season than it was before. So, I could take over the coaching of the All Blacks tomorrow, and they might beat Western Samoa in four weeks' time, but what measure is that of me as a coach?

In order to make sure that the Australia team was always better after he had worked with the players, Dwyer focused on all the details, and on making sure his players got everything right in training. 'Practice does not make perfect,' he was fond of saying. 'Only perfect practice makes perfect.' If you practise doing something in an imperfect way, you only become good at doing it imperfectly. Dwyer was fond of breaking the match down, and working on individual and unit skills with the players.

'Before a home test, we would do about six hours of practice on average, and no more than twenty minutes of this training as a team,' he said. 'No rugby match is a single entity – it is merely a collection of individual incidents and what we need to do at training is practise those individual elements.'

In addition to understanding the importance of focusing on details, Dwyer also understood that it was important to strike that difficult balance between creating a settled and relaxed side in which players could learn to play with each other and build into a successful team, and the importance of taking sufficient risks to make the team as effective as possible.

Dwyer had a policy of not making too many changes too

quickly. He said that he believed inconsistency was a sign that a team had potential but lacked experience. He spoke to coaches Bob Templeton and John Bain and they came up with a list of players who should be dropped or selected. Dwyer would frequently look through the lists they produced and make sure he was considering all possibilities for the team.

When they arrived in Britain, Dwyer said, 'We could detect in the air the promise of greater things.'

There is no doubt that the Australian Institute of Sport provided the Australia coaches with a valuable resource. It began working with rugby players in 1989, and developed so quickly that today the majority of players joining the Wallabies have been through the AIS. One of its immediate values was that it had a central base full of experts in different disciplines who were not exclusive to rugby. This meant that rugby players could access experts who had come from outside the sport and had a broader base of knowledge than those who had previously been involved.

What were Australia's key strengths in 1991?

1. Belief
Bob Dwyer worked hard to instil self-belief in the players. His rallying call to them a year before the World Cup final is a fascinating example of that, as is the way he underplayed England's home advantage in the competition. He worked hard to plant the idea firmly in the subconscious minds of the players that the cheering for England at Twickenham was actually a motivational spur for Australia.

2. Good basic skills
Australia's basic skills were outstanding because Dwyer had worked hard at breaking everything down and getting all the details right. On the Thursday, two days before the final, the Australian management cut off the media's access to individual players. Only Bill McLaren was given access, in order that he could familiarise himself with the players about whom he would be commentating later on. 'Those boys were passing the ball with

such speed,' said McLaren. 'Their handling skills were exceptional – I watched them for a while and realised that I couldn't even see the ball, it was going so fast.'

Dwyer was fond of saying: 'Preparation, preparation, preparation . . . no amount of talent, courage and determination can compensate for poor preparation. It will affect performance in the match as well as how long it takes you to recover afterwards.'

3. Exemplary conduct

Players were level-headed, disciplined and humble off the field. They had been told that they must wear a shirt with a collar, long trousers, socks and shoes (not running shoes) even at breakfast. 'This results in an across-the-board discipline and respect for members of the public which is reflected in the discipline of the team's play, and the respect they have for teammates and opponents.' Nick Farr-Jones gave his team moral leadership off the field as well as leadership on the field.

4. Leadership

When Dwyer became national coach in 1988, his first task was to find a captain for the team. He went for a man who lacked experience, but had what he described as 'certain personal qualities' that marked him out as a potential leader. Farr-Jones had not captained a representative side before, but Dwyer recalls noticing 'the respect and admiration' that other players had for him as a captain. 'His influence on the team in all its activities on and off the field has been vital to its success. Without it I am sure we would not have won the World Cup.'

5. The coach

Dwyer reckons a good coach is worth around a 7 per cent difference to a team. I suspect it's worth more. I think a good leader, in any situation, is an incalculable benefit. A strong coach, leader and manager defines the very culture of an organisation. Every point in this list of reasons why Australia won is due, in some part, to Dwyer. But, even if it's 7 per cent – it's the difference between first and second place. Dwyer was confident, experienced and determined. His sessions were well run and thorough. He made a difference to the team – he made them better, and he is part of the reason that they won.

6. Fitness
Forty-five elite players had been working on a detailed, scientific programme for two years, having started it in 1989. 'More than anything else,' insists Bob Dwyer, 'getting the players involved in such a detailed programme so early on made the difference between ourselves and the rest of the world when it came to the World Cup.'

7. A crucial defeat leading up to the World Cup
When they lost to New Zealand. 'With hindsight, I'm glad that happened,' says Dwyer. 'It gave us a chance to reassess, think things through and make sure everything was on track.'

8. The players
The players, including the essential triumvirate at the heart of the team (Campese, Lynagh and Farr-Jones) were, obviously, essential in the victory. Dwyer set out to find, through his battery of physical tests and his team of advisers, who the best players in the country were in each position.

9. The importance of the non-playing members
Dwyer said: 'My abiding memory at the end of the match was of the unrestrained joy of the non-playing members of our squad. I realised how important they were and how this was their victory, too. If they had been different, it could all have been different.'

10. Dwyer had a big vision for the team that he communicated very clearly
He emphasised the importance of them being task-focused rather than goal-focused, and is convinced that it was Michael Lynagh's ability to understand what this meant that got Australia through a sticky patch in the quarter-final against Ireland. 'The figures on

there cannot change what is happening on the field,' he explained, urging players not to look at the scoreboard and to try to sneak a victory, but get their heads up and get focused. 'The things that enable you to score when the scoreboard says 0–0 are exactly the same things that enable you to score when it's 100–0. Any team needs to focus on the task in hand.' This is very similar to what David Kirk said in 1987: the tries and points are a by-product of playing well – that has to come first. The other important part of Dwyer's vision was CNEs – Critical Non-Essentials.

PART THREE: 1995

Colours of the Rainbow Nation

12

The return of South Africa

If the game is run properly as a professional game, you do not
need fifty-seven old farts running rugby.

Will Carling, 1995

Cars flew past the Hilton Hotel in Paris at quite terrifying
speed. I looked out at the busy Avenue de Suffren, lying in
the shadow of the Eiffel Tower, bathed in midwinter sunshine.
Little French cars zoomed and zigzagged round each other with
not a thought for their own safety, or indeed anyone else's, hoot-
ing, beeping and making a terrific noise. It was like wacky races
out there – with the accompanying fist-clenching, shouting and
whizzing. Dodgems for grown-ups.

'Here it is,' said the helpful porter, indicating a beautiful,
shiny, expensive-looking coach.

'No, no,' I said, with absolute certainty. 'That won't be ours.'

I walked round to the front of the coach, and saw the driver in
his peaked cap as he polished the door handles. A closer look at
the glistening paintwork and lovely clean-looking seats inside
confirmed everything. This was far too flash for the players'
wives and girlfriends. In the windscreen was a sign saying 'RFU
Committee Wives'.

'There,' I said to the porter, indicating the sign.

'I see,' he replied. 'I call you when another bus is coming.'

In the period between the 1991 and 1995 World Cups, I worked for the RFU as match-day PR manager to the England team. It was a role that involved, among other things, making sure the wives and girlfriends were 'looked after' properly (though a group of women who less needed 'looking after' it is impossible to imagine).

These were the days when the RFU committees were all-powerful. The esteemed committee men travelled at the front of the plane while the players were shoved at the back. They had the best seats, the best hotels and the best treatment. On the more exotic trips, there would be infinitely more committee men than players in attendance.

Along with the committee men, of course, came the wives; and as their husbands enjoyed superior treatment to the players, so their wives enjoyed superior treatment to the players' wives and girlfriends (Wags, as we called them then, back in the early 1990s, despite subsequent claims by the *Daily Mail* that they 'invented' the term). The committee wives stayed in better hotels, their lunches were more extravagant and their treatment in all respects was superior. Even their coach was bigger, shinier and cleaner than the one assigned to the players' partners.

When I first starting working with the team, I was pulled aside by a couple of the committee wives and told that I simply must keep the players' wives in order. They should not speak unless spoken to, and should be respectful at all times.

'They really should be more dignified. Don't they realise the company they are keeping? Some of the committee wives have very important husbands.'

Of course, not all of the committee members were so arrogant and self-aggrandising – some were thoroughly decent people, working hard within a system which constrained them as much as it lorded them. But, en masse, the RFU committees of the late 1980s and early 1990s had much more control than their contribution or skills deserved. And the fact remains that players were treated appallingly. I still don't understand why. They were not being paid, why not make the whole experience utterly delightful, and give them the best of everything? Instead, expenses were clamped down on and all expenditure was checked and double-checked. Even after playing for England, players were limited in the food they could eat and were not supposed to order room service. If they were deemed to have been excessive, the bill would not be paid by the RFU. There were dozens of stories of players phoning up reception and pretending to be Dudley Wood so they could order sandwiches in their rooms. The hotel staff had been told they could not put late-night snacks on to the players' room bills. Why? Would the whole system have crashed if a few hundred quid of the millions made every year had been spent on feeding the players?

And yet the England players rarely made a fuss or tried to get round the system. They were a decent bunch, and every time I left them, at the end of a Five Nations weekend, I walked away feeling that they deserved better. It would have been nice if the committee men had summoned up the dignity, grace and confidence in their own position, to allow the players to feel important, cherished and respected once in a while. It would have been nice if they'd stepped aside and offered the weary players their seats in first class, or insisted they took the smarter coach and ate the best food. But it didn't happen.

It didn't happen for the women, either. When the coaches arrived, the committee wives' coach was bigger, better and cleaner. The players' wives and girlfriends coach would be dirtier, less impressive and contain a driver who had no idea where he was going. While the committee wives headed for a lavish drinks function before lunch, the players' wives were left waiting on the roadside for theirs. The whole performance appeared to be a deliberate effort to make them feel less cherished, less worthy and less important than the committee members. Perhaps this was all in the name of conserving amateurism. The less worthy they felt, they less demanding they would be. We will keep the workers down by means of dirty coaches.

'It was like they expected you to call them sir,' lamented Brian Moore. 'I never quite knew why.'

When Jason Leonard was injured, in hospital and unable to

work, he wrote to the late committee man Dr Sir Peter Yarranton. He asked whether there was any fund to help players, or whether there was any way in which his mortgage could be paid while he was in hospital. Yarranton replied that Leonard had not addressed him properly and until his titles were properly used, he would not reply. Leonard received the letter in hospital, tore it up, put it in the bin and decided to cope without their help.

And it wasn't just in England that there were problems – all over the British Isles, players and coaches fought an uphill struggle against the sport's governing bodies. In Ireland, when the team needed a new scrummage machine, it was a hell of a job securing the money to buy it. The team manager had to go to London to find out how much the machine he wanted was. He returned and announced that the cost would be £3400. Then he had to report to a committee meeting and a subcommittee meeting, before enduring a separate one-to-one with the treasurer to justify his planned purchase. The week afterwards, the entire committee and wives flew to Italy for a match at a cost of £175,000. The Ireland team could have had dozens of new machines for the cost of their trip.

There's no question that, by the time the World Cup came round in 1995, rugby union was spinning helplessly towards professionalism, and had divided itself into alarmingly disparate groups on its whirlwind journey – those ready to embrace it and those offering absolute resistance. It had created such a divide between the two camps and there was such tension between the players and the RFU committee men that it was bound to explode at some stage, and it did. Three weeks before England left for the World Cup, Carling was interviewed by Greg Dyke for Channel 4 television. The thirty-minute interview would be shown as part of the channel's *Fair Game* series. Once filming had finished, the two men sat and chatted. In their conversation, Carling said that there were 'fifty-seven old farts' in charge of English rugby. The only thing that appeared wrong with this statement, to most people, was that there are actually fifty-six.

Not according to the RFU. They were furious about his comments, and did what any self-respecting bunch of old farts would do in such a situation – they called a committee meeting at the East India Club. When Carling was alerted to the furore being created in the highest echelons of English rugby, he thought he'd better ring Dennis Easby, President of the RFU, to apologise, and explain the background to the quote. Carling had been chatting casually, off-the-record. What he said was wrong, but he would never have said anything like that on camera. He was very sorry. Carling called the President and was told that Easby was in a meeting, so Carling sent a fax explaining the circumstances. He rang the following morning to talk Easby through the situation properly. Halfway through Carling's apology, the President stopped him in his tracks. 'I'm sorry to tell you, you've been relieved of the England captaincy. You'll still be able to go to South Africa as a player but not as captain. Thanks for all you've done,' said Easby.

That might have been the vainest, most self-indulgent and utterly stupid decision made by any sports committee ever. To travel the world on the funds of the Rugby Football Union working for the betterment of the game, and then take such a decision, that would adversely affect the international team just before the World Cup, was stupid beyond stupid. There's no question that taking the captaincy away from Carling would affect England's chances in the tournament. Bookmaker William Hill lengthened odds against England from when the announcement was made.

It was also grossly unfair to take such draconian action without even allowing Carling to put his side across. Easby and the RFU committees appeared to be managing the whole thing with the sophistication of a kangaroo court.

Yet I knew Easby – he was on the Berkshire committee when I worked as a development officer there. I liked him, admired him and felt he always behaved with such dignity and decency. It seemed astonishing that he had got himself embroiled in such an unseemly situation, apparently driven by the egos of a bunch of middle-aged men. How could Easby have done this?

The RFU announced their decision to fire Carling at 11.30 a.m. on the morning of the Pilkington Cup final. Brian Moore recalls watching Gary Lineker announce on *Grandstand* that Carling had been sacked as captain. He says he felt shocked at first, then confused. Did the committee men not realise that there was a World Cup in a couple of weeks? Then, he says, he laughed, because it was so utterly preposterous that he could think of nothing else to do.

The Cup final started, and the crowds could be heard, chanting for Carling. The next day, the Sunday newspapers roundly mocked the RFU committee. The following week, the RFU tried to find a new captain, but the England players, one by one, refused to take the captaincy. First Andrew refused, then Richards. Moore said no, and Leonard said no. They asked Ben Clarke who had not heard about the boycott so said 'yes' then called them back within minutes to change his mind.

The RFU had made a quite spectacular miscalculation of public opinion, and had grossly underestimated the players' support for their captain.

Jon Holmes, Carling's agent, went on to Gary Newbon's radio show to talk about the situation, and Easby came onto the line. There was no question that the RFU were in a mess by this stage so Newbon suggested to Easby that he might reinstate Carling if the former England captain apologised for his behaviour. 'Yes,' said Easby, and suddenly, as if by magic, an olive branch had appeared. The apology was made and a painful press conference followed, in which the RFU reinstated Carling.

It was a silly episode, of course, and one which had little to do with any offence caused by Carling's comment. The incident was the crystallisation of a power struggle between the committees and the players. It was, in some respects, a class war. It was a battle between the old and the new, the bourgeoisie and their unpaid workers. It was about clean coaches and dirty coaches; it was about rank, superiority, age and position. It was the desperate action of a group of men who felt their power slipping away from them.

Easby is the name most commonly associated with 'fartgate'. But, to his credit, he became the one conciliatory member of the group. When the others from East India Club realised the mistake they had made and dived for cover, at least Easby stepped in to sort it out. By swallowing his pride and phoning the radio station he ended the saga with his dignity restored. The dignity of his committee, however, to the extent that they were perceived to have any before the crisis, was eroded altogether.

While rugby in the northern hemisphere bumbled along – the players coping as best they could with the hobnailed boots and handcuffs that amateurism created for them, big things were happening in South Africa: Nelson Mandela had been freed from prison in 1990, and, on 15 August 1992, the Springboks returned to international competition. They lost narrowly in their first match, going down 27–24 to New Zealand at Ellis Park, and nearly ruined their return to the international game by failing to observe two distinct conditions imposed by the ANC. First, *Die Stem* (The Call) was not supposed to be played before matches because it was the white national anthem. Second, Mandela himself had requested a minute's silence in memory of all those who had died during the country's unrest. But there was no silence and most of the crowd broke into an impromptu version of *Die Stem* amid lavish waving of the old flag. The ANC were so incensed that they immediately withdrew their backing of the South African Rugby Football Union (SARFU).

The Wallabies were due to meet South Africa the following Saturday in Cape Town, but the Australians refused to play without the ANC's official clearance. Mandela relented after reassurances from SARFU and many apologies, with the proviso that South Africa rugby would be banished again if the events of Ellis Park were repeated. This time the silence was observed, and *Die Stem* was not sung. But the Springboks were beaten again, and many feared that international rugby had moved on so far since their isolation, that they would never catch up.

One of the problems facing rugby in the new, free, united South Africa was that the sport was seen as being both a very middle-class game and closely associated with apartheid. Rugby had nothing to do with 80 per cent of the people and simply did not exist in the townships. Football was the sport of the masses.

Indeed, rugby was so closely linked with white supremacy, that the Springboks were actively despised by non-whites, and on their rare visits to watch games, blacks would support any visiting teams against South Africa. The Afrikaans leaders used oval ball metaphors to explain their stance. 'We whites – despite the fact that we are in the minority, are in a position of control. This is due to our discipline, unity and advanced technology ... The struggle to gain the support of the population can, therefore, be compared to a rugby match. He who wins the scrum and controls the ball, scores the try ... We need to work and stay strong for each other. Just like a winning rugby team.'

Then, on 10 May 1994, Mandela was inaugurated as President of the new Republic of South Africa and he promised to change things. Whether he could or would bother to change the image of rugby as a white man's sport was to be seen. Certainly there were other, infinitely more important things to do. He inherited a country in which unemployment stood around the 40 per cent mark, and where attacks on farms were 700 per cent higher than attacks on farms in any other country on earth. The country was also riddled with violence. In the year that Mandela was inaugurated, the Medical Research Council of South Africa reports that there were 32,382 murders in South Africa, and 31,000 attempted murders. As a comparison, in the same period, there were 886 deaths recorded as murder by the police in England and Wales.

Bear in mind that there are fewer people living in South Africa than in England and Wales. Indeed, based on these figures, taking into account the population differentials – there was one murder per 1000 people in England and Wales, and fifty-nine murders per 1000 people in South Africa.

The next World Cup would be held in the Republic in 1995. Few had any idea how the different sections of society in the host country would react to the tournament, or what the outcome of it would be.

While South African players were delighting in their grand return to the international game, Wales were going through a dismal time. Indeed, it would be fair to say that the Welsh team was in a complete mess by the time the tournament came round, due in no small part to the number of players defecting to rugby league. Morale was not helped by the fact that Wales had to qualify for the 1995 tournament – the first of the founder International Rugby Board members to have to do so. They played Romania, Spain, Portugal and Italy to go through as the team from Europe 1. In addition to the humilation of this, they lost 22–10 at home to South Africa.

Indeed, as Wales left for South Africa, they had lost their previous five internationals and experienced a whitewash in the Five Nations Championships. Australian Alex Evans had been brought in as coach just weeks before the World Cup began, and had to do his best to motivate a team that had scored only three tries in their last nine games.

Scotland arrived at the 1995 World Cup in 'a most positive frame of mind', according to Gavin Hastings. They expected to reach the knockout stages with their experienced team, containing captain Hastings and brother, Scott, as well as Craig Chalmers, Tony Stanger and Damian Cronin – men with a great deal of knowledge and understanding of top-flight rugby. These were the players who had created a resurgence in the sport, but Scotland needed to take that resurgence onto the world stage, and make a mark at the World Cup.

Ireland had struggled in the Five Nations prior to the tournament, losing heavily to England, Scotland and France and managing to avoid the wooden spoon by beating Wales in Cardiff. In May, they had lost to Italy, a minor rugby nation. The 1995 World Cup appeared to have come at exactly the wrong time for them.

So, once again, it was on the shoulders of the English players that British Isles hopes rested. England had won a further Grand Slam in 1992 – the first back-to-back grand slam since Wavell Wakefield's team achieved two consecutive victories in 1923 and 1924.

Geoff Cooke left in 1994, and Jack Rowell, the successful coach of Bath, took over as the new coach of England in time for their summer tour in the same year.

'My first impressions were of him trying to niggle people, challenge them and put doubt and confusion in people's minds,' says Moore. 'It worked well – people started to feel unnerved and I'm sure they worked harder as a result. I remember Jack walking into one meeting and saying "Okay, what's happening here? What are we doing?" He got the players involved in running sessions, making decisions. Rowell is one of the best coaches I have been involved with.'

England were better prepared for the tournament in 1995 than for any previous one. They had played six Test matches leading up to it, and Rowell had taken the players for a variety of squad sessions. The players had their own personal training routines and many of them had their own fitness advisors – independent of the clubs and the national team. 'We'd done a stack of sessions at Marlow and, at the time, I couldn't see how it was possible for a team to be better prepared for the World Cup,' said Leonard.

'Players weren't embarrassed about training like they had been in the past,' said Moore. 'We knew the route to success lay in the hard work put in behind the scenes, so we did it. You didn't feel stupid doing extra training, you felt good.'

Kyran Bracken says he decided to work on his passing before the 1995 tournament, so he went to talk to Richard Hill, recognised as the best passer in the game. He asked Hill what work he did to improve his passing. Hill said that he usually practised by doing 200 passes off each hand, four times a week. Bracken decided he would do 201 passes off each hand six times a week.

In 1994, England played South Africa, and the players had the chance to meet Mandela for the first time.

Dewi Morris was a bit nervous meeting him, and I was standing next to him [recalls Leonard]. We were told that we could actually ask Nelson Mandela a question and Dewi got so nervous about what he had to ask him, I mean he was literally shaking. And he was shaking Nelson Mandela's hand and he literally just said 'Um, um, do you have road tax over here?'

He asks the most important man of the twentieth century if he has road tax over there and I'm in tears. Me and Brian Moore were wetting ourselves laughing, so I actually think I was bent over double when I got introduced to Nelson Mandela because I was laughing so hard.

I was sort of wiping tears away while saying 'Very nice to meet you and what an honour and privilege it is' and I was just smiling and giggling from ear to ear so I don't know what he thought about that. That must be the funniest thing I have ever heard. I was thoroughly embarrassed for Dewi and he's still not lived it down to this day.

In the 1995 Five Nations Championship, England beat Ireland 20–8 in Dublin, then they beat France 31–10 at Twickenham a fortnight later.

Spirits were high as they gathered in Richmond before leaving for the Wales game in Cardiff. The players went to The Sun, then on to Park Avenue nightclub before returning home in the early hours of the morning. Bracken recalls drinking seven or eight pints in an effort to keep pace with Jason Leonard.

'That was when I realised I couldn't. Jase was still sober and I could barely see straight, so at about 3 a.m., Mike Catt and I went back to the hotel.'

As he walked in, he heard noises coming from the team room. He was drunk enough to think it would be a really good idea to go and investigate, so put his head round the door. Rowell and Cusworth were sitting there, watching a Wales game on television. Bracken rushed out before the coaches could see him and headed up for bed. The coach called a meeting early the next morning and Jack asked who it was that had come in at 3 a.m. and opened the door to the team room. 'With an important game on Saturday, it's a disgrace,' said Rowell. No one would say, so the players all filed out. A few people looked at Leonard. 'It wasn't me,' said the England prop defensively. 'Why does everyone think it was me? I can prove it wasn't me because I was in Park Avenue till 5 a.m.'

'Interesting defence,' mumbled Rowell, as the players filed out of the room.

Despite the late-night cavorting, England went on to beat

Wales 23–9 in Cardiff, proving that the days when they were unable to win away against Wales were well and truly over. Ubogu led the celebrations after the game, declaring 'The champagne's on me.'

His magnanimous gesture was explained later when he confessed that, before the match, he had noticed that bookies were offering odds of 10–1 against him scoring the first try of the game. He called a friend and asked him to put a bet on for £100. Victor duly scored the first try, and didn't tire of telling people that he had just won himself £1000. Victor treated the squad to a great night out on the town. The next day, he called his friend to collect his winnings and his friend admitted that he hadn't put the bet on because he thought it so unlikely that Ubogu would score. He'd used the money, instead, to buy himself a match ticket.

Three wins out of three took England to the Grand Slam, Triple Crown and Championship decider against Scotland. They won it 24–12, to take the title in World Cup year, and headed to South Africa brimming with confidence.

13

The story of the pools

You ought to be ashamed of yourselves – playing against children.

A South African journalist comments on the mismatch
between New Zealand and Japan in the 1995 pool games

19 May 1995: corrugated iron huts shimmered in the after-noon sunshine on the sparse landscape, as cooling gusts of wind swept down the hills and across the dusty ground, nudg-ing litter into the air and swirling it towards the small bony children hunched on the sun-drenched hill face. The children looked out towards the town centre, occasionally playing with stones, sticks and old twigs – throwing them at the dogs who ambled past, looking bedraggled and unkempt. There were hun-dreds of animals – mainly dogs, but cats as well: all as thin, stray and as desperate as their tormentors. The scene was horrible – a reminder that, on the eve of the 1995 World Cup, with Nelson Mandela out of prison, the ANC in power, and South Africa on the verge of a bright and glorious return to international relations, the past remained. Even as the future was being written, apartheid's legacy was not erased – it sat quietly in shantytowns and on hillsides around Cape Town, providing scenes of desper-ation, suffering and sadness that would contrast so bitterly with the opulence of the sports tournament about to be held. Apartheid may have been dead, but its corpse was still very warm.

Sixteen international rugby teams would convene in this city the next day to enjoy a luscious banquet before the glitzy World Cup tournament kicked off. The event would announce South Africa's triumphant return to international sport. In the eyes of the world, South Africa's policy of segregation and degradation was in the past – consigned to the history books.

Meanwhile, on the hillside, children with sticks and stones continued to wait, hoping against expectation that the adults would arrive soon with food. It was hard not to keep watching, just to check that the little boy with the soft black curls and the desperately sad eyes got fed that night. To make sure that some-one returned to look after him and protect him from the cold night, slowly closing in. As the winter sun dipped below the crest of the hill, the little boy, and many others like him, were still sit-ting. Still waiting.

Later that day, Nelson Mandela announced his joy that his coun-try would be hosting the 1995 World Cup. He said that sport had the power to change the world. Many of us who had stood and watched those children and seen their empty, desperate lives, hoped and prayed that he was right. The South African Rugby Union announced that 40 per cent of its share of World Cup prof-its would go to help under-privileged areas. Perhaps he was right.

20 May 1995: officials at Cape Town airport paced around, check-ing their watches in a state of mild panic. They had convened early to ensure that all plans were in order. They'd studied the arrival times and briefed all ground staff. This would be one of the most challenging assignments in the airport's recent history. They wanted nothing to go wrong. Now it was 10 a.m., and they looked out of the window at the grey, rainy day. Sunshine would have been much better, but at least it wasn't foggy or windy, so the flights should arrive on time. From 11.30 a.m. until 12.15 p.m., eight flights carrying fourteen squads of players for the rugby World Cup lunch would land at the airport. The players had to be dispatched to the buses waiting on the tarmac as quickly as pos-sible, to get them there on time. There would be 416 players from

sixteen nations at the function, taking place in a giant marquee at the Groot Constantia Estate. The vast majority of those players would come through Cape Town airport. The staff had been warned that this was the first event of the World Cup, and that many of the people attending the function would remember their first impression of the country, so it was essential that nothing, nothing went wrong. The players and their entourages must see only efficiency, smiling faces and supreme professionalism. The staff of Cape Town airport must not let their country down. Nothing must go wrong.

Edward Griffiths was the Chief Executive Officer (CEO) of the South African Rugby Football Union in 1995, and to him fell the final checks, confirmations and further checks before the opening match of the tournament. The day before the first game, he wandered around, and considered what on earth was left to check; everything had been organised to perfection. He took a final walk down to see the announcer and to make sure that the music was all organised and ready. To his horror, he discovered that the wrong version of the South African anthem was on stand-by. In an almighty panic, he was forced to ask the Drakensberg Boys' Choir and singer P.J. Powers to re-assemble in the middle of the night before the opening ceremony to re-record the song. At 1.30 a.m. over two dozen boys and Powers assembled in a studio in Cape Town, and finished the recording in the early hours of the morning before the opening ceremony.

Griffiths had one further saviour-like task to perform before the tournament kicked off. The CEO had held five tickets back until the last moment in case a VIP suddenly called. Since no one phoned, after the opening ceremony, and with less than quarter of an hour before kick-off, he came out of the ground, clutching them in his hand. In front of him were a couple of young boys. He called them over, and gave them a ticket each, then handed the others to three Springbok supporters walking down the street. The music sorted, his good deed for the day done, and five boys falling to their knees in joy, and it was time for the first match of the 1995 World Cup.

*

The opening game in Pool A was, as tradition dictates, between the holders, Australia, and the tournament hosts. It was a crucial game for South Africa as they set out to prove to the rugby community that years of isolation had not dimmed their abilities on a rugby field. Kitch Christie, the South Africa coach, knew that the eyes of the world would be on his team, and that it was important for them to get the best start possible. He had analysed the Australians to the bone, and had devised a series of moves that he thought would be good enough to beat them. The players were instructed to learn the moves on the field at Silvermine where the Springboks practised. Every session was planned meticulously. Gysie Pienaar, assistant coach, David Waterstone and Hennie Bekker, the technical assistants, had offered considerable feedback on all the Australian players – advising on their strengths and weaknesses. All this information had been processed to produce the Springboks' game plan for this most crucial of opening matches.They had identified that two Wallabies were likely to cause the most trouble – George Gregan, the scrum-half, and David Campese, the wing. Waterstone, the most senior of the analysts, had provided a detailed report on Campese which suggested that the wing 'runs well off the ball – quick over the first ten metres, suspect defence, inclined to run without support, but – aged 32 – he can be beaten on the outside.'

'I don't think we've ever spent so much time preparing for one game as I did preparing for that game against Australia,' said Christie. It was a must-win game – the winners would contemplate opposition such as France, Argentina and Western Samoa on their path to the World Cup final, while the draw would probably condemn the losers to a quarter-final against England, finalists in the last World Cup, and a semi-final against New Zealand. The stakes were high for South Africa, but they were seriously lacking in experience. Because of the apartheid ban, their total number of international appearances was 126, which was just thirty-one fewer than Michael Lynagh and David Campese combined. No one expected them to beat Australia in the opening game, but then no one accounted for the difference that home advantage and inspiration would make to the team.

No one accounted, in particular, for the sixteenth player in the South Africa team – Nelson Mandela. There is no question that his influence and inspiration gave the South African players further impetus and determination to win. Mandela visited the players the day before the game against Australia to wish them luck. While he was there, Hennie Le Roux grabbed a Springbok cap from Japie Mulder's head and handed it to him as a souvenir of his visit. When he walked into the stadium the next day, he was wearing it. Mandela sat next to Paul Keating of Australia during the game, punching the Australia Prime Minister on the arm every time South Africa scored.

Australia, for their part, were determined not to let the passion and excitement of the occasion get to them. They were desperate not to relinquish their position as champions of the world, and knew that they had a talented team and were more than able to compete with the hosts. Their entire campaign to retain the trophy was code-named REPEAT – Relive at Ellis Park the Elation At Twickenham.

The game was one of unrelenting excitement and drama. South Africa won 27–18 through sheer passion. After the game, at Morne du Plessis' suggestion, the players and their partners went on a tour of Robben Island, including a visit to the prison where President Mandela had been held. It was another exceptionally sensitive piece of management. 'Our visit to the island proved a humbling experience. We peered into the small cell where Mandela had spent so many years – it was awful. You wondered how he'd managed to survive, and we all wanted to do something to pay him back,' said Pienaar. James Small wiped away a tear from the corner of his eye. South Africa were moved and further inspired.

The victory over Australia made life much easier. For weeks before the tournament, Christie and Morne du Plessis, the manager, had planned two roads through the World Cup – the high road following victory in the opening game, and the low road which would follow defeat. The Boks were on the high road. At the outset, the management had told the players there would be two separate teams – green and gold. The gold team was a first team to play Australia, while the green team would then play Romania and Canada – the other two teams in the group. 'The green team was effectively the second-best side in South Africa, and I was backing them to beat both Romania and Canada at home,' said Christie. 'Some people thought I was taking a massive gamble, but I didn't regard it as a gamble at all because the other opponents were far weaker than Australia.'

It was a tough draw for these two smaller 'weaker' teams – they had little chance of qualifying with two heavyweights to fight past first. Gareth Rees, Canada's captain, described it as being the pool of death. 'As captain I was furious because, having been quarter-finalists in 1991, we felt that we were in the top eight in the world and so were hoping to get a seeding. But because South Africa hadn't been in previous World Cups, they weren't seeded, so we found ourselves in the group containing the winners from 1991 and the team that would go on to win in 1995.'

Romania was South Africa's next opposition. Vladimir Vlad, the team liaison officer for Romania, was under no illusions about the magnitude of the task facing his players as they ran out against South Africa, but he was determined that they would not want for commitment. 'You can compare us to kamikaze pilots,' he said. 'The players will give their all.' In the event, Romania provided stern opposition, but lost valliantly – 21–8. After the match, the South Africa team attended a cocktail party in the Presidents' Room at Newlands Stadium. They were standing near the door when the Romanians arrived, carrying their kit in plastic bags from a local supermarket. Pienaar was appalled, and contacted kit supplier Adidas who had provided the Springboks with so much gear. Gavin Cowley of Adidas agreed to provide the Romanians with kit and bags before their next game.

After the official function, the South African players joined Rudolf Straeuli to celebrate the birth of his first child – Rieze. The celebratory evening culminated with several players buying a fish, and putting it into Mark Andrews' bed. As the days passed and the fish rotted, Andrews found it and decided to move it to another player's room. Over the course of the pool games, the fish made appearances in several beds, including those belonging to Straeuli, Hannes Strydom and McNeil Hendricks.

While the players were having their fun, the coaches were getting a little concerned. The strength of the Romanian players had surprised them. Should Christie continue with his plan to send a second team out to play Canada, or abandon such thoughts and send his best XV out to ensure they stayed on the high road? Christie decided to stay with his original plan, but to include Pienaar in the team to lead them. South Africa moved to a 20–0 lead after seventy minutes. The game plan against the very physical Canadians was simple and straightforward – safety first, zero-risk, punting the ball deep, playing in their half and seizing every chance. The aim was to avoid provocation, avoid injuries and conserve as much energy as possible while winning the match. The road to disaster is paved with good intentions. Lots of injuries and a mad 90-second frenzy, and the Springbok campaign almost came off the rails. A brawl broke out, and James Dalton, Gareth Rees and Rod Snow were sent off and banned for thirty days. The Canadians were unaffected by the ban because they were on their way home in any case, but for South Africa it was looking devastating. The entire South Africa squad was demoralised by the decision. Dalton had been third man in (he claimed to be breaking up the fight) – thus was banned for turning a punch-up into a brawl. 'Everything was falling apart,' says Pienaar. 'All focus was gone when we came off the pitch. Everyone was so cross.'

The next day, the South African players were due to be at a barbecue with local rugby officials who had gone to the trouble of laying a tarmac road so the team bus would be able to reach the venue. The players didn't want to go and du Plessis decided that it would be better for them if they spent the day alone, so he contacted the officials and explained that the players would not be there. The barbecue hosts were so upset that they later filed a damages claim against the SARFU.

The players decided that they wanted to go to Fish River Sun golfing and casino resort – to relax and forget about what had happened, refocus and prepare for the quarter-final. It was agreed that they could go, and du Plessis made the arrangements. The bus would take them in the morning and return at 6 p.m., but Pienaar and a few of the players wanted to stay on to have dinner with the resort manager. They were told they could stay, but were asked to return straight after dinner.

'Fine,' said Pienaar. But the South Africa captain was feeling out of sorts and looking for distraction, so he made the most of his time – he drank and went to a casino before thinking about heading back. In fact he, Andre Joubert and Gavin Johnson eventually arrived back at the team hotel at 3 a.m., to find Morne du Plessis pacing across the floor and looking anxious and fed up, panicking because he thought the players had been involved in a car accident. He told Pienaar how worried he'd been, and Pienaar said he resented being treated like a child. The close bonds between the triumvirate at the top of South African rugby – Pienaar, Christie and du Plessis – were starting to fray.

'In my mind, everything was twisted and blurred,' explains Pienaar. 'It wasn't going to plan. I was fed up. I had become sullen and silent and was making no contribution to the team at all.'

Something needed to be done. The next day, Christie and Pienaar spoke about the way the captain was feeling, and a team meeting was arranged. Pienaar promised to pay a fine for being late back and apologised to his teammates, and the matter was put to rest. 'After that meeting, it felt like everything was back on course again,' said Pienaar. 'We went out and had a fantastic training session – the wheels were back on. The World Cup was in sight once more.' With just forty-eight hours before their quarter-final match against the runners-up from Pool B, they finally turned their sights on the match, and were talking about rugby again. Then, some more bad news – the RWC directors had studied the video of the Canada match and announced that they were intending to cite more players for foul play. On Monday morning, as they travelled from Port Elizabeth to Johannesburg for the quarter-final, Hendricks was found guilty of kicking and punching and suspended for ninety days. Hendricks' misfortune meant that Chester Williams – now recovered from a hamstring injury –

could come back in to the side, as the South Africans were given permission, bizarrely, to substitute their banned player. Williams arrived soon after 10 p.m. and in Cape Town a factory worked overtime to produce his Springbok tracksuit in time for the quarter-final.

England, runners-up in the 1991 World Cup, were based in Durban for the 1995 tournament, staying at a hotel just metres away from the Indian Ocean. There was a confidence to the side – they'd won six matches in succession in a nine-month unbeaten run before arriving in South Africa. They won all of their games in Pool B – beating Western Samoa, Italy and Argentina to go through to the quarter-finals.

The England players were fit, trained to the peak and surrounded by a plethora of support men ranging from a doctor and physio to a psychologist and dietician. Along with them were Jack Rowell and Les Cusworth – two of the best coaches in world rugby. Even the playing conditions were in England's favour. There were no midday games in the scorching 80 degree Natal sunshine, and accompanying humidity – instead, their first two games were played at 5 p.m., and the third at 8 p.m. when the temperature had dropped and the humidity was blown away by the gentle breezes.

The squad seemed relaxed throughout the competition – nominating a 'dick of the day' who had to wear an outfit consisting of a cowboy-type denim shirt which had a pattern of three cowboys riding across mountains, plus a hat and a belt containing a toy gun. 'Today the doctor is the winner because he was caught drinking wine from a Coke can,' announced Moore, as he handed over the prize.

England had the best all-round pack of forwards in the competition – with three giant locks in Martin Bayfield, Martin Johnson and Richard West. They won 24–18 against Argentina, despite not scoring a try, then beat Italy 27–20, with each team scoring two tries. Neither match contained any startling displays of rugby, and they were performing at a standard way below their Five Nations form. But, still, there was a quiet confidence about them, and to win when not playing at one's best signified the chances of great success once they found their form.

In their final group game, they beat Western Samoa 44–22, confirming their progress to the quarter-final stages at the top of the group. Western Samoa followed them, in second place. To qualify for the second time running was a great achievement for Western Samoa, but there's no question that the 1995 World Cup was a difficult one for them; because they had done so well in 1991, the burden of expectation was upon them. Western Samoa had a strong squad in 1995, and had done a lot of fitness training over the preceding year, making them faster and stronger in the set pieces. They beat Italy in their first match, and knew they would struggle against England in their final pool game, so qualification really depended on victory over Argentina. In what was the match of the pool, they beat Argentina, 32–26. 'We were relieved,' recalls Pat Lam. 'We didn't want to have to go into the game against England having to win in order to qualify, so the victory over Argentina was the start of huge celebrations and some memorable parties.'

No sooner had the winning sides, Western Samoa and England, packed up their things and travelled to Johannesburg for the quarter-final, than David Campese, the Wallaby winger, launched a withering attack on Will Carling and the whole England XV, describing them as 'boring'.

High on the veldt, in Ellis Park, Johannesburg, the rugby world stopped and stared as a rugby tornado swept into town. Weighing 19 stone and measuring 6 ft 3, Jonah Lomu burst on to the World Cup scene. He was the youngest player ever to run out for the All Blacks – a New Zealander who would come to dominate the tournament. For Ireland in Pool C, facing them in New Zealand's first match of the tournament, it was a baptism of fire. Things weren't helped by the fact that before the players left for the game, a fax arrived in the New Zealand players' team room. It was addressed to Lomu and was apparently from Richard Wallace, the Irish wing who would be charged with tackling the no. 11. The message said that Wallace was going to waste Lomu in the match, and that Lomù might as well just not turn up. 'When the big boy read this I thought his eyes were going to pop out of his head,' recalls Eric Rush. Needless to say, they all discovered afterwards that it was not from Wallace at all, but was a wind-up.

'Yes, very funny,' says Wallace in a way that implies it was all about as humorous as having a needless operation without anaesthetic. New Zealand won 43–19, and Terry Kingston, Ireland's captain, was asked what Ireland might do if faced with Lomu again. 'We would get a shotgun,' he said.

But, despite Lomu's astonishing impact on the tournament, he says that he was absolutely terrified. 'Ohhh man. So scared,' he says. 'Just really scared and being really ill.' He suffers from nerves before matches, but has never known anything like that night, when he was retching and vomiting all evening. In the match, Lomu scored his first try in the black jersey when he crashed over after a pass from Graeme Bachop. Laurie Mains had talked to Lomu before the match, and said, 'Don't take any prisoners, Jonah. If you feel it's on, just go for it. Have a crack from anywhere.'

Jonah-mania started as soon as the match finished. He had played like a one-man battalion, and everyone wanted to talk to him. Sir Brian Lochore said: 'The press were always wanting a piece of Jonah and we were conscious of the fact that he was a young guy and that there was a limit to how much any one player could do. Even with all the attention, he was a wonderful member of the squad. He never regarded himself as anyone special – not like some sort of idol. Nothing went to his head. He was a valuable member of the team both on and off the field.' Ireland took on Japan next, winning 50–28.

Wales were also in Pool C, and played their first game against Japan, winning 57–10. They were based in Bloemfontein for this opening match. The victory helped Wales to a good start, but there was no hiding the fact that Wales was a team in disarray. So many of their players had gone to rugby league – guys like Jonathan Davies, Scott Quinnell, Allan Bateman, Scott Gibbs and John Devereux. Wales came into the World Cup having been whitewashed in the Five Nations and suffering the indignity of having to qualify for the World Cup. Still, things were looking up after game number one, and it was a long time since Wales could say that.

Sadly, it didn't last too long. Addressing a press conference called to announce the Wales team to play New Zealand, Geoff Evans, the team manager, chose to tell the assembled media that Wales were bigger, stronger and fitter than the All Blacks, an interesting suggestion, since Wales hadn't beaten New Zealand since 1953, and all the comment was likely to do was rouse the All Blacks to a greater performance. Evans compounded the whole thing by having the New Zealand team thrown off the Ellis Park pitch after they turned up for a light run out the day before the match. 'That really got the boys going,' said Sean Fitzpatrick: 34–9 to New Zealand.

The match between New Zealand and Japan was a mismatch of quite staggering proportions. The All Blacks won 145–17, with Marc Ellis scoring six tries. One South African journalist was moved to complain: 'You ought to be ashamed of yourselves – playing against children.' Shiggy Konno, their former chairman and spokesman for forty years, said at the press conference: 'I am always saying the same thing – we are simply not big enough.' All World Cup records tumbled in this match – with New Zealand setting new 'bests' for most points, most tries and most conversions.

With New Zealand top of the table, the shoot-out for second place took place between Wales and Ireland. Everything hinged on this for the two teams. The winner would go through to the quarter-finals, the loser would be on the plane. Wales were desperate not to go home before the quarter-finals again, but they were beaten 24–23 in what Ieuan Evans describes as one of the most disastrous matches in the previous ten years of Welsh rugby. For the second time running, Wales had failed to pass the pool stage of the tournament. The players were mocked and humiliated, and several declared they were too scared to go home until the furore over their early exit had subsided, so they stayed on in South Africa until the heat died down. The match was a dreadful exhibition of European rugby, and one that no side deserved to win. Vernon Pugh, chairman of the Welsh Rugby Union, said that he would resign unless comprehensive changes were made to the structure and coaching of the sport in Wales. It was a disastrous day for rugby, but nothing like as disastrous as the dreadful fate that befell a young electrician from the Ivory Coast called Max Brito.

TIME TO GET SERIOUS
David Kirk leads out the All Blacks
during the 1987 World Cup.

NEW ZEALAND DELIVER
John Kirwan scores during the 1987
World Cup final against France.

HEADING FOR A FALL
Gary Pearce and Wade Dooley
during England's 1987 quarter-
final defeat against Wales.

THAT'S FOR YOU
New Zealand skipper, David Kirk
(left), hands over the Webb Ellis
Trophy to Andy Dalton, to thank the
former skipper for his help during
the tournament. Dalton missed the
World Cup through injury.

CAUGHT IN A TIME WARP
England's old-fashioned training techniques let them down at the 1987 World Cup.

WALES ON TOP
England wing Rory Underwood is tackled during England's 1987 World Cup quarter-final defeat to Wales.

FIJI FLUMMOXED
Fiji escaped a military coup to get to the 1987 World Cup, but couldn't fight off the powerful New Zealanders in the pool stage of the tournament.

BLANCO GOES FOR BROKE
Serge Blanco, the brilliant Frenchman, was one of the stars of the 1987 World Cup, scoring the try of the tournament in his side's semi-final victory over Australia.

ABOUT FACE
Welsh fans dress up as Western Samoans before their side's quarter-final defeat in 1991.

YOU BEAUTY!
Nick Farr-Jones raises the Webb-Ellis Trophy at Twickenham after winning the 1991 World Cup final.

WALLABY WONDERS
Stand-in captain Michael Lynagh
scores the crucial try which leads
Australia to victory over Ireland
in the 1991 quarter-final.

CAPTAIN'S SALUTE
Will Carling acknowledges the
crowd after England's defeat in
the 1991 World Cup final
against Australia.

LOMU ON A WING AND NO ONE HAS A PRAYER!
Rob Andrew becomes one of many players to see Jonah Lomu zip down the wing for New Zealand during the 1995 World Cup.

CAN'T CATCH HIM EITHER
Jason Leonard, the most capped World Cup player in history, can only watch as Lomu crashes over for another try.

THANKS MR PRESIDENT
Springbok captain Francois Pienaar
receives the World Cup from South
African President, Nelson Mandela.

ON TOP OF THE WORLD
Francois Pienaar salutes the world
after his team's victory over New
Zealand in the 1995 World Cup.

PARTY TIME
Hundreds of balloons are
released as dancers perform
in the closing ceremony of the
1995 World Cup at Ellis Park.

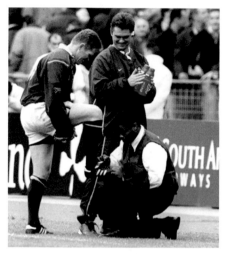

THE BOOT MAN
Jannie de Beer has his boots
worshipped after his dropped
goals took South Africa to
victory over England in the 1999
quarter-final in Paris.

ARGENTINIAN BEEF
Argentinian players celebrate their quarter-final play-off victory over Ireland in 1999.

A BLACK DAY FOR NEW ZEALAND
The pre-tournament favourites are brought down to earth with a crash by a re-galvanised France team in the 1999 semi-final.

YOU BEAUTY! (PART TWO)
John Eales, the Wallaby captain, gets a hero's welcome on his return to Sydney.

WOODWARD'S WAY
England's fitness levels at the 2003 World Cup were the best they had ever been.

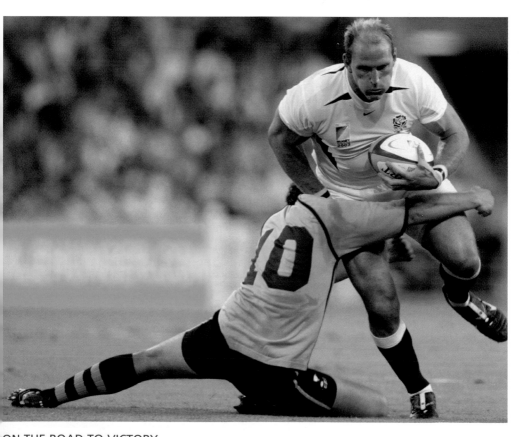

ON THE ROAD TO VICTORY
England's Lawrence Dallaglio helps England to victory in their 2003 World Cup pool game against Uruguay.

THE POINTS MACHINE
England fly-half, Jonny
Wilkinson, lines up another
penalty attempt.
It went over . . . as if you
doubted it.

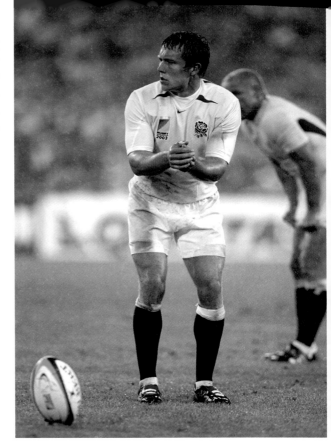

THE POWER AND THE GLORY
Martin Johnson dominates
the 2003 World Cup final
against Australia.

SOMETHING TO SHOUT ABOUT
England's Matt Dawson, who delivered the crucial pass to Wilkinson for the fly-half's winning drop goal, celebrates with Ben Cohen.

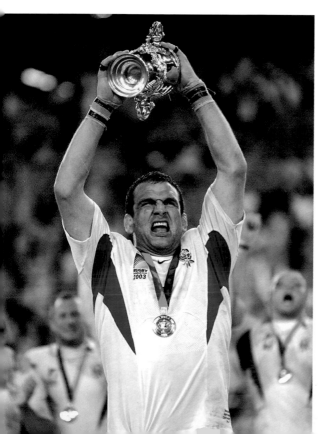

CAPTAIN FANTASTIC
Martin Johnson, one of the most influential players in the history of the game, holds the World Cup aloft.

BY ROYAL APPROVAL
England's coach, Clive Woodward, is congratulated by Prince Harry at the Olympic Stadium in Sydney.

VICTORY PARADE
England celebrate with fans at Trafalgar Square following their 2003 World Cup victory.

SMOOTH OPERATOR
Jonny Wilkinson heads out of the team's plush hotel to celebrate his team's World Cup victory.

14

Tragedy hits the World Cup

When we play in the World Cup, we hope most of all not to be ridiculed. We will apply the option to play positively and I hope that people will see we are trying, and I hope that we will not be ridiculed.

Claude Aimé Ezoua, Ivory Coast selector

In May 1995, Max Brito was a 24-year-old electrician having the time of his life. He was an Ivory Coast rugby player heading for South Africa on an entirely unexpected adventure from West Africa. No one expected Ivory Coast to qualify for the World Cup. They had never qualified before, and they haven't qualified since, but in 1995 they managed surprise defeats over Zimbabwe and Namibia in the qualification tournament to go through to the world's premier competition from the African zone. For Ivory Coast players it was a dream come true. 'This is mind-bogglingly exciting for us,' said their captain Athanase Dali, with the breathless anticipation of a child.

Brito enjoyed putting in the big hits – indeed the fearless tackles from the 6 ft, 11 stone 7 lb winger were one of the highlights of the Ivorian team. He was distinctive – with his big, lumpy dreadlocks that bounced along as he ran around the pitch from his position on the left wing, and a passion for the sport that others described as 'contagious'. He had three caps for his country, having made his international debut a year before the World Cup. When not playing for Ivory Coast, he played for Biscarosse on the south-west coast of France, and had happily settled there – just south of Bordeaux – with his wife and two children.

Rugby in the Ivory Coast, and their team, known as *les éléphants*, is new. The union was not formed until 1990, the same year that it joined the International Rugby Board. The sport is popular among school children, but the playing population is small, with only 10 clubs and around 11,000 registered senior players, many of whom, though registered, do not actually play the game. Football remains the dominant sport in the country by a considerable margin. Indeed, such is the infatuation with the round ball game that on one occasion, when the Ivory Coast football team was eliminated from the African Cup of Nations, the squad had to be detained by the military authorities for their own protection on their return. The footballers were taken to an army camp following their elimination, because of the fear of possible reprisals by angry fans. It couldn't be more different in rugby. 'The problems they have in football come because everyone loves it too much, but the problem we have in rugby is that no one cares at all,' said Dali.

The lack of interest in Ivory Coast rugby from within the country is echoed, say the players, in the rugby community at large. So in 1995, they were eager to use their first appearance at the World Cup to emphasise that they desperately needed help.

'If the International Board don't help the little countries like us, rugby will die,' said Dali, during the tournament. 'Few people play rugby in the Ivory Coast. The IB must help to bring more people to the game. We cannot play World Cup qualifiers alone. We need experience in the top echelons.' The Ivory Coast coach, Claude Ezoua, added: 'We need to play to prosper. Not the likes of England or the Springboks, but the smaller nations, such as Italy and Romania.'

Brito, Dali and their Ivory Coast teammates began their World Cup adventure with a match against Pool D rivals, Scotland. No one expected them to beat one of the oldest rugby nations in the world, but the defeat by nearly ninety points (89–0) hurt. 'The teams are harder than we thought,' said Dali. 'They are very much better than we are. We have much work to do.' The record defeat led to some questioning the presence of the minor teams at the tournament, but when they managed to score eighteen points against France, losing with a more respectable score line of 45–18 in their second game, the questioning temporarily stopped. Côte d'Ivoire lost the game in the forward battle, and through inexperience. When their fly-half Camara left the field, they played without a fly-half for at least five minutes before eventually sending Dali onto the park as a replacement.

Next, Ivory Coast faced Tonga, and the competition took a turn into the sombre, as two consecutive tragedies struck. First, on the day before the game, there was the terrible news for Dali that his brother Maxime had died. The Ivory Coast's liaison officer, Camille Anoma, announced that 'Maxime Dali died in an Ivory Coast hospital on Friday. He had been suffering from mental problems for several months.' The players ran out for their match against Tonga the next day, wearing black arm bands in support of their captain. Maxime Dali, a sports teacher, had played rugby himself before his mental problems ended his career in the sport. He had played in the African qualifying group for the 1991 World Cup, winning three caps, and also played for France in Caen. His father, François Dali, was one of the founders of Ivorian rugby and a former national coach. The Dalis were the most important rugby family in Ivory Coast rugby, and the death of Maxime hit everyone in the country's sport very hard.

Then, another tragedy . . . three minutes into the game against Tonga, Brito was running out of defence when he was tackled by Ionke Afeaki, a Tongan flanker. Several players fell on top of him, leaving him prone and motionless on the ground. He was taken to intensive care in Unitas Hospital, Pretoria, under the care of Etienne Hugo, the Pool D doctor and an orthopaedic surgeon. Brito was breathing unaided but unable to move. An operation to defuse the vertebrae was planned for the following day – to stabilise his fourth and fifth vertebrae. He was left paralysed from the neck down with total quadriplegia.

Brito is still confined to a wheelchair. He lives in France, watches rugby, and is delighted to be invited to the World Cups every four years. He didn't want to be interviewed for the book because, as his friend wrote, 'He is having operation soon and he is not for pity from everyone. He is alive and he has friends and family and the world of rugby around him, so he is happy.' I spent weeks tracking him down – through the Embassies of Ivory Coast and France, through the Unions of France and Ivory Coast, through clubs and, finally, through the school he went to. The hospital that treated Brito in Pretoria, while incredibly helpful, could not ultimately be of any assistance because their archives only go back five years. At points in my research it looked as if Brito had dropped off the edge of the earth. A few players, like Harvey Thorneycroft, had taken it upon themselves to go out and play in games to raise money for him, but no one had any idea what he was doing now. SARFU, the South African Rugby Football Union, said they had no contact with him. When I expressed surprise at this, considering that he was injured in their country, during their tournament, and treated in one of their hospitals by their medical staff, there was silence at the end of the phone.

'I suggest you try the Ivory Coast,' I was told. Obviously, in a country which boasts so few players and clubs, the Union does not have a manned phone. Calls and emails went unanswered and the race to find Brito was taking on a life of its own. The International Rugby Board tried to help, and eventually put me in touch with Marcel Martin, a former Rugby World Cup director. He is charged with looking after Brito, but no interview could be arranged through him. Damian Hopley, CEO of the professional Rugby Players' Association, became incredibly frustrated with the way Brito was being treated. 'We became involved in money-raising events for Max, but there was very little support from Rugby World Cup,' he said.

I am delighted that I tracked him down, though disappointed not to have spoken to him. I am delighted that he seems well, but disappointed that no one in the governing bodies of any African nations or France had any idea where he was.

The cost of the emergency treatment given to Brito was borne by all the unions from a general fund. If a player is injured today, it is the responsibility of the individual country. Obviously, they are encouraged to take out insurance coverage but clearly this is something they simply can't afford.

Although injuries like that sustained by Max Brito are rare, a tough collision sport like rugby union is nevertheless likely to result in injuries to participants. Dr John Best, medical coordinator for the 2003 World Cup, says that, by looking at the injury patterns from the World Cup tournaments held to date, it is possible to predict what injuries will be sustained in future World Cup tournaments (assuming that numbers of participants and coaches remain the same and the sport does not materially change in any respect). An average of four injuries are predicted to occur per game (an injury being defined as 'significant medical treatment or a player leaving the field of play'); 20 per cent of these are likely to be to the head or face and 45 per cent to the lower limbs. Ambulances are on stand-by for all matches, but the authorities expect them to be used in one in ten matches. At every World Cup match now, there is a sports doctor, orthopaedic surgeon, dentist, anaesthetist, X-ray nurse and plastic surgeon, as well as those provided by the visiting teams.

But when injuries like that suffered by Max Brito occur – injuries demanding a lifetime of treatment and care – who is responsible? The Ivory Coast? How can they be? They can barely get an international team together, and to add that financial burden to their tiny resources would take competition in the World Cup out of their reach.

Ivory Coast lost the game against Tonga, but the scoreline was irrelevant. Neither team would progress in the tournament regardless of the outcome – a fact which adds an air of pathos to the tragedy that occurred. The winners from the group were always going to be France and Scotland, the question was which way round they would finish. Scotland had arrived for the 1995 World Cup in very good heart, and hoping to reach the quarter-final stage. They had a squad that had created a resurgence in

Scottish fortunes, having consigned a dismal record of nine consecutive games without a win to the history books with a run of four wins in a row, over Canada, Ireland, France (their victory in Paris was the first for Scotland in twenty-six years) and Wales. They had also beaten Romania and Spain.

Their first game, against the Ivory Coast, had given Gavin Hastings a new world record of 44 points in the 89–0 victory. Scotland played Tonga next, and were expecting a hard time from them. Tonga had arrived at the 1995 World Cup having been reprimanded by King Taufa Ahau Tupou IV of Tonga, for being beaten 75–5 by Canterbury in the Super-10 series. The King of Tonga was a big rugby fan who wanted to see the national rugby side doing well. They had a tight five averaging 16 stone 8 lb, and a 16-stone right wing. Their tackling was legendary. Scotland beat them 41–5, and found themselves with 130 points and sixteen tries to their credit after their first two victories.

France beat Tonga 38–10, but it was not enough for coach Berbizier, who declared himself unhappy with his team. 'There are too many vain egotists in the French side who fancy themselves. They are too interested in the TV cameras and the photographers. They just want to look good, as if they are thinking "Take my photo, bring the camera to me." They love themselves a bit too much . . . In the end, we just showed a whole lack of respect for the event itself.'

France and Scotland then played to see who would come top in the pool and who would come second, and thus face a next match against New Zealand in the quarter-finals. Scotland led 13–3 in what was one of the best matches of the tournament, until France replied with a flurry of scores to win 22–19.

As the Pool stage of the tournament ended though, the abiding memory was of the young Ivory Coast player lying in a hospital bed.

15

It never rains here at this time of year!

The French team are now close to drinking champagne, but at the moment we are struggling to get the cork out of the bottle.

French coach, Pierre Berbizier

Once the heavy hand of disaster had touched the rugby World Cup, there is no question that the tournament was indelibly marked. Many people who had expressed doubts about a World Cup in the first place, and all those who had strongly resisted the concept because of their fears that it would make the sport too professional, had been slightly encouraged by the notion that the tournament would help to bring on the smaller rugby nations. The idea of raising the profile and financial aid for the development of the sport around the world was extremely compelling. It stopped the tournament from becoming a month-long glorification, and instead promoted a nobler ideal that was more in keeping with the sport, its history and its people. Investment back into the grass roots of the sport in the smaller countries, coupled with offering them the chance to play against the world's best sides in front of massive TV audiences and packed stadia would give them a genuine lift, and be of value to the world of rugby.

Then, Brito was injured and the questions came crushing in on the sport, burying it under a mountain of accusations and assertions. What was the sense of having teams like Ivory Coast that barely played, competing on equal terms in a tough team sport against teams with 100 years of experience and big, serious players? Who was responsible for the decision to send the All Blacks out against Japan? Where was the value in matches that allowed one side to win by 100 points? And, in doing such a thing, weren't the tournament organisers culpable when something went wrong?

'This was a tragic and freak accident, but we are very concerned about spinal injuries in rugby. Law changes have depowered the scrum, but the tackle is still a major problem,' said Etienne Hugo, chairman of the South Africa medical committee. Brito's injury came a fortnight before specialists met in Sun City for an international congress on rugby medicine. While the lawmakers discussed possible changes to make the sport safer, and the coaches contemplated the padding, headguards and other security measures suggested, the players thought of Brito – one of their own – now lying in a hospital bed instead of playing in the tournament.

Brito was visited by five members of the Springbok squad – du Plessis, Griffiths (CEO), Hennie Le Roux, Garry Pagel and Andre Venter. The men went to the hospital on the outskirts of Pretoria to check on Brito and present him with a Springbok jersey and several CDs as gifts. The players were ushered into intensive care where Brito lay on his back, motionless, his body wrapped in foil. In order that Brito might see the gifts they had brought, du Plessis held the jersey directly up above the man's eyes. He saw the emblem on the shirt. 'The whole squad is thinking of you,' said du Plessis.

'*Merci mille fois*,' said Brito, looking up at the shirt. His voice was a whisper, so soft they could hardly hear. They moved in closer and saw a tear roll slowly down his cheek. 'That was tough,' recalls Venter. 'We'd liked to have stayed there longer because he seemed happy to see us.' But the nurse was insistent that the South Africans left straight away, so that Brito might get

some rest. 'We walked out,' said Venter. 'And everything we had
been through – all the things that had seemed like such big deals
at the time, like the sending offs, and the frustrations in the
camp – they all seemed trivial by comparison.'

The South Africans climbed into their car to drive back, feeling stunned and horrified by what they had just seen. But as they
pulled up in front of their hotel, there was further bad news waiting for them – one of their security officers, Douw Schoeman
(known as Magnum to the players) had been shot in the stomach
while driving an unmarked Springbok team bus. He was still
alive in hospital but very unwell. 'I felt as if we were being bat-
tered from all sides,' said Pienaar. 'And there were only three
days until the World Cup quarter-final against Western Samoa at
Ellis Park.'

For some reason, not immediately clear, the organisers of the 1995
World Cup decided that all players in the knock-out stages of the
tournament should stay in Johannesburg and travel down to their
match venue on the eve of each game, returning to the country's
capital afterwards. This was fine for the South Africa players
whose matches would take place in Johannesburg but for other
players, it added a huge amount of travelling into an already
tiring schedule. It also meant that, with so many rugby players all
staying in the same vicinity, there were a few uncomfortable hotel
double-ups. When the Springbok camp moved to Johannesburg
in advance of the quarter-final against Western Samoa at Ellis
Park, they discovered they were in the Sandton Crowne Plaza – a
nice hotel, except that the Australians were staying there too, in
advance of their quarter-final in Cape Town against England. The
players walked in, looked at each other and turned to walk away.
'This was really not going the way we imagined it would,' says
Pienaar. 'It was all amounting to a real problem for the team.'

The problem, it seems, was exacerbated by the fact that the
hotel staff had put the two team rooms next to each other. So, the
rooms that represented the players' sanctuaries, and the place
where all important tactical decisions were made, sat right next to
one another. 'They were so close that I'm sure they could hear

what we were saying.' The Australians were as disappointed with the arrangements as Pienaar and his players. They demanded a separate gym from the Springboks, and asked whether they could eat in different areas of the restaurant. On one occasion a South African player reached out to take something from what he thought was a public fruit bowl, and an Australian voice shouted: 'Don't touch our fucking bananas.' The Australians thought the South African players were deliberately trying to wind them up, and impinge upon their space, while the South Africans were feeling more and more cross with what felt like a million things going wrong all at once. It was all very tense in the hotel, and it practically shivered with resentment in the two closely located team rooms.

Against a background of all this hostility, the South Africa management called a special meeting soon after 9.30 on the Tuesday morning with the quarter-final now only four days away. Christie had called Pienaar and asked the captain to meet him. 'Ten minutes,' said Christie.

The two men met, and Christie looked deep into Pienaar's eyes. 'The fact is that we're three matches from winning the World Cup in front of our own fans,' he said. 'It's time for this squad to stand up and be counted.' Pienaar agreed, and the two men decided to talk to the squad. They urged the players to start thinking about the once in a lifetime opportunity that lay ahead of them. 'The atmosphere changed in a second,' said Pienaar. 'This started to feel like a winning side again because you could feel the bonds building back up between the players as they realised the magnitude of the opportunity that lay ahead of them, and the chance in a lifetime that we might be throwing away.'

On the bus on the way to training, they started playing a joke on du Plessis. The manager's phone rang and the players listened as a man introducing himself as Jacob said he was phoning from Soweto. He asked for tickets to the match, insisting that he needed twenty for young rugby players at the club and that the boys would be desperately disappointed if he couldn't get them. The conversation ran for ten minutes before Balie Stewart admitted it was him and laughter could be heard from the back of the bus.

They took it easy in the days leading up to the first of the knock-out matches, playing golf at the River Club on Thursday, and playing ten-pin bowling on the Friday. On the Saturday, they beat Western Samoa 42–14 in the World Cup quarter-final after dominating the game.

After everything the team had been through, it was a massive relief, but they didn't escape those crunching Western Samoan tackles and returned stacked with injuries. Chester Williams made his return on the left wing in the match and scored four tries, two in each half – a record for his country.

While South Africa enjoyed a relatively comfortable victory, France had a struggle to exert themselves in their quarter-final match against Ireland in Durban. They were infuriating, declared Pierre Berbizier, utterly infuriating. Berbizier's tough training regime at a military-style camp before the match had prompted the players to shave their heads in protest. 'They do not like to work,' said Berbizier, shaking his head. 'Not at all.'

The French players replied, not to Berbizier, but quietly to anyone who would listen, that they felt the trashing they had been given in training before the match had been the reason for their poor showing and, despite winning 36–12 against Ireland, they'd felt utterly exhausted throughout. To be fair to them, they looked jaded – showing no flair or élan in this match. 'The French team are now close to drinking champagne, but at the moment we are struggling to get the cork out of the bottle,' announced their poetic coach. 'We were there [in the final] in 1987 and we want to go that one step further. We will definitely work on the mistakes we made today, for instance our handling of the ball, but that is not serious. None of it is serious. We have the style to win if the players will play it.' Cue raised eyebrows and rude gestures from the players. 'It is his fault,' declared Abdel Benazzi. 'How can we play stylish rugby when we are all exhausted?'

For Ireland it was another disappointing World Cup. They had expected to do so much better after almost beating Australia in 1991.

Simon Geoghegan, the Ireland wing, said:

It was a very disappointing tournament for us, and an odd quarter-final in many ways. It started off strangely when the French players all turned up with shaved heads – apparently they did it because before they came away they had been to a training camp where they felt they had all been treated like convicts. Then, they did not play well and complained of being exhausted, but we still lost, so had to go home. It was an anti-climax. I would have liked to have stayed on to watch the final, but I had to go back to work.

So, it would be France and South Africa in the first semi-final, and the quarter-final battles for the two remaining semi-final places would take place the following day. The quarter-finalists were England against Australia and New Zealand versus Scotland.

Pretoria was the scene for Scotland's gentle introduction to the world of Jonah Lomu.

We spent a lot of time thinking about how we were going to stop him [said Gavin Hastings]. It doesn't sound very sophis-ticated, with hindsight, but we thought the best thing would be to grab and fall with him, rather than trying to knock him back in his stride. After our pool games in 1995, we had a day or two's relaxation planned at the Mala Mala game reserve on the outskirts of Kruger Park. After seeing Jonah on television, we spent our time practising our tackling on elephants and rhinoceroses. Seriously though, we knew he was going to be incredible. We'd built him up into this man mountain in our minds, and that's exactly what he was like. If I remember rightly in that match, from his first touch of the ball he ran around our winger, Craig Joiner, and then went round my brother Scott who missed a tackle on him.

I thought to myself, right, sonny, you're not getting past me – but when I lined him up, he just ran right over the top of me. Hell, I'd been round international rugby for nine years. I was 6 ft 2 and 15 stone – not exactly small for a full back – but it was such a totally different proposition to play against him rather than simply watching him on television. Until you actually faced him and witnessed first hand that power and explosiveness, that strength and size, you just had no idea what you were up against. After that game I loved watching him play. I mean, you literally laughed when he got the ball in his hands. It was the excitement and anticipation, like what's he going to do next? I didn't laugh all that much when we played him though.

Hastings was playing in his sixty-sixth International in the quarter-final of the 1995 World Cup and, as he led out his team for what would turn out to be his last international rugby match, he knew that the odds were against a Scotland victory. The Scots had not beaten the All Blacks in seventeen starts. New Zealand had to play in white jerseys to avoid clashing with the dark blue of Scotland. It was captain Fitzpatrick's 100th appearance in a New Zealand shirt, so for both captains, the match was a significant one. Scotland did exceptionally well against a very tough side. They disrupted the All Blacks flow and forced them into uncharacteristic errors. There were even two special moments for the captains, as Fitzpatrick scored at the end of the game, and Hastings converted his brother's try to score his last points in a Scotland jersey.

New Zealand won 48–30. 'It's incredible to think we've scored thirty points against New Zealand, including three tries, and yet we've still failed to become the first Scottish side in history to beat them,' said Hastings.

On the way back to the team hotel, after the quarter-final, Lomu was summoned to the back of the team bus by Richard Loe, the All Blacks hard man. The back of the bus is sacred territory – reserved for the most senior All Blacks. Loe said he wanted to chat to Lomu, so off the youngster went. 'What were you doing this time back in 1976?' asked Loe. 'I'd just had my first birthday,' replied Lomu. Loe said that he had just played his first game of senior rugby in that year. 'You can go now,' he said, and Lomu walked back to his seat, knowing that he had been accepted into the bosom of the All Blacks. He was determined to make a big impression on the team in the next game – the semi-final in Cape Town.

New Zealand's opponents would be either England or Australia, as the two finalists of the last World Cup slogged it out for a place in the semis. The fact that the two teams had met in the final four years previously and, on that occasion, the Australian players had mocked England for what they perceived as being 'boring' rugby, had created friction. Jack Rowell knew that he had to give England a psychological edge as they went into the game, so he dispatched Austin Swain, the team's psychologist, to act as a spy in the Australia camp. Swain dressed as a backpacker and sneaked in to watch Australia's last closed training session before the quarter-final. He befriended the groundsman and drank some of the Australia players' isotonic drinks at the side of the pitch before leaving with a notebook filled with information about Australia's strike moves and defensive patterns. Australia went through their pre-match routine unaware that there was a spy in the camp. When Swain returned, he showed the England players which way Australia preferred to attack from certain areas of the pitch, and who they saw as the key men in different moves. As a psychological boost it was excellent for the England team.

This psychological advantage was developed by Swain, as he asked every player to write down why he thought another player was great, and why he was glad that player was in the side. Swain put the pieces of paper under the doors of the relevant player's room the night before the match, to remind them how well-respected they were in the team.

The match was extremely close, and sat at 22–22 as the time was ticking down. Then ... three minutes into injury time, England were awarded a penalty just short of the halfway line. Catt kicked for touch and England set up an attacking line-out. Moore threw perfectly; Bayfield took the ball at the top of his jump, then Ubogu drove in, next Morris, then Andrew. It was roughly at that point that time stood still. All the clocks stopped, telephones were cut off and dogs stopped barking. Up into the air he belted it, and every English man and woman with breath in their body, shouted at the television and urged the ball to sail over. It did. With it, England sailed into the semi-final of the rugby World Cup. They had won themselves a semi-final encounter with New Zealand, and Campese and his fellow Aussies were on their way home. Life was sweet, very sweet.

Campese, a man of startling talent and stunningly quick thinking on the field, does have a habit of leaving all his finer skills and graces behind him once he crosses the touchline. What started out as pleasant enough fun – with his simple jokes about how useless the England team were – had developed into all-out aggression and rudeness towards individual players and the team as a whole at every available opportunity. Some of his insults were personal, all of them were becoming excruciatingly boring. England had revenge in spades when Andrew booted Australia out of the tournament, and won a further revenge when the bus of the England players' wives and girlfriends mistakenly pulled up outside the Australia team hotel, and Campese leapt aboard thinking it was the Aussie team's official bus. The women went berserk – screaming and shouting at him as he looked around in horror, jumped off the bus, and ran for his life.

'That was the greatest game I have ever played in, and I have never seen anything like Rob's kick. After the match, he touched Dewi's bruised leg and cured it and later in the evening we found him having a walk in Cape Town Harbour,' said Carling.

Australia, naturally enough, were not quite so complimentary. Bob Dwyer said: 'When teams play England, they often end up wondering "How did they beat us?" Well, in our case, it was the combination of the rolling maul and Andrew's kicking. It's up to each nation to play the way they want, but I don't like England's style and I don't find it exciting. Mind you, they have changed. They kick the ball up the middle rather than to the corners. On balance, I think their 1991 side were superior.'

Saturday, 17 June. Semi-final day dawned grey over Durban. South Africa would play France at King's Park that afternoon. Kitch Christie awoke to the sound of rain pattering against his window and peered out into the greyness. This was not good. He was confident of beating France in dry weather but he was not so sure about how they would cope in the wet. These conditions would bring in an element of chance, which was when France were at their most dangerous. By 12.45 p.m., the rain was pelting down still harder. What would happen? He really didn't need any more calamities. The injuries sustained against Western Samoa turned out to be quite serious, with André Joubert worst hit. He had broken his hand in three places and it had required an operation just three days previously. It had been a major procedure, involving the placing of a wire through the channel in the bone usually filled with bone marrow in order to hold his shattered hand together. Still, the full back was determined he was going to play. He'd trained with the team and declared himself fit. Christie was worried, though – what if he wasn't ready?

Now it was raining. Raining! In Durban, in June? It never rained in Durban in June. Yet on the morning of the semi-final the rain poured until the streets were gushing, the drains were flooding, and everyone connected to the semi-final game stared disconsolately out of windows around the city.

There was chaos everywhere. Even the aircraft bringing fans in for the match were affected, and had to circle for up to an hour before landing.

Christie went back to his notes and tried to focus on the game. He had spent every moment since South Africa and France knew they would meet in the semi-final, assessing the threats imposed by the French. His video-watching extravaganza earlier in the week had alerted him to the height of Abdelatif Benazzi and Marc Cecillion at the back of the line-out . . . how would he counteract them? It seemed the Frenchmen could ensure a stream of possession which would cause real problems if the French were on song and able to use it effectively. Christie had sent his squad home for three nights after the quarter-finals, and he had headed for his home in Midrand as he pondered possible solutions to the problem.

By the time the squad had arrived back at Sunnyside Park in Johannesburg on the Tuesday before the semi-final, Christie had told his fellow selectors of his controversial decision – he would play Mark Andrews, the lock, in the back row because he needed to get some height at the back of the South Africa line-out. He called Andrews to his room.

'Mark, can you play on the flank?' asked Christie.

'No,' replied the lock.

'What about number 8?'

Andrews says he looked at his coach and considered the options. Christie had not looked pleased when he'd said that he couldn't play on the flank. He was worried about saying no again in case he lost his place.

'Yes, of course,' Andrews recalls telling Christie, even though he hadn't played there since he was at school.

'Great,' said Christie. The two men smiled, and Andrews walked away, reconsidering the wisdom of offering to play completely out of position in the biggest, most important, highest-profile match of his entire career.

'What?' said Pienaar.

'I'm very serious about this,' explained Christie, as the captain looked on askance. Christie wanted Kobus Wiese to jump at number two in the line-out, Strydom at four, and Andrews would leap at the tail against Benazzi and Cecillion. The problem was that this plan would mean dropping Rudolf Straueli who had done nothing wrong.

'You'd better tell him,' said Pienaar.

Christie went to Straueli's room and knocked on his door. There was no one there so he asked another player whether he had seen Straueli. 'Heading for Mark Andrews' room,' came the reply. Christie rushed down the corridor towards Andrews' room, fearing conflict and accusations, but when he got there, Christie discovered the two men deep in conversation.

'Sorry, coach,' said Straueli. 'I know you've been looking for me, but I thought I'd better run through some of the back-row moves with Mark. He should know them.'

Straueli continued to stand by the team and to publicly back his coach's decision. When the press reacted with amazement, asking why such a risk would be taken before a semi-final, Straueli shrugged. 'Because it's a semi-final,' he said. 'The probability is that we will find ourselves in this position only once in our careers so we want perfection. This is not the time to be safe. It is the time to follow your instincts and back your judgements. That's what we are doing.'

Now it was match day, and the rain continued to fall; throughout the morning, through breakfast and as the players travelled to the ground it was getting heavier. When they arrived at the stadium, it was torrential. Joost van der Westhuizen and Joubert went to talk to Christie – they had concerns about their shirts. Following normal practice, they had cut the sleeves from their shirts because it was more comfortable that way, but now they'd seen the conditions, they decided they'd rather have their shirts with long sleeves attached to help control the wet ball. They asked the manager for another set of jerseys but Christie knew there were none there, and to send out for some would take longer than the time available to them.

'Change jerseys with the replacements,' he suggested. The replacements relinquished their fully-armed jerseys in return for the shortened ones, and du Plessis began writing a revised team list by hand to take into account the new numbers on the players' backs. The list was handed to the match officials. The rainfall continued. World Cup officials decided to delay kick-off from the scheduled 3 p.m. to 4 p.m. in the hope that the weather would clear.

The most important task now was establishing what to do with the pitches, and how to clear the river of water that was sitting on the pitch from the morning's downpour. They contemplated using the water-soaking machines from the Durban Country Club golf course, or police helicopters to hover above the field and blow the water away. Then, at 3.30 p.m. the rain temporarily stopped, and the solution seemed obvious – send ten rotund black women on to the field, clutching brooms and mops, to sweep at the puddle in front of the posts at the southern end. It was one of the more peculiar sights in modern sport. It had been odd enough to find that, against all the climatic constants which state that it never rains in Durban in the middle of winter, it had pelted down all day, but now this – a highly technological approach of middle-aged women and their brushes striding bare-foot through the lapping waves.

While the women swept, officials met with the referee just before 4 p.m., and announced that if there was no more rain, the semi-final would kick off at 4.30 p.m. The South Africa players were utterly relieved. If the pitch had been declared unplayable, France would have gone through on their disciplinary record because they hadn't had a player sent off. In the France dressing-room, there was considerably less eagerness to see the back of the rain.

Three minutes before the team was due to head for the field, Derek Bevan, the referee, came to the Springbok dressing room and told them they couldn't go out with their shirts numbered the way they were. They were told they would be disqualified unless they wore the right numbers. They had to change their jerseys back round. Eager not to forfeit the match, and keen to get out there as soon as possible, the South Africans swapped their shirts back, and ran out on to the field, determined to score a try first just in case it rained again and the pitch was declared unplayable after all. After twenty-seven minutes, they scored. By the time there were four minutes remaining, South Africa led 19–15 but were being put under immense pressure on their own line. James Small literally threw himself on the goal line to prevent the charging Benazzi from scoring what would have been the match-winning try. The final whistle provoked bedlam. South Africa had defeated France 19–15, and in doing so, had qualified for a place in the World Cup final.

Pienaar is convinced that the difference between the two sides that day was their psychological preparation. South Africa were all geared up in the changing-room, wanting to play, wanting the rain to stop – or they would lose the game. The French wanted the match to be cancelled so they would qualify without having to go on the field – so South Africa were much happier, much more 'up' for the game when it was declared on.

After the game, Christie went to the changing-room and watched the five members of the squad who had neither been in the XV nor on the bench. They were walking around, slapping people on the back and shaking hands. 'In a very real sense, these people were involved, were part of the victory. This was not a team, this was a squad. In fact, this was not simply a squad, this was a family – just as Christie had intended,' said Pienaar. 'I looked around the room, and I saw heroes in every direction.'

'I felt sorry for France,' said Christie. 'To be honest, it was a bun-fight out there, and we were just lucky to finish with the last bun.'

Philippe Saint-André, France's captain, said that his men had found it all incredibly difficult.

To keep stopping and starting like that [over whether they were going to play the game or not] made it very difficult for me as captain because we were stuck in the changing-room for two hours.

Now that I am a coach in England, I can see that English people don't prepare in the same way. It's more relaxed and more quiet. But in France we have a lot of speeches and a lot of mental preparation and each time we got ready to start, the game was delayed for ten or fifteen minutes more. It was not easy, because we built the pressure up and when the pressure was ready, the game was cancelled! The pressure goes down, we build it up again, the game was cancelled . . . but that's life. I think I made my speech three times – and had to change it every time in order to get the team's attention.

16

Jonah Lomu
makes his mark

Lomu is a freak . . . The sooner he goes away, the better.

Will Carling

Lomu just ran straight over me. I didn't know before the match just how big he was.

Mike Catt

How do you stop Jonah Lomu? I've no idea. I suppose an elephant gun might help.

Bob Dwyer

On the hotel's fourth floor, a big man was stomping backwards and forwards – pacing across the carpet like an expectant father in a 1960s film. Up the corridor, turn around, back down the corridor, turn around . . . It was 3 a.m. but he couldn't sleep. He never could at a time like this. Instead he trudged back and forth, staring ahead, muscles pumped and his fists clenched. He'd been wearing a track through the plush hotel carpet since 11 p.m., and would continue to do so through the night. There had been a couple of diversions – out to the car park to pace around there for a while, and even a short spell sitting in the foyer, wringing his hands and mentally rehearsing the match to be played later that day. One of the security officers watched him in amazement. 'I knew exactly who he was. We'd all been keen to meet him earlier in the day. This huge superstar. He was an awesome size. But when I saw him in the night, by himself and just sitting there, staring ahead – I felt so sorry for him. He seemed small and lonely there.'

The man, of course, was Jonah Lomu, the 20-year-old wing whose bulldozing impact later that day would be directly responsible for England's exit from the 1995 tournament. Lomu insists that this is how he spent the night before he tore the heart and soul out of England's World Cup dreams – by pacing up and down the corridors instead of getting a good night's sleep.

By 8 a.m., Lomu knew his roommate would be awake, so made his way back up to his floor and did a final march down the corridor to let himself back into his room. Still lying in bed was Frank Bunce. 'Where've you been? What have you been doing?' he asked.

'I've just been walking up and down the corridors,' said Lomu, as if it were the most natural thing in the world. 'I couldn't sleep. I'm going to get a shower.' Lomu disappeared and Bunce sat up. He wondered whether the young lad was okay. Was all this pressure getting to him? The last thing they needed was for Lomu to collapse with nerves at this stage. He decided to keep an eye on him in the semi-final that afternoon. A lot was expected of him – he'd make sure he was there if needed.

The teenage rugby sensation emerged from the shower and turned to Bunce. 'Coffee?' he asked.

Bunce said yes. Best to keep things as normal as possible on the morning of a big game. The unlikely duo had struck a great friendship during the tournament. Bunce acted as adviser to Lomu on all aspects of New Zealand and All Black culture and history, and Lomu lapped up the information. In return, Lomu tried to make Bunce feel as comfortable as possible. It was Lomu who had the smaller bed in the room even though his feet hung over the edge. It was Bunce who chose what programme went on the television. Bunce looked after Lomu on the pitch and Lomu looked after Bunce off the pitch – that was the All Black way. He ran Bunce's bath, and Bunce ran through the workings of the All Blacks hierarchy. On the pitch, he shouted advice and watched Lomu's back. 'You okay?' he asked his protégé.

'I'm good,' said Lomu. 'I didn't sleep much, but I'm good.' After coffee, Lomu says he remembers eating a healthy amount of cereal, yoghurt and toast. 'More than most people, I guess,' he says. 'But not as much as I eat sometimes. I love food. I can eat and eat and eat.' Then he went back upstairs and stood by the window – staring out at Table Mountain and down to the streets below where thousands of South Africans went about their daily business. He thought about what he'd read in the papers that week. Rory Underwood had said 'I'm sure that Lomu will have been thinking about Tony [Underwood] running at him, and, in a one-to-one, I'd put my money on Tony.' Mmm, thought Lomu. Then, he thought about what he'd read from Tony Underwood. The England wing had said he thought he could run rings around the big New Zealander. Lomu turned around and looked at the cutting stuck to the mirror . . . I can run rings around him, he said to himself. He'd read the cutting every day since it appeared. Today, he stared at it one last time. 'It was huge motivation,' says Lomu. 'I looked at the cutting and realised what these English guys thought about me, then I thought about the All Black shirt and what the silver fern meant to me. I could feel myself getting more and more angry until I thought I might explode. I knew there was only one way of making myself feel better again. I had to perform on the pitch.'

Lomu recalls going down for lunch that day and sitting next to Zinzan Brooke. He needed something to relax him and take his mind off the game. Brooke duly obliged by staring at a large basket of muffins on the table in front of them. 'How many do you reckon you can eat?' asked Brooke.

'I can eat loads,' said Lomu. 'How about you?'

'Let's see,' said Brooke, and the two men stared at each other as they ate – matching each other bite for bite, muffin for muffin. Once Lomu had eaten seven, he sat back in his chair.

'Can't do any more,' he said.

Brooke took another bite – sealing his victory. 'I'd have eaten the whole basket if I'd had to,' said the famously competitive number 8. 'I was always going to take one more bite than him.'

Lomu's tale about Brooke reminds me of the lovely story about former England cricketer, Ian Botham – regarded as one of sport's more competitive beasts. He sat around with like-minded friends one evening, long after he had retired from the game, and looked at the wine bottles sitting in the middle of the table. 'How much do you think you could drink?' he asked the assembled guests. His friends shrugged and said they didn't know. But Botham wouldn't let it rest. 'Go on,' he chided. 'How much could you drink if your life depended on it.' Being used to Botham's ways, his drinking chums knew that they had to give an answer or face an evening of inquisitions. 'Four bottles,' replied one friend. 'I don't know – about the same, maybe five,' said another. Then they asked Botham: 'So, how many do you reckon you could drink?'

'One more than you,' said Botham. 'However much you drank, I'd drink one more.' It seems competitive spirit does not wither too much with age. Perhaps, like other energies, it is simply transferred but never extinguished. Brooke will always be a 'one muffin more than you' sort of person.

Lomu says he is not like that. He is madly competitive. Certainly, he wants to win on the field, but doesn't feel duty bound to rise to every challenge and go hunting for duels like some of his teammates. 'I'm a laid-back sort of person off the pitch, but I want to win when I'm on it. Some people are always wanting to prove that they are better than others. That doesn't interest me.'

Considering they were preparing to play New Zealand – their nemesis – there was considerable confidence in the England camp before the World Cup semi-final. They had beaten New Zealand back in 1993 – an occasion when Carling had managed to rub salt into the New Zealand captain's wounds when they sat at dinner after the match. Carling wondered who the large woman on the table was. 'Who's that woman there?' asked Carling. 'The really, really fat one.' Fitzpatrick looked unamused. 'That's my mother,' he said.

But the confidence appeared to dissolve when England left their hotel bound for Newlands Stadium. Carling looked around at his teammates, and admits that he was worried – no one was talking: it was all so quiet . . . again . . . as it had been when they lost to New Zealand in 1991. Perhaps the spectre of New Zealand and the image of them as all-conquering and heroic in status was more enduring than he had realised. Or was it that the emotion and effort of beating Australia had taken too much out of them?

Carling's sense of foreboding continued into the changing-room. 'It wasn't anything massive,' he says. 'There were no major problems, I just had a feeling that things weren't right – that they weren't how they should be. It was just a feeling.'

Lomu ran out on to the field for the semi-final against England feeling pumped up and raring to go, despite his lack of sleep. When asked by the coaches how he'd slept, he says he just told them what they wanted to hear – that he'd slept like a baby and was fully refreshed. He joined his teammates for the haka.

'Then, at the end of it, I looked over at Tony Underwood and he gave me a little wink,' says Lomu. 'A wink! I was so mad. The haka is a challenge. Tony was being disrespectful by mocking it. All I could think was "I'll show you, I'll show you. I'll stop you winking".'

And, to be fair to the guy, he did. Lomu's one-man show of strength, power and determination was the most significant factor in a match which saw him suffocate England's World Cup chances in one almighty squeeze. 'I never set out thinking "I'm going to smash 'em today, I'm going to score heaps of tries and bust them all over the place". I don't think any player does. Rugby's a team game. Sometimes play doesn't go your way. Other times, everything clicks,' he said. Lomu scored four of their six tries, the first of which came after he had crashed past three tackles less than three minutes into the match. Final score 45–29. England were on their way to a miserable third-place play-off against France, and New Zealand were in the World Cup final.

The last time New Zealand had made it to the final, they had won. Hopes were high. Lomu described himself as being 'in fairyland' when he came off the field.

Tony Underwood went up to him and asked the NZ wing whether he wanted his England shirt, knowing that there was no way that Lomu would hand over his. Lomu concedes that this was 'a mighty big gesture. I knew in that minute that I'd got him wrong. In my mind, I'd built him into something that he wasn't. He seemed okay really.' There is no question, though, that Lomu's perception of Underwood before the game was a source of considerable motivation. 'Oh yeah – he got me all wound up and raring to go, man,' says Lomu.

The other players say they were also motivated by the fact that England had beaten them two years previously. Brooke describes that victory in 1995 as being the most satisfying victory of his career. Brooke, rather improbably, dropped a goal from the halfway line in the match. 'We'd lost to them a couple of years earlier at Twickenham and some of the guys weren't happy about how certain English players had been mouthing off afterwards. By the time the semi-final came along, there was still a nucleus of players on our side – and England's – who had been involved in that game and we desperately wanted revenge. It was nice to get it.'

Lomu says he recalls seeing the 1993 match on television and watching the sad faces of the players as they trooped off. He had no desire to present such a sad face himself, he says. 'And that's why I was up all night and worried. I didn't want to let anyone down.'

Lomu thoroughly ripped through England in Cape Town. His extreme power and utter domination indicating that, while rugby was more sophisticated than ever – a sport in which fitness was keenly embraced and cleverness, clear thinking and intelligence rewarded – the fact remained that, if you stuck a great big fast bloke on the wing and got him to bosh everyone out the way, you'd score every time. There was almost something refreshing about it – as if nature had won out over sports science and sports psychology. Men bounced off Lomu. Tony Underwood's reaching in vain for Lomu's disappearing ankles was like something out of a comedy sketch. In fact such was the comic potential of the thing that the scene was appropriated by a pizza restaurant company and used in their advertising campaign. 'It wasn't just his strength and his speed that made him such a formidable athlete. His balance was also special. He could step off either foot,' Carling said. 'That was the best side I've ever played against . . . It was like fifteen-year-olds against men.'

Rory Underwood says that the Lomu threat was discussed before the game, but that the players

> didn't want to become embroiled in a discussion about him, because they had fourteen other good players on their team. We didn't want Lomu to affect how we played as a side. Our approach was to try and close him down as quickly as possible; half-stop him and then the next person could come in and help. For the first twenty minutes he got the ball in space and with time to run. He was like a howitzer and my brother Tony got swatted and dragged and scragged. But Mike Catt got trampled over too and, in fact, not a single player managed to tackle him. Gavin Hastings had got the treatment in the previous round.
>
> Having said that, I don't think that our performance was all doom and gloom. Take away the first twenty minutes of the semi-final and we played just as well if not better than New Zealand. But we were blown away in those first twenty minutes. It was the first time we had played against Lomu and we got blitzed. After that opening he was just another player and we sorted him out, but in the first twenty minutes we didn't. Concede three or four tries in the first twenty minutes of a game and any side would have crumbled [NB New Zealand scored two tries in the first twenty minutes]. But we actually won the second half. At the end of the day we didn't play that badly. We were gobsmacked at the end but we lost to a very good New Zealand side.

For Carling, Richards and many other England players, the match marked the end of their pursuit of the Webb-Ellis trophy. They had experienced near-glory in 1991 and had hoped to go all the way this time. Their elimination from the tournament marked the end of their World Cup careers. For England players who had led a resurgence of the game in England – Carling, Richards, Moore, Underwood – this had been their last chance.

For Lomu, the end of the game signalled the beginning of superstardom as he was courted by clubs from around the world. His former manager Phil Kingsley-Jones was working round the clock to take calls in relation to his protégé who was being heralded as one of the greatest players the world had ever seen. For Lomu, it was all rather startling. He rushed back to the comfort of the team and continued as normal, making coffee for his roommate and wandering down hotel corridors all night. Then, it was time for the World Cup final. Two further indignities for England first, though: after the semi-final defeat, they had to travel back to Johannesburg on the same flight as the All Blacks. The New Zealanders were in first-class and England were in economy. Then, it was time for the third-place play-off.

'It's so hard to get up for the game,' moaned Victor Ubogu, as he contemplated a meaningless match against France to ascertain which team had finished third and which one was fourth. 'It will be a test of our resolve,' agreed Rob Andrew. Across town in Pretoria, the French were trying to put a braver face on it. 'We are going to make pleasure on the pitch,' said Philippe Sella, which rather made one wonder what they were planning to do. His fly-half and old sparring partner in the centre – Franck Mesnel – was in upbeat mood. 'We are going to run it,' he declared, ambitiously. 'We will run it from everywhere.'

After the battering in Cape Town, England were far from enthusiastic about this game against France, and any residual enthusiasm seeped away as news filtered to them that the French had been out drinking and having a good time.

'That is never great,' said Jason Leonard. 'If the French are off drinking together and bonding, they can be tough to play against – they become more cavalier, more dangerous.'

Arguably, France wanted this victory more, since they hadn't beaten England in seven successive games. They won it 19–9. Philippe Saint-André reflects: 'Only Sella and Mesnel of my team have had the delight of beating England, so it was gratifying for the younger generation. I have always lost against Will Carling, so I took special pleasure in shaking hands with him with a smile on my face while he stared at the grass.' Berbizier was finally pleased with his team: 'Now that we have overcome England after seven years, and have qualified automatically for the next World Cup, we can take our summer holiday relaxed and assured.'

'We wanted desperately to perform,' said Will Carling afterwards. 'There was a challenge there for us tonight and we didn't respond.' England manager Jack Rowell simply pointed out the magnitude of the experience his players had gone through in the preceeding eleven days. 'To play Australia, New Zealand and France within such a short space of time is asking a lot,' said Rowell. 'We hit a brick wall last Sunday against the All Blacks, which is when our World Cup effectively ended. I think you saw that tonight.'

After the third-place play-off defeat, the players cheered themselves up by holding an evening court session. Rowell and Les Cusworth were fined for working 'like the locals' and had to wear bib and braces and leather flat caps. The doctor was fined for impersonating a doctor and prescribing such wonderful cures as mentholyptus for earache. As his punishment he had to wear an outfit like the one worn by the doctor in *Star Trek*. Carling was punished for being on the phone all the time, so he had to pull a Direct Line phone on wheels behind him wherever he went.

'Afterwards we went to a bar,' says Rory Underwood. 'The French were at the same bar and it was a bit interesting to start with. But after a few beers there was soon an *entente cordiale*. We played some drinking games and had a sing-song, and it broke down a few barriers. At the end of the day we were all rugby players and I think that post-match session had a huge benefit for Anglo-French relations.'

17

Mandela's new shirt

Stuff the haka. That's where it starts for them. Stuff the haka, and stuff the All Blacks. This is going to be our day.

Kitch Christie, the South Africa coach, in his address to the team before the final against New Zealand

If New Zealand do not beat South Africa and win the rugby World Cup at Ellis Park, Johannesburg next Saturday, there will have to be a steward's inquiry.

John Mason, Daily Telegraph

Russell Mulholland toyed with his coffee, cupping his hands around it and savouring its warmth as he contemplated the day ahead. He had been working with the South Africa players as their team liaison officer throughout the World Cup. Now his time was nearly over. It had been one hell of an experience. Just one match to go: the big one. He sat back in his seat at the breakfast table and glanced at his watch. He needed to get back up to his room to make sure everything was ready for the final game. He finished his coffee and eased himself to his feet, as his mobile phone rang in his pocket. Scrabbling to find it, he had no idea that the call he would take would lead to the creation of the most iconic moment in the history of the rugby World Cup, a moment loaded with political, historical, cultural and emotional meaning.

'Mulholland,' he said.

It was Mary Mxadana on the line, Mandela's private secretary.

'Hi,' she said. 'Listen – the President would like to wear a South African jersey when he comes to the game this afternoon. Can that be arranged?'

'Of course,' said Mulholland. 'They're for sale in sports shops all over the country. I'll arrange for one to be sent over.'

'No,' said Mxadana. 'What he really wants is exactly the same jersey as François Pienaar.'

'I'll sort it straight away,' said Mulholand, rising to his feet. 'Just leave it with me.'

By 11 a.m. that morning, Mxadana was in a car on the way to the Sandton Sun hotel to pick up the jersey that would appear on the front of most national newspapers across the globe the following day.

The build up to the World Cup final had gone remarkably smoothly in the South Africa camp, considering the array of disasters and problems they had encountered en route. Christie and du Plessis began the week by studying the schedule and making plans. 'First of all, we wanted to get away after the semi-final,' Christie said. 'I knew there would be huge demands from the media, so we decided to spend a couple of days at Sun City. We would be able to play golf and just settle down.' In the concrete paradise of Sun City, Christie decided that his intention was to keep the same team that had won in the semi-final against France, but he recognised that he would need a different game plan against New Zealand. They had different strengths, different players to watch out for. Beating them would be a very different prospect. He decided on a plan that he thought would truly amaze the watching world, and throw the New Zealanders off their game.

After a relaxed golf day on the Tuesday, the coach gathered his squad to his room on the Wednesday morning and proposed they adopt the 'brains game' for the final. This was the fast and loose strategy which the team had used effectively before to counteract good sides. In a knockout tournament it was particularly effective, and Christie believed it would be perfect in the World

Cup final. In essence, the plan involved playing every move at double pace; it created a frantic and fast game, but would hand all the control to South Africa because they were going into the match knowing what would be done, and having practised for it in the week-long build up.

'We have the skills to execute this plan,' Christie told his players. The team sat there in total silence. Christie continued – he told them that if he ran through the team from 1 to 15, there was no question that 'we are brighter than they are, we have the brains. They don't. This game plan will catch them completely unawares. No one will believe that any team would dare take such a strategy into the World Cup final.'

The players went away feeling a little confused and concerned that they were being asked to do something that none of them felt completely comfortable with, in the run-up to a World Cup final. Still, at fitness training that afternoon, the spirit in the South Africa team had reached an all-time high. Pienaar remembers a training session in which the back-line players were sweating through bench steps, counting loudly as they did so. The forwards were doing sit-ups nearby, and began counting loudly as well, working to outpace the backs. They all felt fitter, more competitive and more confident than ever.

On Thursday, though, things started to crumble, as they put in some serious practice sessions with the 'brains game'. They were getting some of the moves spot on, but Christie detected that there was a lack of conviction. By Friday morning, when things seemed to be getting worse, Christie backed down. He told the players that they should forget the 'brains game' and go back to their normal tactics. There was a general mood of relief all round.

While the South Africans had been trying to make the 'brains game' work, the question being asked by everyone else was 'what on earth were South Africa proposing to do about the threat posed by Jonah Lomu'. The giant All Black wing had appeared unstoppable in rampaging over the England defence in the semi-final at Newlands, and he was the undoubted star of the tournament so far. Centre Hennie Le Roux proposed that James Small be charged with marking Lomu. Christie agreed that this was the best strategy, and added that Small should strive to stay on the outside of Lomu and drive him infield, herding him towards the covering defence. Lomu was virtually unstoppable at speed and he appeared to get crucial speed when he passed outside the defence and was able to hand off any defender who came near him. If they could stop him doing that – they might nail him.

Shell, the oil company, had caused a little disquiet by announcing that they would pay SARFU R5000 every time Lomu was cleanly tackled. SARFU accepted this on the grounds that the money could be used to provide new jerseys and equipment for an entire rugby club in an underprivileged area. The All Blacks expressed their disappointment and described it as being in bad taste.

It wasn't the only thing the All Blacks were expressing their disappointment about, nor, as it turned out, would it be the only thing to leave them with a bad taste in their mouths. The New Zealand players had faced a less than perfect build up to the game. For a week since the semi-final they had suffered fire alarms being set off in the hotel, cars blasting their horns and phones ringing in players' rooms through the night.

> The first night a car alarm went off, then it kept going – every couple of hours. I asked the hotel why they couldn't do anything about it, and what was going on, and they replied that it would be too difficult to move the car because of the fear of bombs [said Sean Fitzpatrick]. My phone rang as well – waking me up all night with someone telling me I was useless and I was going to lose. The hotel weren't supposed to be putting calls through to the room, so I went and asked them why they had. They always gave the same excuse – that someone new had been on that night, and hadn't realised he wasn't supposed to be putting calls through.

This was hugely disappointing to the All Blacks management team who had been eager to keep things as smooth and unhassled as possible for the players. To this end, they had tried to keep exactly the same routine that had been so effective for the players up until this point, and that included going back to the same hotel that they had been in previously, even though they were strongly advised to go to the Sandton Sun hotel that had been pre-booked by the tournament organisers. Indeed, the only thing that changed at all was the management's decision to provide a separate dining room with food prepared specifically for them, in order to allow the players to relax while eating, away from autograph hunters and watching fans.

Then, after eating on the Thursday night before the Saturday game, the players felt sick. Overnight it got worse until, by Friday morning, half the team were suffering.

'It wasn't just one or two,' recalls Lomu. 'We were all being sick. People said it was like a war-zone in the hotel, with people being sick all over the place.'

Lomu says he wasn't too badly affected. He felt rough, but nothing like as bad as some of the other players felt. They had severe food poisoning and, before they'd even taken to the pitch, the debates were raging about whether the poisoning was accidental or deliberate. Was this a ploy to weaken them in advance of the match and gift victory to the South Africans? Or, even an intervention by bookies looking to fix the match? Half of the 36-strong squad suffered a debilitating outbreak of food poisoning before the final. Jeff Wilson was clearly struggling on the day and had to be taken off the pitch.

Something was definitely done to us [says Zinzan Brooke]. Forty-eight hours before the big day, and eighteen of us, plus management, go down with food poisoning. That may be coincidence, but I don't think so. For every game before then we had made a point of eating in public restaurants to avoid being targeted. But in the week of the final we isolated ourselves in a private room. When we realised what had happened we thought about pulling out, getting the game postponed. However, we decided to use it to motivate us even more. Unfortunately, things didn't work out as we had hoped.

While the All Blacks were struggling to cope physically and mentally with what had happened to them, South Africa headed out for their last training session of the tournament at a university playing field in Melville. Pienaar was taking his boots off when his phone rang; Mandela had called him to wish him and the team luck. He had called before the opening game, before the semi-final and now before the final. 'I thought at the time that it was one final shot of inspiration,' said Pienaar. 'I had no idea what was waiting for us at the stadium.'

On match day, the South African team boarded their bus, and Pienaar decided to break with tradition. Usually the journey to the ground is silent, but Pienaar put on some music. He walked to the front of the coach and put on 'If' by Roger Whittaker. Players had been worried what would happen *if* they dropped a pass, *if* they missed a kick, *if* they missed a tackle, and so on. He wanted to stop worrying about the 'ifs' and concentrate on the bigger picture – winning the World Cup for South Africa. He says he wanted that journey to be different to all others. 'I made sure my own preparation for the match was different,' he said.

Pienaar says that years prior to the 1995 World Cup final his brother Kobus said that, every time Pienaar had his hair cut before a game, South Africa lost the match. His brother's remark had stuck in Pienaar's mind, so he never cut his hair before a game, just in case. But before the 1995 World Cup final, he decided to change with tradition, and cut his hair. Also, he never shaved before matches, because he knew his skin would be more resistant to cuts if it was rough. But before the 1995 final, he shaved. 'To this day – I don't know why I did that,' he says. For some reason he felt the need to separate this match out from all others.

The team arrived at the stadium and Pienaar walked out on to the pitch to savour the atmosphere, before walking back to the changing-room. By the time he got there, Mandela was standing at his place, wearing a no. 6 jersey. The President beamed and stretched out his hand and the two men shook hands. Outside, a crowd of 63,000 was packing into Ellis Park, while an audience of 145 million watched on television. The players changed and, for the last time, Christie rose to address them. He pulled from his pocket a scrap of paper, the same paper on which he had written his remarks before the opening match of the tournament against Australia.

> Guys, we have travelled a long way together [he read]. I want to say that I have no doubt what is going to happen this afternoon. I believe you're going to win the World Cup for South Africa, and for yourselves. You're going to do that by showing the All Blacks no respect at all. They're a good team but they're not a great team. Let them know what you think of them. Stuff the haka. That's where it starts for them. Stuff the haka, and stuff the All Blacks. This is going to be our day.
>
> And we're going to win the World Cup by getting the basics right . . . Every final I have been a part of, at every level, has been won by the team making fewer mistakes on the day.
>
> Guys, over the years, it has generally been true that New Zealand has sneezed and the rest of the world has caught a cold. I think it is all going to change this afternoon. We will sneeze, and we will let everyone else catch a cold from us. This is our opportunity to set South Africa apart as the top rugby community on this planet.

Pienaar stood, too, and told his men: 'If we all come off the field having given everything we have, then I'm convinced we'll be world champions.'

When the players came out of the changing-room, it was the first time Small had seen Lomu, as the New Zealand team came out and lined up alongside the South Africans. Small was staring at Lomu, thinking how big he was, when Chester Williams walked towards him and said: 'Don't worry, mate. All you've got to do is hold him until the rest of us can get to him.'

As the match got under way, the Springboks' ability to smother Lomu at every stage became obvious. Every time the big wing got the ball, he was submerged in green and gold. By half-time, South Africa was leading 9–6, having utterly ridiculed the predictions of an All Black walkover. The defensive pattern was holding firm.

When Ed Morrison blew the whistle for full time, it was 9–9. Pienaar gathered his team around him: 'Whenever you feel tired, just look at the flags in every corner of this stadium. This whole country wants to win the World Cup, and we must do it for them,' he said.

As the players regrouped, and prepared themselves for extra time, high up in the stadium sat Gareth Rees with two of his Canada teammates. 'There were these guys in the stands talking about how important it was for South Africa to win in extra time because the tournament rules dictated that disciplinary records would be taken into account if the scores were tied after extra time. The three of us Canadians slunk down in our seats and hoped that no one would notice us. It was against Canada that South Africa had the players sent off, and if they'd ended up losing the World Cup final because of it, we'd all have been mobbed!'

With seven minutes of extra time left, Joel Stransky kicked the soaring drop goal that won the World Cup. It was the most important three points ever scored in the 105-year history of the game in South Africa. The final score was South Africa 15, New Zealand 12. The whistle brought a nation to its feet and the players to their knees. Scattered images remain in the memory from that surreal post-match euphoria. Pienaar on his haunches with tears in his eyes. Mandela and Pienaar in a hand-holding huddle. Then the moment when the captain showed such grace. Approached by a TV commentator within seconds of the final whistle, he was asked what it felt like to have such fervent support from 63,000 people. 'We didn't have the support of 63,000 South Africans today. We had the support of 42 million,' he said, as the 63,000 in the stadium cheered their approval. Mandela, still wearing his Springbok gear, handed the cup to Pienaar.

'Thank you very much for what you have done for our country,' said Mandela.

Mr President,' replied Pienaar, again with a statesmanlike dignity, 'it is nothing compared to what you have done for our country.'

Back in the changing-room afterwards, before the media poured in, Christie told his players to be humble in victory. 'Guys, you're all heroes today and you'll probably be heroes forever,' he said. 'But I am determined that you should all be humble tonight. We know how close this game was – I think it was our destiny to win, but the All Blacks have come desperately close. Let's keep our feet on the ground and behave decently in victory.'

Just a few years earlier, the country had been perilously close to racial war. Now, it seemed so different as the black President and the white captain stood, united. A symbolic representation of the new country. The children on the hillsides and labouring in the shanty towns did not get fed by the drop goal that clinched the World Cup, nor were they given homes, security and a happier life, but the step that South Africa took that day – albeit a symbolic one – appeared to be a step towards such a goal.

It seemed significant that it was rugby that had brought the country together in that moment because, during apartheid's half century, the sport was always perceived by black South Africans as 'the oppressors' sport' – as evocative a metaphor as any for the bullying humiliation to which white South Africans had subjected black South Africans ever since the arrival of the first European settlers in 1652 – but especially since 1948, the year the apartheid system was introduced and racism became law.

South Africa's image changed dramatically that day – but were there any real changes as a result of the World Cup? Mandela said 'Sport has the power to change the world' and it would be a brave person who chose to stand up and disagree with him, but what have the real changes been?

When Chester Williams wrote his autobiography, he described the show of unity among the players as being 'a lie'. Williams was the only non-white member of the 1995 World Cup winning team, and said that he had suffered heavy racial abuse from James Small, the international wing (and the player who was charged with tackling Jonah Lomu). 'Small called me a fuck-ing Kaffir,' said Williams. 'Then he shouted "Why do you want to play our game? You know you can't play it".'

As I write this in 2007, the Cape Town daily newspaper *Die Burger* is suggesting that Springbok players and management staff may have their passports confiscated if the team for rugby World Cup 2007 does not have enough black players in it. South Africa's chairperson on the Committee of Sport, Butana Komphela, has threatened the Springboks may not take part if the team is not fully representative. He said that the six black players in the World Cup squad are not enough. 'We are polite about this but deadly earnest,' he said.

Racism has reared its ugly head a few times since 1995. The most famous incident was when lock Geo Cronje allegedly refused to share a room with black teammate Quinton Davids. A SARFU inquiry into the allegation did not find conclusive proof of racism, but there is no question that the incident left a sour taste behind, as one was left pondering exactly what was going on behind the closed doors of the South Africa rugby team. The ANC was quick to condemn the situation. 'We are appalled and disgusted by Cronje's actions and we believe he deserves nothing less than being excluded from the rugby fraternity,' said an ANC spokesman. 'Cronje must never be allowed to play a role that ele-vates him to a hero while he undermines the very essence of our democracy.'

Then there was former coach André Markgraaf who was filmed using the word 'Kaffir'.

In every instance, there was disgust expressed within South Africa and across the rugby world – perhaps that is the lasting legacy of the 1995 World Cup triumph – a zero tolerance policy.

Danie Gerber says that things have changed dramatically in South Africa since 1995, and that he has never judged a colleague or an opponent by the colour of his skin. 'I grew up when every-thing was changing,' he said. 'Maybe older people were more worried about stuff like that [playing in the same team as non-whites]. When I was at primary school, the team was mixed. From then on, everything was mixed. The older you get, the less of an issue it becomes. You trust the player next to you. When I played in the Currie Cup, race was never an issue.'

When Gerber was a young boy, sporting sanctions kept South Africa in the international wilderness. 'There weren't any Springboks,' he said. 'Your only aspiration was to play in the Currie Cup. My father had an album of old radio recordings from Springbok games that we used to listen to. It was a huge moment when we came back. There would be no cars on the streets when the Springboks played – everyone was inside watching it on TV.'

The 1995 World Cup changed the image of South Africa, and gave the people of the country a vision of how life could be, but it was all largely cosmetic – it represented a starting point from which genuine changes could be made. When those changes have been achieved, rugby can be immensely proud of itself for being part of the story, but it would be wrong to think that it was the whole story. Perhaps sport does have the power to change the world, but in this instance, I would suggest that sport had the power to provide a country with the opportunity to change itself.

18

New Zealand gets sick and South Africa rejoices

We had grown together to a point where our relationship could more easily be recognised as that between a father and a son than between a rugby coach and his captain. I had felt the benefit of his support and advice like the rays of the sun on my neck. I knew he supported me, I knew he cared for me. He never let me down . . . In silence, I stood in front of the coffin. The coffin seemed so small, so final . . . Life would go on. Kitch would never be heard on the end of the telephone again but, for as long as I draw breath, I know he will never be far away.

François Pienaar, the former South Africa captain, in Rainbow Warrior *remembers coach Kitch Christie, who died in 1997*

The 1995 World Cup final fell on a crisp June afternoon. Morne du Plessis had stood on the touchlines afterwards and looked out at the flag-waving crowds. Winning had meant so much; it was as if beating the All Blacks, one of the most formidable rugby sides ever seen, was a validation of every individual South African, and the nation collectively as the new Republic of South Africa. While New Zealand had hurled teams out of the competition at every stage, unleashing Lomu and standing back to watch sides chase their tails in his presence, they hadn't been able to beat the hosts. There were many reasons for South Africa's victory – the presence of Mandela and the enormous backing of the nation among them. The President's unwavering support had been a gift to the South Africa team throughout the 1995 tournament. To have one of the most highly respected men in the world appearing on the day of the biggest match, wearing the team's colours, was a massive boost to morale, and conversely, created a real obstacle for the All Blacks to overcome. New Zealand must have felt as if they were playing against the very notion of what is good and right and proper – all dressed up in green and gold.

The 1995 World Cup final was about the power of place, history, politics, culture, determination and a squad of players eager to play their part in the rebirth of a nation. It was not just about the physical strength of the South Africans against the physical strength of the All Blacks – high-level sport is rarely so simple, and never less so than in the 1995 World Cup final. Caught up in the battle for victory were a host of powerful social and racial issues. The sights at Ellis Park, where once black fans had been penned in away from the whites, and invariably supported the visiting team, were spectacular. Blacks and whites supporting together. Whatever happened afterwards and whatever had happened before, there was a feeling of equality in the stadium that day. The final was about the projection of that feeling to the world. And it wasn't just about the freedom of black people from oppression and degradation, it was also about the freedom of white people from fear. A fear that had kept them chained to and constrained by destructive thought processes about native South Africans. A fear that was sometimes inherited and sometimes learned but never did them any credit and had led to their country being isolated from the world. Now, though, here they were, in front of the world – showing the world that everything was okay. The oppressors and the oppressed united in support of South Africa; the jailed and the jailors stood in the stadium, long after the players had left, banging the same drum.

So, in the attempt to analyse why South Africa won the 1995 World Cup, it is necessary to dwell for a short while on the implications of this highly emotive landscape. How much does their victory owe to the power and passion of a nation backing its players? How much additional strength does such support give a team? Can that be calculated? And what of Mandela? Is it possible to quantify the impact of the President in the Springbok shirt on the South African team? Most significantly of all, would they have beaten New Zealand without all that support? New Zealand have only played South Africa on one other occasion in a World Cup match – in the quarter-final in 2003. On that occasion, New Zealand won 29–9.

There is no question that environment and the support of a nation has an impact on a team. After his team's victory in 1991, Bob Dwyer said that the enthusiasm of the Australian public had helped Australia to victory. When the public started to believe in the team, it led to the development of the team's belief in themselves. When a group calling themselves the Wallabies' Supporters' Group began holding a lunch before each international, and the players heard about it, Dwyer recalls that it had the effect of lifting the players, and making them feel that they really could win the 1991 World Cup. As public confidence grew, there was a commensurate growth in the confidence of the players.

In 1987, the All Blacks were motivated by the New Zealand public in a very different way. They became determined to prove to rugby fans that they were all still good, honest and decent people and that the New Zealand team was still capable of being the best in the world, despite all that had happened on the Cavaliers tour. The All Blacks were eager to prove that rugby was still a valuable sport.

In 1995 there were obviously a host of other reasons for South Africa's victory. The coach and captain and their relationship was a vital constituent. The separate skills of Pienaar, as captain and Christie, as coach, were central to South Africa's success. And their relationship, and the one they would develop with Morne du Plessis when he came in as manager, created a strong du Plessis–Pienaar–Christie three-way axis at the centre of the team. This was vital for all three of the men who had support, feedback and checks on their performance throughout the tournament.

*

Pienaar and Christie first met in 1993, as coach and captain of Transvaal. Together, through two seasons, they won seven trophies. 'We worked together, played together and did rugby together. He was a very important man in my life,' said Pienaar.

Christie was appointed South Africa coach in 1994, after the former incumbent, Ian McIntosh, was dismissed following the unsuccessful 1994 tour to New Zealand. Pienaar remembers calling Christie to congratulate him on his appointment. The first question the coach asked of Pienaar was whether the South Africa captain thought they could win the World Cup. 'Do you?' he asked. 'Do you think we can do it? Have we got the right players?' Pienaar admits to being slightly thrown by the directness of Christie. The coach wanted immediate and frank answers to all his questions, as he fought to assess what the problems were and how they might be immediately eliminated. Pienaar recalls that Christie had already identified key areas that they would have to work on if they were going to lift the trophy:

1. Fitness
Christie thought it vital for South Africa to be the fittest side in the tournament, so brought in Ron Holder and gave him responsibility for getting the players fitter than they'd ever been.

2. Management
He wanted a powerful manager to work alongside him. It would have to be someone the players respected and would turn to if they were concerned. He needed a manager who would be his eyes and ears in the team, his biggest ally and confidante. He brought in Morne du Plessis who had an enormous impact, was more effective, more involved and more of an inspiration to the players than Christie could have dreamed of him being.

3. Self-belief
Christie identified early on that for a team that had not competed in a World Cup tournament before, and was short of international experience, self-belief was going to be crucial. He did not want his players to start thinking that they couldn't do it. They had to

believe that they were going to win the World Cup. Obviously, the way the South African people stepped up to support, and the utter belief shown by Mandela, would help foster this essential quality.

4. Relationships among the players

Christie felt that the players needed to become more like a family. Throughout this section of the book, you may recall Christie's thrill when the players stepped up to the mark for each other and helped each other. On every occasion he would remark 'We are a family now'. This was a burning passion for him, and he felt that great teams were teams where the players had great respect, admiration and love for one another. Indeed, a quick look back at Christie's career illustrates the importance of this to him. He resigned as coach of Transvaal because he did not think that plotting to beat players on the club scene one week, then asking them to become a family with him in the international team the next was possible.

Once, when on tour to the UK two players, Uli Schmidt and Rudolf Straueli, set off a load of fireworks in their hotel room and did £800 worth of damage to curtains, bed clothing etc. The squad all put in £25 each to pay the bill, with no one complaining that the guilty players should have to foot the bill themselves. He delighted in this. Those who knew him well say he never tired of telling the story of the day the players stepped up to the mark and supported each other so freely – like a family.

5. Discipline

Christie thought that to succeed at the highest level would demand discipline, so he looked for this quality and fought to develop this trait in all the players he worked with. On one occasion, he dropped Andre Joubert and James Small, both established players, when they missed their flight and arrived late for his first squad session. He refused to take Small on tour to Britain in 1994 because Small had a fight outside a nightclub after a woman allegedly pinched his bottom. Christie's focus on discipline was taken to extremes, and he would punish those displaying a lack of discipline in a variety of ways – many of which one may describe as 'questionable'. For example, when Tiaan Strauss was late for a morning training run, he was forced to bend over so that each member of the squad could smack him on the bottom.

6. A clear vision and a unique approach from the coach

Christie had a clear vision before every game and was clear with the players about what would be needed from them. He was very keen on breaking the rules, throwing out tradition and thinking of new ways of doing things. Playing a lock in the back row in the semi-final, and his plans for the 'brains game' in the final would fall into this category. The fact that he didn't pursue the brains game approach was testament to the strong three-way axis of control that he had established – it gave him checks and measures and limited his excesses, but it didn't change the fact that he was a visionary.

It is interesting that this need to do things differently rubbed off on Pienaar, too, who prepared himself psychologically for the final by making changes. He cut his hair and shaved before the World Cup final – two things he'd never normally do. Then, on the way to the ground, he made a point of breaking with tradition by putting music on in the coach.

'I liked the feeling I got from the players in the run-up to the final,' said Christie. 'They were separating this match out from all the others. They were behaving differently towards it – making it special.'

7. Target key individuals and key team weaknesses

South Africa were gunning for Campese in the opening game; they knew all his strengths and weaknesses (he's not great in defence or under pressure), then they did the same with Lomu in the final – limiting his impact by realising that he was virtually unstoppable at speed and he appeared to get crucial speed when he passed outside the defence. They kept him inside and managed to contain him. Also, there was the understanding of the team qualities: Christie knew the Australians liked to control the game from the line-outs and the kick-offs, so it was imperative that South Africa won their kick-offs. He did his research.

8. Attitude
South Africa vowed to show the opposition no respect at all, and to be ruthless and aggressive while on the pitch, while being humble and show respect for everyone off the pitch. The ability to combine these skills and be competitive on the field and humble off it was, according to Christie, a measure of greatness.

9. Get the basics right
Christie emphasised to the players that most matches were lost through too many mistakes, most of them simple, avoidable errors. He urged them not to lose the game by giving away penalties, and told his players to force opposition sides to kick the ball out and not to lose valuable possession by kicking the ball into touch themselves.

10. Enjoyment
Christie built in trips away, team-building sessions, emphasised the 'happy family' qualities in the team and was described as being 'a father figure' to the players.

One final point on the subject of why South Africa won. The question entered my mind, while researching the various reasons for their victory, that I should add 'because the New Zealanders were poisoned'. Whether deliberate or accidental, the New Zealand team claim that their ability to perform in the 1995 World Cup was greatly affected by their health. Clearly the strength of the opposition can be a fundamental reason underpinning a rival team's success. But since there is little a team can do to affect the health and fitness of a rival team (allegations of deliberate food poisoining aside), I have not included it here in this list, and tend to place the health of a rival team in the same category as injuries to a rival team – as luck more than anything else.

So, in attempting to establish what attributes a winning team has, it would be ludicrous to select 'plays against sick teams' as an attribute worthy of consideration. So, the illness to the New Zealand team, though it may have affected the pattern of the game in this instance, and though most in the New Zealand team believe that it absolutely affected the outcome and that they lost the match because of it, is not in this list.

Before leaving the 1995 tournament, it is worth looking briefly at the whole issue of the poisoning and how the allegations that it was deliberate came about. When 18 of the 36 players in the New Zealand squad fell ill on the Thursday night before the Saturday game, there was a belief in the All Blacks camp that their food must have been tampered with in some way, because it came on the back of other interruptions to their training – such as the car alarms going off all night and phone calls being put through to the players' rooms. Such initial thoughts appeared to be given credibility when Laurie Mains, the coach, left the tournament and still felt uncomfortable about what he had witnessed. He decided to investigate further, and hired a private detective to look into what had happened to his players that night. The detective reported back that a waitress called Suzy had been hired by the Crowne Plaza hotel, where the players were staying, and that it was she who had poisoned the players on instruction from a Far Eastern Betting Syndicate. The private detective said that Suzy had put something into the players' water that had made them ill and thus made it likely that they would lose the match, leaving Suzy's employers free to bet millions on a South Africa victory. The theories of food-tampering and 'Suzy' were backed by Sir Brian Lochore and Colin Meads.

Further credibility was given to the story when Rory Steyn, the security officer who had been assigned to the New Zealand team for the World Cup, added his voice to the debate. Steyn, a South African, was a credible source: a former police officer and head of security for Nelson Mandela, he was a passionate South African, with no connection to the New Zealand team other than he had worked with them as their security officer. He seemed to be as objective a witness as one could hope for. He remains convinced that the All Blacks were poisoned before the final. He describes the New Zealand team as being laid back when he first met them, and very happy to have him along with them. 'But as soon as the finalists were determined, the entire South African contingent on tour with the All Blacks was ostracised,' Steyn says. He advised them to go to the Sandton Sun hotel, but instead they were eager to return to the Crowne Plaza where they had previously been staying, because they wanted to change as little as possible about their preparation. Steyn said this was against his advice. Also against his advice was the idea of a separate dining room to keep the players away from the public glare. Until then, the All Blacks had been eating in the main dining room, in a cordoned-off section. The hotel was packed, and anyone looking to poison the team would have had to poison all the guests as well. By isolating themselves, they made themselves more vulnerable.

On the Thursday evening, Steyn took the players to the cinema after dinner. He watched the film with Richard Loe, who turned pale during the screening and wanted to go, so Steyn led him out.

> I said I would go and tell Goldie [Wilson] that I would come back for him. As I approached the doors to the cinema, he came out clutching his stomach, almost doubled over. I immediately knew we had a serious problem. We raced back to the hotel. Loey didn't even make it to the flowerbed. He vomited all over the driveway. When I got upstairs to the doctor's room, it looked like a battle zone; like a scene from a war movie – players were lying all over the place and the doctor and physio were walking around injecting them. Now, I was a police officer, I worked with facts. What my eyes told me was that the team had been deliberately poisoned . . . There is no doubt that the All Blacks were poisoned two days before the final.

Compelling stuff. But, there are conflicting stories about what happened. Just before the 2003 World Cup, a man called Tony Rubin decided to speak up. He had been a senior hotel executive at the Crowne Plaza hotel and he said that the players had eaten out of the hotel on the Friday night. He added that the mysterious waitress, Suzy, simply did not exist. The players, he claimed, had gone to a seafood restaurant on the night before the World Cup final, but when they got sick they decided to keep this unauthorised trip from Mains, as they feared his wrath. 'I have never met Suzy, there was no Suzy. She didn't exist. We knew what had happened [players going to the restaurant] but Southern Sun took a decision not to talk about the incident,' he told the South African newspaper, *Sunday Independent*. Further debates ensued about the timings, with Steyn saying this was rubbish and remaining adamant that the players were already suffering illness by Friday, well before the alleged trip to a restaurant because he was with them when they became ill on Thursday.

It is unlikely that we will ever know exactly what happened in the period leading up to the 1995 World Cup final, and while the story has died down with the passing of the years, it remains one of those little mysteries that sits, nestled in World Cup history, and interpreted either as a silly overreaction by the New Zealanders or as a criminal act that deprived a hugely talented team of their rightful position as world champions.

'The New Zealand players were bitterly disappointed although their reaction to the defeat did them no credit,' said François Pienaar. 'The allegations of deliberate food poisoning before the final rumbled on for several years, but without ever producing any shred of evidence to substantiate the claims. Some of their players might have been suffering from an upset stomach of sorts, but we had players on the field with broken hands and cracked ribs.'

It was 9 p.m. by the time the South Africa players arrived at Gallagher Estate for the official World Cup closing dinner. Dr Louis Luyt, President of SARFU, was furious that they were all late and the other squads present were bored with waiting. Luyt said the victory confirmed that if South Africa had played in 1987 and 1991, they would have won then too. Then he gave a gold watch to Derek Bevan, referee in the South Africa v France semi-final, instead of Ed Morrison, the man who had refereed the final. The English players were mocking Luyt openly and the New

Zealand players had begun heckling him. Mike Brewer was jeering so loudly that Luyt could hardly be heard at times. So incensed were they with his callousness and self-aggrandising that the New Zealand and England players left before the main course arrived.

The South Africans stayed until it was polite to leave, then headed off to find something less formal to enjoy.

That night, François Pienaar, Garry Pagel and I got the bus to drop us and our wives at a really good night spot in Jo'burg called the Rattlesnake Diner. We had our sports bags with us, with our medals inside, but when we tried to get in it was so packed that we ended up standing outside on the stairs [said Joel Stransky]. People absolutely mobbed us, buying us drinks and congratulating us. We were stuck on the stairs for half an hour and eventually decided we would never get in, so we left. There was no chance of getting a taxi, so we actually hitched back to the hotel carrying our bags, medals and all.

When they made it back, they each jumped, one after the other, into the hotel pool – fully dressed.

PART FOUR: 1999

Bowled over by professionalism

19

One fine day in Paris

You know – I spent all my career campaigning for us to be able to make money out of rugby but my friend, who plays at Richmond, tells me that all professionalism means is that players do nothing more all day except wank and dye their hair.

Brian Moore

You didn't have to be Sherlock Holmes to work out that something quite astonishing had happened at the Ambassador Hotel in late August 1995. The thing that gave it away for me was the sight of a well-known committee man banging his head against a brick wall. Ah, I thought – now he knows how we've all been feeling for the past decade. Next to him, stood a fellow committee type looking twice his real age (about 180!). 'It's gone,' he was muttering. 'Gone.'

Inside the hotel, there was an eerieness – a sense that something quite monumental had happened. A little like the feeling you have in a room when you are told that someone died there – suddenly the room takes on a personality of its own – becomes more than the sum of its walls, ceiling and assembled furniture. The Ambassador felt less a hotel and more the scene of a crime.

But all that had taken place in this beautiful Parisian hotel was a committee meeting. Surely nothing could have happened at that? Nothing ever happened at those things.

I was Features Editor of *Rugby World* magazine in August 1995, and just about to become Editor of the title. I was in Paris to interview a player – Jean-Pierre Rives, no less. It had been an interview like no other. Rives had been stark staring mad, to be honest, as he showed me round his artwork. Some of it was as sublime as the rugby he once played. Much of it was as incomprehensible as the man standing before me.

'Fiiiiisssssssshhhhh,' he kept saying, for reasons he didn't explain, his nose just an inch from mine. I'm only 5 ft 3 so he had to crouch a little every time he did it, and as he pulled himself up to his full height, his back creaked and he looked at me quizzically as if I were deliberately being small on purpose. It seemed churlish to suggest that he just stopped muttering 'fish' at me all the time – then we'd both be much happier about life.

It was only on a whim that I swung past the Ambassador before heading back to London. I'm glad I did, because this was the day on which rugby became a professional sport. Vernon Pugh had stood before the rugby world and made the announcement that every rugby follower was expecting, but that all were surprised to hear. Rugby union was to become a professional game. It had been talked about, written about and argued over. Everyone thought it would happen. Rugby was bound to become a professional sport eventually; one day. But rhetoric and action seem so far apart. Rather like a girlfriend who tells you she's going on a diet – you don't actually expect her to lose weight.

The moment of rugby's transformation was swift and simple – the process considerably less so. The announcement seemed to toss aside the cloak of amateurism in one fell swoop, but what it actually did was set fire to it while everyone was still wearing it. Officials in the northern hemisphere refused to take it off even after the announcement was made – hopping around from one foot to the other as it smoked and smouldered on their backs. In the southern hemisphere, it came straight off and on they got with the professional game.

The essential difference between the way in which the southern hemisphere and the northern hemisphere dealt with professionalism was a startling revelation about the essential differences between the two halves of the rugby globe, and an indication of just how far down the road to professionalism the southern hemisphere countries had already gone. In the northern hemisphere, the reluctance to leap straight in remained, even after the announcement. A moratorium year was declared during which time there would be a 'freeze' on professionalism while the governing bodies, clubs and players came to terms with the turn of events, and worked out what to do next. In effect, it was like going on holiday for a year and leaving the front door wide open. The declaration that rugby union would become a professional sport attracted commercial interest immediately. Were the big businesses going to wait until the end of the year-long moratorium before acting? Were they hell. They weren't going to wait until the end of the week.

Sir John Hall was first in. The 62-year-old multi-millionaire had bought Newcastle Gosforth rugby club within 72 hours of rugby union going professional. His plans for the club were formally announced on 5 September, nine days after the Paris announcement.

'The moratorium was a mistake,' says Cliff Brittle, the management board chairman. 'It was introduced in September 1995 and took the RFU's eyes off the ball, allowing others, with different agendas, to stake their claims for changes.'

There were many claims staked during that eventful first few months following the announcement. In October, Vinnie Codrington, President of Richmond Rugby Club, received a call from a Monte Carlo-based millionaire called Ashley Levett who wanted to invest. Levett went on to buy 70 per cent of the club.

The RFU were alarmed by the developments. Clubs issued a vote of no confidence in the RFU's seven-man commission, set up to establish guidelines for the new open era. The clubs formed themselves into their own organisation and threatened to split from the union. It took until May 1996 for a peace deal to be thrashed out. While the clubs and the union fought, so there was infighting within the union, because committee members had strong affiliations to clubs themselves and each man was eager to ensure his own club was going to be okay. So it wasn't even as simple as being 'them and us' with the clubs and the union, there was fighting within the factions as well.

But, not content with battling against the clubs and each other, the RFU decided to take on the world! They signed an independent TV rights deal with BSkyB and found themselves expelled from the Five Nations because of it. They were allowed to rejoin when they offered to put a percentage of their £87.5 million windfall into a communal pot, meaning they wouldn't have the income they needed to meet the clubs' demands. They couldn't win – it seemed that whichever way they turned, they got slapped in the face. It was difficult not to feel a little bit sorry for them as they staggered around like drunk teenagers at a party, groping for the answer. Difficult, but not impossible. The whole situation was of their making and the endless problems were eminently avoidable. If they had opted for action over inaction, and been proactive instead of passive, they would never have got into such an unseemly and damaging mess.

The reaction to the sport turning professional in South Africa, Australia and New Zealand was quite different because, in many ways, like the World Cup tournament itself, it was they who had been at the forefront of it – leading the way. At the end of the 1995 World Cup Louis Luyt announced that Australia, New Zealand and South Africa had done a deal with Rupert Murdoch for a southern hemisphere equivalent of the Five Nations. There would also be a lower-tier competition to be called Super 12 for the provincial sides. The countries would share US$550 million over a ten-year period. The northern hemisphere sides looked on in awe and wonder.

In addition to the giant sums being offered to the unions by Murdoch, there were also rumours circulating in the 1995 World Cup about a rugby circus – backed by Kerry Packer, Murdoch's big rival. 'I heard rumours,' says Will Carling. 'Some of the New Zealand players seemed to have been asked to join a rebel organisation, and the South Africans too, but it was supposed to be top secret.'

Things had started in the week before South Africa's quarter-final match against Western Samoa. François Pienaar was at the Sandton Holiday Inn when a call came through from Ian MacDonald, a Transvaal player, who asked Pienaar whether he would talk to 'the organisers' of a fantastic rugby project for the future. Pienaar agreed to attend the meeting with MacDonald, and was taken to meet Harry Viljoen, the former Transvaal coach. It would be to discuss a proposal from the World Rugby Corporation (WRC).

Viljoen outlined detailed plans for the launch of a professional rugby championship, staged outside the official structures of the game and funded by Kerry Packer. Every major national team would take part. It would be Pienaar's task to sign up the entire South Africa squad if he wanted to get involved. He would be paid handsomely for his efforts. Pienaar said he could do nothing until after the World Cup. Viljoen said he understood, but requested that Pienaar come and meet Ross Turnbull. This meeting was arranged for a week's time, before South Africa's semi-final against France.

Pienaar reiterated that he would not talk to the other players until after the World Cup, but took away one of the World Rugby Corporation contracts to read through. It said that basic salaries for Springbok players would range from R400,000 (around £45,000) to R1.5m (around £160,000) per year. Similar deals were being put to similar players from countries across the world. Sean Fitzpatrick, Phil Kearns and Will Carling were also approached, as WRC sought to sign up the star players from the world's leading teams, and a good proportion of those outside the top echelons.

Gareth Rees, Canada's captain, says he was approached and handed information about what would be on offer to him as a player in the WRC tournament. 'I thought it was a bit late for me. I was approaching retirement, and I wasn't sure what the guys in Canada would get out of it, but I didn't dismiss it. I took all the stuff, read through it and promised I'd think about it all.'

By the time South Africa won the tournament and became champions of the world, WRC organisers were more eager than ever to get signatures on forms. But Edward Griffiths, CEO of

SARFU, had discovered what was going on, and addressed the players during the team meeting straight after the World Cup final to outline an alternative vision of the sport.

He told them about the US$550m television rights deal signed by SARFU, NZRFU and Australia RU with Rupert Murdoch's News Corporation and said it would result in massively increased salaries for the players. He warned them not to sign contracts for any kind of unofficial rugby circus without first seeing what SARFU could offer.

Griffiths' bold move may have saved the sport from the WRC tournament. But, at the time, Pienaar was still convinced that the contracts handed to him by WRC would be better than any that SARFU could offer, so he gave them out to the players and, within a week of the final, twenty-seven of the twenty-eight players had signed with WRC, but they urged Pienaar at least to listen to what SARFU had to say about the tournament they were proposing before handing them over.

South African players arranged to meet Luyt to have a thorough discussion on the state of play at 9 a.m. at his Ellis Park office. The evening before, the players all gathered at Pienaar's to discuss what they would say to Luyt. They compiled a wish-list to be handed to the union.

In London, Will Carling was summoned to see WRC, in the form of Ross Turnbull, in his suite at the Ritz. Carling took Andrew Harriman, Brian Moore, Rob Andrew and Jon Holmes. Turnbull explained the plan to Carling as he had to Pienaar, and asked him to sign up the players. Carling wasn't sure. 'We'll pay you £1 million over two years if you come on board,' the England captain was told. Carling was asked to get players' signatures onto letters and keep them in a bank vault – as Pienaar had been asked. Carling refused to sign, but most of the England squad did. The contracts were all put away for safe-keeping and the players began to look forward to a lucrative future away from the paternal, patronising hand of the RFU.

But, in South Africa, panic was starting to set in at News Corp, the company that had just committed US$550 million to televising rugby in the three southern hemisphere countries. They were becoming anxious that the leading players in those three countries were being poached to perform beneath the banner of News Corp's bitter media rival – Kerry Packer. They were becoming increasingly frustrated that the governing bodies didn't seem to be able to do anything about it.

Pienaar was contacted late one night at home by Sam Chisholm, head of News Corp in London. 'What's happening in South Africa?' Chisholm asked. Pienaar admitted they were seriously considering the proposal from WRC. Chisholm asked Pienaar how much money he was being offered and when Pienaar told him, Chisholm said he completely understood why he had acted the way he had. He asked Pienaar if he would be interested if News Corp made a similar offer.

Pienaar felt caught in the crossfire. He wasn't overly sure about the validity of the WRC offer, and was aware that many of the players felt uncomfortable with it. But there was an enormous amount of pressure on Pienaar from WRC because without the World Champions on board, the tournament would not work. A satellite link-up had been organised by WRC between representatives of all the nations whose players had been given contracts. They were very eager for Pienaar to appear on the link-up and tell the other nations that South Africa had signed, thus prompting them all to sign as well.

Chisholm asked Pienaar not to participate in the link-up, and that News Corp would match whatever WRC were paying. News Corp were effectively offering the best of both worlds – stay playing the way they always had, but earn money from it. Luyt confirmed this. He said to Pienaar, 'I'll match Packer. We will contract all the World Cup players.'

The players voted overwhelmingly to go for the SARFU contracts, so South Africa were out of the WRC. 'It dealt a fatal blow to the WRC venture,' says Pienaar. 'I realised that we'd wrecked it all for them by pulling out, but there was nothing I could do.'

Across the rugby world there was a feeling that the Springboks had let everyone else down. They had taken the best offer they could get and in doing so had messed things up for the rest of the world.

The tournament never happened, but the negotiations that had taken place, and the terrifying spectre of Kerry Packer looming over the sport, forced the administrators to think seriously about whether amateurism was sustainable. They decided in August 1995 that it wasn't, and rugby union braced itself for professionalism.

20

But what about us? The minnows' stories

This will kill island rugby. For a long time we have had a special relationship with Australia and New Zealand but now we have been cut adrift at the first sign of money. I thought rugby was supposed to be one big family. Well, if it is – this is child abuse.

Bryan Williams, Western Samoa's coach, laments the arrival of the Tri Nations and the Super 12 tournament

'**W**e just want an even playing field,' Rob Andrew had complained in those weary amateur days. 'That's all we're after.'

And who could blame him? Andrew just wanted to make sure that British teams had the same opportunities to make money from their association with the sport as their colleagues in the southern hemisphere. There had been strict laws governing the payment of players in the amateur era, but all laws from the IRB were open to interpretation by each individual governing body. So, even though the sport pretended to be entirely amateur, the definition of 'amateur' varied considerably depending on where in the world you lived. Some players could earn money and others couldn't, meaning some had to work full time and others didn't, so some could train full time and others couldn't. Yet every four years they were pitched against one another and we were supposed to believe they were all amateurs with the same constraints.

When the sport finally went professional and all the top countries paid their players, allowing them all to train full time and compete equally with one another, finally they had the level playing field that Andrew had craved.

But, while everything may have been fair and equal for the leading rugby nations in the new professional era – what of the smaller ones? How were the minnow nations, who could barely afford to send a team to the World Cup once every four years, supposed to compete with fully professional teams? They simply didn't have enough money to pay players. In short, they couldn't afford to be professional, and they couldn't attract the big sponsorship deals to facilitate the move from amateurism. Furthermore, they couldn't see how on earth they could ever become successful enough to attract big money to the sport when the leading nations were now paying their players and investing in equipment, coaches and performance-improvement strategies, so would always be one step ahead. Surely professionalism would just allow the major rugby nations to develop away from the rest of the sport, making the gap between 'haves' and 'have nots' even greater. How on earth could sides from Romania and Argentina compete? They are both dedicated rugby countries (they are two of only four nations outside the Six and Tri Nations sides to have played in all five World Cup tournaments) but without the finance of the major European and southern hemisphere sides. And what of the Pacific Island teams? How would they cope in this new, bright, dynamic era?

Romania struggled enormously when the sport went professional, losing nineteen of its best players to French clubs. The players simply couldn't make a living in Romania, so headed off to France to play. By signing with French clubs, they ruled themselves out of the World Cup because the French clubs said they would dock their weekly payments if they left their clubs and went to play for Romania in the tournament. Romania was unable to make up the shortfall.

In the end, the Romania Rugby Union says eleven of those players who did not make the trip to the World Cup in 1999 would have been first-choice players. Basically, professionalism ripped the heart out of the Romanian team, and the selectors were left picking players who could not make it into the French club sides.

Professionalism came at a difficult time for Romania. The game was on its knees after the revolution to overthrow the Ceauçescus. It had been the much-disliked communist regime that had supported the sport by giving the players jobs in the army or the police, enabling them to earn a living and train all day. Once the regime went, so did the support. The lack of backing for the players ran alongside a lack of basic equipment. There was one scrummage machine in the whole of Romania leading up to the 1999 tournament, and no tackle bags.

Yet, despite these shortages, they manage to create players that are good enough for the French clubs to sign. It's a constant frustration for the Romania Rugby Union.

Romania players who travelled to the 1999 World Cup were paid what amounts to £10.41 a day. By the end of the tournament they had earned around £208 per man. Compare this to the Australian players who were awarded £3750 a game, and a bonus of £8500 for winning. So, at the end of the tournament, the Romanian players went home with the tiniest fraction of what an Australian player got for every game. England were thought to be on to make £100,000 if they had won the final, plus many times that again in lucrative advertising and sponsorship deals.

But it is not just the problem of keeping hold of players and paying those they can keep hold of that has become a major issue for minnow nations since professionalism. The other problem they have faced is the change of emphasis from participation to competition, making it harder for the smaller nations to get regular tough opposition. Countries like Samoa have found it hard to play any of the bigger nations with any regularity. I travelled out to New Zealand soon after the sport went professional and spent some time talking to the former All Black, Bryan Williams, who was the Samoa coach at the time. He was horrified about the deal that had been signed by Murdoch for a competition between Australia, New Zealand and South Africa. To cast the Pacific Islands out of regular competition with the formation of the Tri Nations and to not include them in the Super 12 was, he said, 'horrific'.

According to John Boe, Samoa's coach in the 2003 World Cup, Williams was right, the signing of the Tri Nations and Super 12 deal has made it extremely difficult for Samoa, Fiji and Tonga.

'If we could get a team in the Super 12 that would be fantastic because we could pay our players, we'd keep them. We could extend our player pool and we'd never look back,' he said. 'We'd be able to play the way we did against England all the time because we'd be playing at that intensity all the time. If we could get into a Tri Nations competition the same would apply. We need finance, so gate shares would be helpful, but I think from my point of view as coach we need a bigger player pool. At the moment it's drying up.'

Boe said that he thought Samoa should be allowed to pick New Zealanders of Samoan heritage who are not likely to be All Blacks. Currently those players are not eligible for Samoa because they are considered kiwis. 'It's a shame for those players and it's killing us,' he said.

Argentina has been feeling the pinch, too. Like Romania, they have participated in every World Cup competition, but they have found it incredibly difficult since the sport went professional.

Wyllie, Argentina's coach in 1999, and the man who was part of the triumvirate to take New Zealand to victory in 1987, discovered as soon as he became involved with the Pumas that they were clinging on to amateurism even after the rest of the world had moved on. The officials of the Argentina rugby union simply did not 'believe in' a professional game. Even persuading them to allow sponsors' logos on shirts was a huge battle, so determined were they to retain the principles of the sport that had attracted them to it in the first place. The trouble was that other countries were all becoming fully professional and Argentina were struggling enormously to compete with them. Alex Wyllie found himself being called 'technical adviser' instead of coach (so he could be a paid employee of the union), and found it difficult to get money for anything because they were so poor, but they refused point-blank to change their conduct and behave in a more professional fashion. 'I suppose in some ways it was refreshing – they weren't at all money-grabbing and wanted to do the best thing for the sport, but I think it made it difficult for them to develop so in the end they had to change.'

Fiji is a country a little like Western Samoa, in that it felt cast adrift when the sport went professional – left to fend for itself. Bob Challenor took over as the FRFU chief executive early in 2000. He says:

Fiji had no reserves. Players began to look for contracts just like their overseas counterparts, and the bottom line was that the small economy in Fiji had no hope of sustaining that.

The FRFU lurched from one year to the next trying to play international rugby without the resources to do so. Virtually all the funding it obtained was consumed by the cost of competing in international rugby, such as player contracts, travel expenses, accommodation, and travelling with larger parties.

Then the IRB expanded the sevens rugby competition to become a series of eleven tournaments around the world. The losses the FRFU incurred from the 2000 Sevens series, Challenor said, were horrific. At the end of December 2000, the FRFU was burdened with accumulated losses of F$933,306.

We owed much more than we owned. It's difficult because even tours are financially stacked against small unions because the visiting team has to pay its own assembly costs and travel to the destination, but receives none of the revenue. You can only make a loss on it.

That works for the large nations because, for example, if Australia plays in England, they lose money on that tour, but when England plays in Australia, Australia makes plenty.

If Fiji goes to France, France makes a packet. France comes to

Fiji and the FRFU loses money because of our small economy. We can't get F$100-a-seat and we have only small stadia. When you get 60,000 people into a stadium at F$100 a ticket that is big money.

The island unions went to see IRB officials jointly – as the newly-formed Pacific Tri-Nations Alliance. 'What we told the IRB is that unless we get an equitable share of the game's revenue, we can no longer afford to tour because we don't have financial reserves,' Challenor said.

'The present international tour agreement is inequitable. A review committee is looking at the matter right now . . .The IRB is quite sympathetic. The South Pacific hasn't had a voice in the past. By getting together with Samoa and Tonga we've now got quite a loud voice.'

Traditionally, Fiji, Samoa and Tonga have played a fiercely contested and greatly entertaining triangular series. In 2000, for the first time, they played a home and away Pacific Tri-Nations series which, Challenor said, instantly established itself as the number three series in the world after the Six Nations and SANZAR (South Africa, New Zealand, Australia) series.

But, he said,

It is not financially sustainable for the very simple reason that we don't have any television broadcast revenue, because we can't put out a picture of international quality. We could sell the games if we could do that. But to bring a crew and equipment into Fiji, Samoa and Tonga is an expensive exercise and too high a risk.

What we are looking at right now is to create a South Pacific OB [outside broadcast] unit not just for rugby, but for any South Pacific event . . . If we want to sell it internationally it has to be first-class, it has to be covered by a minimum of six cameras and hopefully ten.

It would mean equipment, a producer, a director and cameraman to train local people. It could be very profitable. What we are looking at is to establish it through an aid programme.

But, professionalism is not all bad news. Officials in Fiji say that now, looking back, they have much to be grateful to professionalism for, because in some ways it has made the organisation and administration of the players a little easier because the players who have signed for foreign clubs can at least be contacted.

'Even though they're thousands of miles away,' says Jeremy Duxbury, the Fiji Rugby Union's director of marketing, 'playing for clubs all around the world – at least they're not on some small island and utterly unreachable like they used to be. Roughly half of our international players are playing in other countries.'

The sport in Fiji is much more professionally run now – thanks to men like Duxbury, and thanks to income from the professional game. All the island players now come together in the Island Zone side. They come to Suva to a High Performance Unit (HPU) for two weeks and if they excel, they are drafted into the squad.

The HPU is a central point for elite training funded by the IRB. There are fifteen full-time staff working there, and players are paid for their time away from their clubs.

Players who head for clubs abroad earn money that allows them to help their communities when they get back. Players come back to Fiji having made money in European clubs, and build town halls, generators and start businesses to employ local people.

A lot of the businesses don't work out because there is not a competitive enough business culture here [says Duxbury], but at least the players are given the opportunity to try and help. I think the players like that – they like that if they are good enough, they will be paid well enough to make a real difference. But there is a downside, too, and one of the downsides is that World Cups aren't as sociable as they used to be. In 1987, the players felt special because they were in the same dining hall as the rugby greats from round the world. They all felt very welcomed. This was very different in 2003, when they were sent home straight after the competition and didn't get to see the closing stages or other players. It would have been nice to have just one function, at least, when all the players were together.

Canada's players have also noticed a fall-off in the old ways of behaving since the end of amateurism, in particular the tradition of shirt-swapping. 'I guess Canada's not the sought-after jersey that we like to think it is,' said Rod Snow, Canada's prop. 'At the end of a match, no one wants to swap, I guess that if they keep their own jerseys they'll make money from them. It's a shame though.'

Canada's David Lougheed went to the New Zealand dressing room with Canadian jerseys after playing them, but had little success and returned empty-handed.

'That's not the only thing to have changed since the sport went professional,' said Al Charron. 'There's less mingling and there's less socialising now. Players are not sitting down to have a drink with their opposite numbers after the game. That's disappointing.'

Coach David Clark senses that this is because of the top teams' attitude towards minnows such as Canada. 'When you come up against the big professional teams, there's a slight arrogance about it; they just snub their noses at those sort of things, which again is a shame, but attitudes have changed. In a lot of people's eyes, it becomes a business.'

21

Pool time

There were occasions when we didn't have enough balls.

Japan's interesting explanation for their shortage of possession against Argentina

The first fully professional rugby World Cup was to be hosted by Wales. Now, when I say Wales, remember this is the rugby World Cup we're talking about, so some matches were in France, some in England, some in Scotland and some in Ireland. Oh – and some in Wales. Certainly, the opening ceremony and the first game of the tournament were held at Millennium Stadium in Cardiff, as was the final. The twenty nations were split into five pools, creating the added complication of a quarter-final play-off round involving the side finishing in second place in each of the pools and the best third-place finisher. So, the five winners went through, and the six play-off teams contested the other three quarter-final berths. Simple? It's as if they have a committee somewhere whose sole responsibility is to think of ways of making the tournament as complicated as possible.

There was a new team in the tournament in 1999 – Spain qualified for the World Cup for the first time, and found themselves in Pool A with Uruguay, South Africa and Scotland. They became the tournament's second 'one-cup wonder' – a team that has competed in only one World Cup tournament. They didn't qualify before, and they haven't qualified since. The Spanish game is modelled on the French style, and is played only in Spain's big cities, with Madrid and Barcelona providing the vast majority of the national team's players. The sport began in Spain in 1923 and it joined the International Rugby Board in 1988, with 212 clubs and around 12,500 male players.

Prior to their qualification in 1999, their biggest achievement had come in 1997, when the team qualified for the Rugby World Sevens in Hong Kong. I remember watching them there – I was editor of *Rugby World* magazine at the time of the tournament, but travelled to Hong Kong with the ITV team to act as an on-air presenter and writer for *The Times*. The sight of Spain had us all rushing for our textbooks. 'Ali – what do you know about Spanish rugby?' came the cry through the press box. I could hear mutterings: 'She's the editor of *Rugby World*, she'll know.' Oh lord, I thought. No, she does not. Even the textbooks were of no help. Still, we found a number for the coach, though we didn't have his name. I decided to call in the hope that his English was better than my Spanish. A gruff New Zealander answered the phone. Thank God. There aren't all that many times when you're thrilled to hear from a gruff New Zealander, but this was one. At least he wasn't going to talk to me in Spanish. Bryce Bevan was his name; he was an Auckland lawyer who'd moved out to coach the game in Spain and was having astonishing success. Two years after the Hong Kong Sevens, Spain qualified for the World Cup for the first time. One decade on since Bevan's arrival there were 200 more teams playing rugby in Spain than there had been when he arrived. He transformed the game but then moved on to coach a club in the region, and standards immediately began to slip. Spain lost all their matches in 1999, but announced that 'by being here, we have won'.

Uruguay beat Spain to come third in the table, with South Africa coming top to win a quarter-final encounter with the qualifiers from Pool B, while Scotland would have to go through the play-off system.

Pool B brought with it a sense of déjà vu. Last time the World Cup had been in the northern hemisphere, England had faced a crucial opening game against New Zealand that had coloured the rest of their tournament. In 1999, they were in the same group as New Zealand again, needing to beat them, again. This time it was more crucial, because the second-place finisher would have to play off for a quarter-final place, so would have played an extra match and had significantly less rest than the team they would face in the quarter-final. Since that team was likely to be South Africa, the reigning world champions, beating New Zealand and thus topping the group, assumed mammoth proportions. But England lost 16–30 to New Zealand and so much had been riding on that game – that losing it felt as if their World Cup hopes had been dealt a severe blow. Martin Johnson had given his trademark scowl – his one-man answer to the haka – but New Zealand scored three tries to one. Tonga finished third, after conceding 101 points to England, and Italy ended up bottom of the table after a desperately disappointing tournament in which they conceded 60 points to England and 101 to New Zealand. Alarm bells were ringing about the sense of having invited Italy to join European teams to create a Six Nations competition.

Pool C featured France, Fiji, Namibia and Canada, so there were never too many questions asked of France. They went through in first place, without conceding a match. But they admitted to feeling worried before their clash with Fiji. 'This will be a tense week for the French team. They have to be very serious, very strong in the forwards against Fiji. They need to keep it tight, not play with traditional French flair,' said coach Bernard Laporte. 'At the moment, they cannot do it,' Raphael Ibanez added. 'Playing wide balls is too difficult for this French team. Too many turn-overs, too many mistakes. There are worries in our head,' he said. Happily for France, those fears remained in their heads, as they won 28–19. The Fijians were desperately disappointed. They had been refused what had seemed like a fair try, and France had been given a penalty try. Without those, Fiji would have won. 'What do they want us to do?' asked Brad Johnstone, the team's voluble, media-friendly coach. 'Here we are – fifteen guys with boots taking on fifteen guys with laptops and mobile phones, and they get given all the breaks.'

Johnstone would repeat his now-famous line about boots and

laptops when his team played England in the play-off. 'It's very hard to compete,' he said. 'I can't tell you how frustrating it is to have a try not allowed at this level – it's soul-destroying.'

That evening, I went out to a café in Toulouse with some fellow journalists and we sat there on that warm evening, talking about the game. As we stood to leave, the lumbering figure of Johnstone could be seen in the distance. 'I have players with more talent in their fingers than half the players in the World Cup would know what to do with,' he announced. 'But the All Blacks are in first-class accommodation and we are in huts, and showering in the yard outside with an old hosepipe. We cannot compete. Put that in *The Times*. Tell everyone that it's all just not fair.'

I was rugby editor of *The Times* in 1999, and I did write about the plight of Fiji – all the journalists did. We wrote most of all about Johnstone himself, though – this fabulous, colourful figure with a memorable quote for every occasion. He had been drafted in to Fiji rugby after they failed to qualify in 1995, and had restored their credibility and vastly improved their game by the time 1999 came round. The problem he faced was limited resources. There was a shoestring budget which meant no staff, so Johnstone had to do everything himself – from the difficult to the comedic.

I sat down with him shortly after the 1999 tournament and he explained. 'I get to work, open the office. If I want to send a letter, I buy the paper to write it on and I arrange to get it on to a boat. The players need looking after and that's my job, too. One wife wouldn't give her husband his passport because he hadn't left her any money, another was arrested before they could fly out of the country because he hadn't paid maintenance.' Before flying to Wales on one occasion, Johnstone found out that there was a warrant out for the arrest of a player who had been involved in a fight on a previous trip to the country. The player concerned was taken away and jailed for three weeks. 'Coaching is just one part of what I do.'

But Johnstone did manage to find time to train the players between his more domestic duties and, under his leadership, Fiji beat Scotland for the first time, and overcame Samoa by sixty points to nil. He was awarded the Order of Fiji on his return from the 1999 tournament and there cannot have been any rugby coach anywhere, ever, who deserved it more.

In Pool D, another Pacific Island team was ready to make a mark on the competition. Samoa would face Wales again . . . and the world held its breath again, to see whether the boys from the Pacific Islands would humiliate Wales on home ground again . . . and they did!

'I've never lost against Wales,' says Pat Lam. 'Isn't that strange? We just always seemed to beat them. We could lose to everyone else, but we'd still beat Wales.'

Wales still managed to top the group though, so avoided the dreaded play-off game, and it was Argentina, not Samoa, who went through to the quarter-final play-offs, after they beat Samoa.

The final group, Pool E, contained Australia, Ireland, Romania and United States. The Australia versus Ireland game was the match between the two strongest teams in the pool, and one which would determine which team finished top, and which second. It looked as if Ireland were prepared to concede this match, when news began emanating from the Ireland camp suggesting that coach Warren Gatland would play a second-string team against Australia because a better route through the competition could be won by losing this crunch game. Since Ireland had not beaten the Wallabies since 1979, that didn't seem to be too much of a danger in any case – whichever team they picked. In the end, Gatland quashed all such theories and said Ireland would be playing to win in all their matches. To be fair to Ireland, they had a strong side in 1999 – coached by Gatland, a former All Black hooker who built his side on the strength of his forwards. There was a strong front row of Peter Clohessy, Keith Wood and Paul Wallace who were the equal to any in the competition.

'If we have an off day against Ireland, we'll be beaten,' said John Eales, the Australia captain.

In the end, it could be argued that the Wallabies did have something of an off day, but they still managed a victory. There was a lack of continuity in the Australian game and they failed to string passes together. By half-time, the Wallabies were only 6–0 ahead, eventually winning 23–3.

So, Australia qualified for the next stage while Ireland were forced to endure the quarter-final play-off. Ireland had done well in the pool section though, having kicked off their campaign with a 53–8 defeat of USA at Lansdowne Road. They were confident that once the play-off match was behind them, they would be able to give France a good run for their money in the quarter-final.

The play-offs. What's to be said about them? They had never appeared in World Cups before, and they haven't appeared since. In 1999, they were a huge pain for many of the teams, especially the British and Irish teams, as three of the four home-nations teams went into the play-off stage to battle against three of the minnow sides. Wales was the only British side to avoid the extra game, along with all of the three big southern hemisphere sides and France. The advantages of the extra rest and not having to peak for another game were massive. Teams avoiding the extra round gave themselves a real advantage in the competition.

England were given a particularly rough ride through the tournament courtesy of the play-off system. They had to play Fiji at Twickenham, having played Tonga a few days previously. They then had to face South Africa in the quarter-final in Paris. 'I've got pains everywhere,' said Jason Leonard. 'You don't want to play those two teams twice in a season, let alone twice in a week.'

Still, they won. The 42–24 victory over Fiji booked them their place in the first stage of the knockout competition. They were followed into the quarter-finals by Scotland who beat Samoa 35–20, leaving just Ireland to qualify by beating Argentina. There was a strong feeling in the Ireland camp that having defeated Argentina, if things went their way, they could beat France in Dublin and be in the World Cup semi-final. Mentally, perhaps, the players and their management had made that classic mistake of not taking each game as it comes – and had projected forwards to the quarter-final.

It's not hard to see why they might have done this. No one would expect Ireland to lose to Argentina. They had played them in the August before the tournament, and won 32–24. This time, though, it was different. Ireland lost 24–28 and failed to make it to the quarter-final for the first time. Argentina's winger Diego Albanese scored the only try as the Pumas came from behind to win a first place in the last eight of the World Cup.

The reaction in Argentina was extraordinary. Florida Street, the principal pedestrian road through Buenos Aires, was filled with people all afternoon – watching the sport on televisions. This football-mad country was warming to rugby union. When Argentina won, the cacophony of sound that traditionally accompanies any success in football, began in earnest – car horns, hooters, people cheering, singing, shouting in the streets. Gonzalo Quesada won the Olimpia de Oro and the players were all awarded Congressional medals for their efforts. The quarter-final became must-watch viewing in Argentina.

It was a slightly different scene in the Irish camp, of course. They flew back to Dublin the next day devastated at their early exit. 'We didn't have an intelligent enough game plan,' complained Keith Wood. 'We can't let this happen again.'

He led his players away, leaving the other home nations teams to the quarter-finals.

22

The road to the final

I thank the Lord for the talent He gave me and I thank the forwards for the ball they gave me.

Jannie de Beer, South Africa's fly-half, after his team's quarter-final victory over England

There was good news and bad news. On the positive side, Wales had the advantage of not having to go through a quarter-final play-off game so, unlike the other qualifying British teams, did not arrive at the finals stage exhausted and labouring under a huge casualties list. But, on the down side, neither did their opponents. Further on the downside, the opponents were Australia, a team that Wales hadn't beaten since 1987 when they narrowly won the third place play-off. Since then the teams had played six times, and on every occasion Australia had triumphed.

Not that this was going to bother Wales. Under the positive leadership of Graham Henry, they went into the match bursting with confidence and, until their pool match defeat to Samoa, they had strung together ten successive wins and felt that, with the benefit of home advantage, they should be able to defeat Australia.

They met on a rainy day at Millennium Stadium under an open roof, despite calls from the Australians that it should be closed. Australia requested the closure because of their desire to release their backs and play an open, running game. In the end, they man-

aged this feat regardless of the rain-soaked ground. They dominated the midfield battle, with Stephen Larkham, Horan and Daniel
Herbert proving far more penetrative than Jenkins, Gibbs and
Taylor. 'Australia are an awesome side, they have great defensive
qualities,' said a heart-broken Robert Howley, the Wales captain.

But Wales had played well, perhaps that was the hardest
thing to come to terms with – they had played well, but lost to a
better side. It wasn't that they lacked determination or commitment – they showed that in spades – but it was not enough. By
the end of the match, Australia had played 320 minutes of rugby
in the tournament and conceded just one try. They won 24–9.

Over to Paris on a pleasant autumnal day for the second quarter-final in which England would play South Africa, the reigning
champions, at the Stade de France. A place in the semi-final at
Twickenham was up for grabs. The two teams met on a pleasant
afternoon, and battled out an opening first half on the sun-dappled
pitch. But it was in the second half that the match's true course
was set, as Jannie de Beer – the fly-half who was only in the side
because of injury, and who had been so frustrated with the South
African set-up earlier in the year that he planned to move to
Britain – kicked a remarkable five drop goals to take his team
through. Four of his kicks were long-range hits – bang, bang, bang,
bang – the whole thing had a surreal quality to it. No player had
previously kicked more than three dropped goals in an international. By the time he had converted tries and kicked penalties, his
personal total was thirty-four points, and South Africa won 44–21.

It was the most astonishing afternoon's rugby, and as we
walked out afterwards, shell-shocked and baffled, I recall turning
to my esteemed colleague on *The Times*, David Hands – a man
who's seen it all, and is not given to hysterical overreaction.

'Did that just happen?' I asked.

'I think so,' replied David, vaguely. 'But it can't have.' That
summed the whole thing up – it simply can't have happened.

As we wandered towards the bowels of the stadium where
the press conference was due to take place, it emerged that Clive
Woodward was standing before the players, and giving them a
talk that would inspire and re-energise them.

The team were feeling terrible, but Clive stood in front of them and told them how well they'd done [recalls Humphrey Walters, the management expert retained by Clive to help work with the team]. He praised them, saying how proud he was of them, and that this was the beginning. They were to forget about 1999, and begin thinking about 2003. He told them they would win the next World Cup. He said this defeat marked the start of something brilliant for English rugby. I've never heard him give a speech like it, and to this day I don't know how he did it. He must have been feeling awful, but he managed to rise above it, and in that moment, the seeds for 2003 were sown. I watched and thought 'he's done it. He's completely turned them round.' I knew in that moment that England would win the next World Cup.

It was England's worst World Cup showing since 1987, but back then they'd done a bit of fitness work and turned up. This time, the shock defeat had cost £8 million and a vast amount of time.

'We knew they had done a lot of work on their defence, so we thought we'd kick it over the top,' said Nick Mallett, South Africa's coach. Suddenly this complicated and refined game seemed no more sophisticated than hopscotch.

Before Scotland encountered New Zealand in the quarter-final of the 1999 World Cup, they had met them in each of the three previous World Cups – twice in quarter-finals and once in the third place play-off – and each time they had lost. Indeed Scotland had not beaten New Zealand in eighty-four years of trying. The tally stood at 20–0 to New Zealand before the match. Sadly, for Scotland, the score afterwards was 21–0.

New Zealand had been relaxing and sunning themselves in the South of France prior to the game, while the Scots had been coping with a physically demanding midweek play-off battle against Samoa.

There was nothing relaxed about their approach to Scotland though – the kiwis came out all fired up, played at a million miles an hour to blitz the Scots and put seventeen points on the board before half the players knew what was happening. But it was not all fantastic stuff from New Zealand and, once they had exerted their authority, they seemed to sit back and take it easy, allowing the Scots to outperform them 15–5 in the second half. The kiwi scrum and line-out were nowhere near as strong as everyone expected them to be but, it has to be said, plenty good enough to beat Scotland.

The last of the quarter-finals, in Dublin between Argentina and France, provided the French with a stage for some dazzling showman-style rugby – running the ball, classic tries, flamboyance and glimpses of the team's traditional flair and confidence all combined to give France a 47–26 win.

'The danger of this French team is that they can wake up in the morning, feel good and produce something special,' said John Hart whose All Blacks would have to play France in the semi-final. 'They looked as if they had lost confidence but they found their way back against Argentina. That makes them dangerous again.'

The first of the semi-finals – between South Africa and Australia – was the battle of the two previous winners of the tournament. For Rod Macqueen, one of his pre-match considerations was how to contain the threat of De Beer and his dropped goals. 'It's very difficult trying to defend against something like that,' admitted Macqueen. 'What we won't be doing is practising charging them down. The answer is to play the game in their half. The answer is to deny him the opportunity to do it. Once he has the space and time to do it – you've had it. We need to prevent him from having the opportunity in the first place.'

Australia went into the game with only thirteen victories over South Africa in forty-four previous meetings, while the Springboks had yet to lose a World Cup match in nine previous outings. But it was the Wallabies who appeared the more attack-minded throughout the contest – battling against a resilient opposition defence. It fell to the boots of Burke and De Beer to keep the scoreboard ticking over, as they swapped spot kicks for much of the match. This was not a pretty Test. But it was an enthralling, monumental battle – defence frequently ferocious and the scoreline equally matched throughout the game.

This thrilling encounter also revealed holes in the Australian team. While Tim Horan was the star, rising to the occasion magnificently, the Wallabies made a number of breaks that they simply didn't finish. They failed to ram home any of their advantages, and breaks by Horan, Roff and Herbert died out because support players did not arrive in time. So it had been left to the kickers to battle it out.

As the clock ticked over, De Beer slotted a penalty over from 35 yards to make it 18–18. De Beer then put South Africa ahead before Burke levelled in the second half of extra time. In the end, though, it was the boot of another, Larkham, that proved the deciding factor. His drop goal sailed over – the first he'd ever struck in an international match – then Burke added another penalty to ensure the win. It was 21–17 to Australia and a place in the World Cup final. Larkham revealed afterwards that his drop-goal from forty-eight metres was kicked despite a strain to the medial ligament in his knee.

After the ferocious battle between South Africa and Australia, little was expected of the second semi-final. To be honest, everyone expected the out-of-form France – bottom-place finishers in the Five Nations, who had suffered a disastrous run of six defeats in eight matches – to be torn apart by the all-powerful New Zealand team – favourites to lift the Cup. In the end, the teams played out one of the most astonishing games in the history of the World Cup. New Zealand started the match at 15/1 on favourites and finished as losers by 43–31.

The French players employed a range of psychological tricks to prevent being overcome by the New Zealand team. World Cup-winning footballers Franck Leboeuf and Didier Deschamps visited the team before the match and told them: 'Create a revolution out there today.' 'So,' says Olivier Magne, 'that's what we did.' Skipper Ibanez recalls: 'We knew we had to prepare for war. Either that or not to have a chance. We prepared for war.'

Three Frenchmen turned their back on the haka as soon as New Zealand began. Then the match started and at first it seemed to be going the way of every prediction, as France slipped 24–10 behind and any hope of an upset appeared to be fading. But in a sudden Gallic turnaround, they added thirty-three points to just seven from the All Blacks for a sensational victory. The star of the match was Christophe Lamaison, who had been overlooked by the selectors prior to the game and only made the starting XV following the withdrawal of the injured Thomas Castaignède. Lamaison went through the All Blacks defence for the first try then did not miss a single kick all match.

It was arguably the biggest turnaround in rugby history. From the 46th to the 59th minute, France harvested twenty-six unanswered points to go from 10–24 to 36–24.

Lamaison's two drop-goals and two penalties in quick succession gave France a realistic chance and New Zealand fell apart. From there, the tries came rolling in. First, Christophe Dominici, then Richard Dourthe, then Philippe Bernat-Salles. The All Blacks were left reeling. Jeff Wilson scored a consolation effort at the death.

'That result will rock New Zealand to the core,' said All Black legend Andy Haden after the match. How right he was. The New Zealand stockmarket slumped for a few months, the Prime Minister was hauled out in front of Parliament to give an explanation for the team's demise and one university offered its students grief counselling. When the team returned they found that the baggage handlers at Auckland airport had scrawled 'losers' in white chalk across all their bags.

'We're devastated,' said John Hart. 'I take full accountability for the loss. We were outplayed today . . . but we should not have lost from 24–10. Devastated.'

'It was awful,' recalls Zinzan Brooke. 'When we lost to France in 1999, the whole country was devastated. The government even lost an election because of it. I know that sounds stupid. It's only a game after all, but it's our game. We're not supposed to lose matches like that.'

*

In a corner of the Australian team room, Scott Harrison, the statistician and video analyst, sat back in his chair and waited for the inevitable. Rod Macqueen came bursting through the door and Harrison smiled. 'You want me to look up all the players in the French side and put them on CD-Rom overnight, don't you,' he said. Macqueen nodded.

Harrison threw the CD-Roms he'd painstakingly prepared on the All Blacks into the bin and started again. He worked for the High Performance Division at the Australian Rugby Union, headed up by Jeff Miller, and was in charge of the computer software system that had been brought in to enable them to obtain astonishingly detailed statistics on all their opponents. Players just had to type in what facts they were looking for – kicks, tackles, passes – and the computer would give information about the number and types of actions, off which hand or foot, where weaknesses were, favoured foot, where they were reluctant to defend, where they usually ran. All the information that the players could possibly want to know about their opposition were available at the click of a button.

The trouble is – you had to search for the right team in the first place, and Harrison had spent days collating information on the All Blacks. The French team were harder to analyse. They didn't have a definite pattern of play like the New Zealanders. They were excellent at taking advantage of any situation, counter-attacking and playing instinctively. That made them close on impossible to analyse, categorise and plan for. Harrison explained the situation to Macqueen and the coach pondered a moment then quoted the philosophy of Sun Tzu to him.

'Do the unexpected by attacking the opposition's strengths,' he said enigmatically.

'Right,' said Harrison. 'So what do you want on these CD-Roms?'

'Give me everything you've got. What the players have to do is force the French into playing a particular pattern and stop them playing instinctively . . . attack their strength.'

Through the CD-Roms that Harrison prepared after working through the night, the coaching team established that the French ability to counter-attack came from the strength of their back row, so the obvious thing to do was keep the ball for long periods of time and attack around the fly-half position, so forcing the back row to tackle continually. In the second half they predicted that gaps would open up around the field. If tighter defence was needed, they would have players on the bench capable of providing that defence. Once the advantage line was broken, they would throw the ball wide.

Australia spent all week before the final practising their new game plan. Macqueen had developed his team over the past two years not to be formulaic and rely on a set way to play. He'd encouraged them to spot weaknesses on the field and attack them rather than go onto the field and follow a prescriptive plan. Never was he more grateful that he'd trained them to be flexible than when France got into the final.

23

A double for the boys from Down Under

We will go in with the necessary humility, and with the pride of champions. But it will be difficult to play two matches like last week, to get the state of mind back.

Jo Maso, France's manager, before the 1999 World Cup final

The Australian players in the team room looked round at one another. Today was the day. Jason Little stood up and read out the words of Herb Elliott, the former Olympic middle-distance champion. 'There is a point of no return where you have laboured so long, sacrificed so much, that you can't go back. You must reach your goal and trample on anyone who tries to stop you.'

The room was silent.

Then Andrew Blades stood up to address the group. It was his last Test. He began his speech then choked up. 'This means everything to me,' he said. 'Everything.' As he looked around the room, half of his teammates were in tears, too.

Scott Staniforth, the winger and the youngest member of the group, rose to his feet. 'This is it,' he said. 'Make sure there are no regrets.'

'Let's go.' John Eales led the players out of the hotel and onto the bus. It wound its way through the packed streets of Cardiff –

past the painted faces of men, women and children. 'It was a chance to make history and we all knew it,' said Little. 'I've never known tension like it. The sense of expectation was enormous.'

'The players were so emotionally charged by the speeches it was hard to imagine that we would lose,' said Eales. 'There was so much passion and all this adrenalin. We had peaked at exactly the right time. We were composed and confident and ready to get out there and play.'

Things were slightly different in the France camp, where Ibanez, the French captain, made different claims for his team. 'We are French. We are always unpredictable, and I don't know exactly what will happen in the final. I don't know what we will do. Who can know? Always remember – we are French.'

Indeed, and only the French, perhaps, could have gone from Wooden Spoon to World Cup finalists in just a couple of months. It is what has made them such a delightful force in World Cup competitions – with their game plan that appears to have been formed and revised on the run. Who knew what we would see in the final? France had shown that they were clever enough to break down defences as tough as the All Blacks'. They could per-form magic and create tries out of nothing. But it could just as easily go completely wrong. History is laced with examples of spectacular self-destruction from the French. Does this make them a good opponent or a bad one? According to Joe Roff, he would rather line up against Lomu than Dominici or Bernat-Salles. 'They're so unpredictable. You know what Jonah's going to do. I admit that stopping him is a bit tough but at least you have an idea what to expect. You don't have a clue with the French players.'

Eight years is not long, but in the life of a rugby player it's a huge amount of time. Many of the players preparing for the World Cup final in 1999 had been teenagers when Nick Farr-Jones led the team to victory in 1991. Only two players remained in the starting line-up from that first victory – Tim Horan and John Eales. Horan was the star of the Australia team in 1999 and Eales the captain.

'I think the whole team felt the sense of history on the

occasion though,' said Eales. 'They all knew how much it had meant to us in 1991, and wanted to experience it for themselves.'

If history was anything to go on, the two teams went into the game keenly matched. Australia had played France twenty-eight times before the 1999 final, and it was thirteen wins to Australia and thirteen wins to France, with two draws. To further underline the closeness, Australia had scored 498 Test points against France and conceded 481. The last World Cup meeting between these sides was the semi-final of the 1987 World Cup – one of the best matches ever played. On that occasion, France knocked Australia out, then went on to lose to New Zealand. This time, they beat New Zealand. Would they now lose to Australia?

Yes. And, they lost for the same reasons – because the enthusiasm that had coloured the semi-final was distinctly lacking in the final. Once under pressure from Australia they became undisciplined, allowing Matt Burke a host of kickable opportunities. As the game headed to half-time, Australia were 12–6 in front. But it was after the restart that things moved forward for Australia – piling the pressure on the French. Australia led 18–12, six penalty goals to four entering the last quarter. With a 21–12 deficit, France were still clearly in the game until the first of two second-half tries. Ben Tune pulled off the killer blow when he ran into the corner virtually unchallenged, before Owen Finegan made the margin of victory even bigger in injury time when he followed Tune's lead to pick a gap in the French defence and force his way over the line. Burke converted both tries as Australia became the only two-time winner of the William Webb-Ellis Trophy with a massive score of 35–12.

Australia had not allowed France – the team that had scored four tries against the All Blacks – to score against them. It was further testament to the Australian defence that had been the cornerstone of the Wallaby campaign. They conceded just one try in six matches.

But this had not been a pleasant game, and Eales had been so angered by French tactics that he told referee André Watson that he'd lead the Australians off the field if the French kept up dirty play in scrums, rucks and mauls. Watson twice cautioned French captain Raphael Ibanez to keep his players under control. Eales, who sustained a torn cornea of the right eye, was one of four Australians who finished the game with an eye injury.

John Best, the Australians' doctor, said Richard Harry, the prop, Michael Foley the hooker and George Gregan the scrum-half had also been the victims of gouging. David Wilson was kicked in the face.

After their victory, the Australians returned home straight away, and to mass celebrations. So, strangely, did the French. Despite losing the final, their victory in the semi-final had been delighted in by a French public who were miserably predicting an early French exit. Some 10,000 supporters turned out Sunday night to greet France's rugby team. The players, in suits and ties, stood aboard an open-top bus which paraded through the streets of Paris. They had no trophy to brandish, but their success seemed as real as if they were clutching the Webb-Ellis trophy. They stopped for a ceremony at the Eiffel Tower. 'It's marvellous to see all these people welcome the French team,' said coach Jean-Claude Skrela. 'I think they're acknowledging the pleasure the team gave them by beating the All Blacks.' The French team, after a disastrous run of six defeats in eight matches, had been given no chance by the French public in the run-up to the World Cup. But the mood turned to one of euphoria after France's remarkable 43–31 semi-final victory over the All Blacks.

The French players acknowledged that the better team had won the final.

'Two weeks ago, who would have imagined that France could get to the final?' said Interior Minister Jean-Pierre Chévènement. 'Not I, not anyone.'

Australia's rugby heroes were treated to parades in Sydney, Melbourne and Brisbane. Each city presented the keys to the city and a special plaque to the Wallabies' team. The Sydney celebration was the largest, with tens of thousands of people lining the street for the ticker-tape parade, while streamers were thrown from office buildings. More than 150,000 had turned out to support the players. There were civic receptions, too, and an endless stream of welcome-home dinners.

How did they do it?

The Australians' campaign to win the Webb-Ellis trophy was nicknamed 'Bring Back Bill'. The campaign had a light-hearted spirit to it, even though it was all organised with military precision, because Rod Macqueen was keen for the whole thing to be based on great team spirit. The players were encouraged to behave as a family, look after one another and respect and admire what they each, individually, brought to the team.

'If you ask me the moment I'll never forget,' said Toutai Kefu. 'It is the day we got there [to Ireland, where they were based for the early stages of the World Cup]. It was 10 a.m. when we arrived. By noon we were on the golf course at Portmarnock and, after the round, we all went to the pub for a team-bonding session.' Joe Roff agreed: 'Having a few Guinnesses that day – talking about what lay ahead, it finally dawned on us what we were about to embark on.'

The story of the Wallabies' 1999 victory is the story of Rod Macqueen's selection as coach of the Wallabies. Many World Cup success stories start with one individual's planning before they broaden out to include teams of people: players, assistant coaches, nutritionists and doctors, as well as events: defeats, successes and national events – all conspiring to put fifteen men on to a field in a successful frame of mind. What is unusual about this journey to victory is that it begins with Macqueen's bid to become Australia coach.

It was 1997 when Macqueen, a self-made businessman and advertising executive, applied for the job as coach of Australia. He had coached New South Wales in the early 1990s, been an Australian selector and was the first coach of ACT Brumbies when they arrived on the Super 12 scene in 1996. Macqueen took over after the resignation of Greg Smith whose tenure ended after Australia's dismal 61–22 defeat by South Africa. No previous Australian side had conceded fifty points in a Test. Macqueen and two other men were invited to interviews for the post. When Macqueen wandered into the room he was clutching a blueprint for the future of rugby in Australia – a seven-point plan that would become the foundation for the Australia triumph in 1999.

He introduced it by pointing out that rugby had improved dramatically since the start of Super 12, but that he didn't think Australia had fully embraced the changes and were in danger of being left behind. He suggested the following seven points:

1. The establishment of a Rugby Business Unit with an independent budget to run all rugby-related activity within the ARU.
2. All provincial teams had to understand their role in helping to prepare the national side. He suggested restructuring to encourage interaction between the coaches.
3. Instigate a plan to take Australia through to 1999 World Cup.
4. Ensure access to relevant personnel – including unorthodox coaches from martial arts and sport psychology, and make sure all research is up-to-date.
5. Instil team spirit and positive attitude.
6. Ensure the players share the ownership of the Wallabies and believe that everyone is working towards a common goal.
7. Establish a controlled communication system to ensure positive responses from all media.

In September 1997, Macqueen was offered the job as coach of Australia, and took the players on a four-day camp. He introduced the philosophies and practices of Edward de Bono – much to the confusion and alarm of his players. He wanted them to think about rugby differently, to challenge what they'd done before in a bid to improve their rugby, to embrace new ideas and seek inspiration and ideas from outside the sport.

Macqueen brought in Jeff Miller (a member of the 1991 winning squad) as assistant coach, and Tim Lane (also a former Wallaby) as back-line coach. John McKay became team manager.

In the spirit of 'doing things differently' the team played with multiple skills instead of traditional training with forwards and backs. He mixed the team up so that every player learnt to work with everyone else. The combining of forwards and backs was known as 'forax'.

The Wallabies' first test under Macqueen was against

Argentina. They performed well on the tour until they lost the second Test. 'Then I realised I had so much work to do. Not because the players had lost, but because I was stunned and embarrassed to see our players lying on the ground after a Test match instead of standing on their feet, people who had just represented their country. We still have a videotape of those images and have used it countless times as a motivational tool.'

Macqueen says that defeat was crucial because he realised the players lacked belief in themselves and had allowed the fabric of the team to break down. 'The best person to be the keeper of the standards is yourself,' he said. Issues like pride, belief, confidence and standards were important to Macqueen. He would constantly remind the players of the heritage of the team they were playing for. He would draw on military references and take them to the graves of Australia's war dead to remind them that men had died in the name of the country.

In December 1997, he called together the coaches and senior players from the three Australian provinces to find out what could be done to ensure their support of the national team. He wanted a coordinated programme from the provinces to ensure that he achieved point two on his original seven-point plan. He walked away from the meeting feeling concerned that they did not put the national team first, so then set out with his management team to visit every club in NSW and Queensland and hold seminars for coaches. He wanted to change the mindset of the coaches in clubs and encourage them to coach rugby as if they were coaching it at the national level – so that the next layer of international players would slot seamlessly into the international team.

Macqueen wanted the Wallabies to be two years ahead of everyone else, and always looking into the future. He called the country's development officers together to make sure a long-term, united approach was being adopted.

Then, when he felt all the mechanics were in place, he sat back with his coaching team and worked out the detail on the way they would play in the World Cup to ensure victory. He worked this out almost two years before the tournament so that if any additional personnel needed to be brought in, they had plenty of time to do so. He decided:

- forwards need to have the running and passing skills of the backs;
- backs need to be able to ruck and maul;
- players need the ability to seek out opposition weaknesses and attack them as the opportunity arises, rather than run onto the field as a programmed unit;
- to achieve the above, players need to take responsibility for themselves and be able to think for themselves on the field (he would need to begin to develop these skills off the field first);
- Australia needs an impenetrable defence;
- to achieve all the above, the players will have to be fitter than any other team in the history of rugby union.

So, two new members of staff were needed immediately for Team Australia: a defence coach and a fitness coach. In the defense corner was John Muggleton, a former Kangaroo forward who played with some of rugby league's toughest tacklers. He came with the aim of turning Australia into the finest defensive unit in world rugby. To do that, he developed a defensive pattern for union based on his experiences of rugby league. Players were taught new ways of tackling and to move up quickly, hit the opposition and drive them back behind the advantage line.

The fitness expert was Steve Nance who was employed, quite simply, to come on board and create the ultimate fitness programme. Macqueen told him that he wanted him to find out just how far the human body could be pushed.

Once his team was assembled, Macqueen found them a permanent base, in the seaside resort of Caloundra. The players would not have hotel facilities – they would have to learn to cook themselves breakfast there, do their own washing, cleaning and ironing. He wanted them to take responsibility for themselves – on the field, and now off it. They also had to look after one another, so he urged them to team up when they cooked and help each other with washing. 'We not me' he would chant at them.

'We not me.' He put up posters declaring: 'For the strength of the pack is the wolf, for the strength of the wolf is the pack.'

While the players burned eggs and ruined their clothing, the coach set about providing them with the sort of notes and agendas more commonly associated with big business. He started with a players' manual, then handed out personal diaries with details of every meeting they were expected to attend, every training session, match and commitment. The diary contained inspirational quotes, fitness, diet and health information, as well as information on a basic playing style. The aim of the diary was to shift the onus of responsibility onto them. The players had the information – they had to be in control of their training and their personal organisation. They had to be responsible, and they had to help each other.

Next, Macqueen produced a mission statement:

- We set ourselves the highest possible standards, never resting in our pursuit of excellence, both on and off the field
- At all times be positive in our approach, while constantly seeking new ideas and innovations
- Keep ahead of the game, making use of the best technologies and resources available to us
- Study and respect our opposition

When it came to selection, Macqueen's mantra was 'people for positions, not positions for people'. He was interested in the balance of the team at all times – making sure he mixed experience with youth and potential. He thought that looking after the players and getting the right men into the right positions in the team was vital. He wanted those he selected to feel special, confident and proud. He did this by always being careful not to change the team too often, understanding that consistency in selection was important for confidence and stability. He also introduced the 'Classic Wallaby' concept, whereby a former Australian player would address the team before each international. The purpose was to emphasise the legacy of the team, and make the players thoroughly proud to wear the jersey and remind them that they were part of something special. The Wallaby visitor would then present John Eales with his jersey and he would present the forwards with theirs. The vice-captain would then present the backs with their jerseys. It became something of a ritual before every game.

He had taken lessons from previous Wallaby coaches on how to relate to the players. Bob Dwyer had said that he always wanted to be around and available to communicate with players over selection. 'We resolved that no player would hear about their selection or dismissal through the media.'

He watched the players closely – always looking for clues about how they were feeling and what they were going through. He made a note of the different reactions he got when telling players that they'd been dropped. Some players would express disappointment but want to know why they'd been dropped, others would express disappointment, resentment and non-acceptance that they weren't good enough. 'We found that by far the greater majority of the former type of player ended up being successful.'

His understanding of his own players he saw as being crucial, but he was also eager to know all about his opposition. He was a targeted coach who would look at forthcoming games, predict problems and establish what the strengths and weaknesses would be. He used the business tactic of SWOT to do this – analysing Strengths, Weaknesses, Opportunities and Threats. He was also very keen that the players keep analysing themselves, so he also insisted that they perform SWOT analyses on themselves frequently.

When his SWOT analysis established that a key strength of New Zealand rugby was the haka, Macqueen set about trying to combat its effectiveness. He decided that Australia should keep their tracksuits on for the haka, then take them off and get themselves ready for the game afterwards, and in their own time, so that the New Zealand team weren't dictating when the game started. They could do the haka and Australia would respect it, but then Australia would take a few minutes to get ready for the match.

When Australia lost 14–13 to South Africa in the Tri Nations, Macqueen was determined to take the positives from it.

'That was probably the biggest learning experience for us and a real milestone,' he said. 'The best way to learn is from your mistakes. You need defeats to keep evaluating. I realised through that game that we had started playing in a very negative way – shutting the game down too soon. It was an important lesson. I emphasised to them that they had to keep positive and keep attacking. That defeat was important. Very important in our development.'

By the beginning of 1999, Macqueen had everything in place. The High Performance Division at the Australian rugby union, with its elaborate and detailed computer software system, was in place. Now he needed to make sure that the players knew just how much support they had from the country. Macqueen began working on a strategy to stir national support. He brought in John Williamson, the popular Australian country singer, to belt out 'Waltzing Matilda' at matches, and make sure that support for Australia was appreciably louder than support for opposition teams.

John Eales was an important figure in the team. He had played in the 1991 and 1995 World Cups. He had a very clear idea of how he thought the game should be played which clashed with Macqueen at the beginning, but the two agreed to disagree in private but never in public. The special relationship that they came to develop, and the mutual respect, was an important factor in the success of the Wallabies.

'Rod understood the importance of detail,' said Eales. 'We all felt confident that he would not miss anything.'

The night before the first game, Macqueen had a checklist of sixty things to run through to make sure nothing was forgotten, the list included everything from spare studs and weather conditions, to when players were due to come off the bench, what they would do in the event of blood injuries and the answer to dozens of 'what if' scenarios. 'I've tried to think of everything,' he said. 'I hope that nothing can happen on the pitch that I haven't considered in some depth.'

The key reasons why Australia won the World Cup in 1999

1. The players were encouraged to 'think differently'

Macqueen was eager for the players to start thinking differently, imaginatively and positively and to play a much more open and lucid game. He introduced 'Forax' so that players had multiple skills, with the forwards and backs training together.

2. The personnel

Australia had great personnel – coaches and experts from beyond the confines of rugby union. If someone could be of use to the team – Macqueen brought them in. The coaches worked well as a team and touched on every possible 'what if' scenario. 'Nothing can happen that we haven't thought of,' said Macqueen.

3. Team spirit

'The strength of the pack is the wolf, for the strength of the wolf is the pack' was one of Macqueen's mantras. This mentality underpinned everything he did with the team.

4. Players could think on their feet

The players had personal responsibility during the game (leadership qualities). This sounds like an obvious skill but the fact that Macqueen worked so hard on ensuring that players attacked opposition weaknesses rather than just went and played to a formula and a series of set pieces, meant that when France got through to the final instead of New Zealand, Australia could cope.

5. Defence

The higher the standard of competition, the more important it becomes to have an impenetrable defence. Macqueen talked to Des Hasler, a former Australian Rugby League representative known for his aggressive tackling, and to wrestling coaches about the ideal way to tackle someone. Australia had just one try scored against them in the tournament, which was an incredible achievement.

6. Fitness

Macqueen knew that all the work he was doing, all the motivational coaches he brought in and all the clever new techniques he introduced were worth nothing if the players weren't fit. It became a vastly important factor and something which underpinned and facilitated everything else that he did.

7. All the non-essentials were taken care of

The players had a regular base, diaries, manuals, mission statements and a coach who cared a great deal for their welfare off the pitch as well as on it. Macqueen established links with the past to emphasise the history of the Wallabies, and what the players were involved in.

8. A crucial defeat

They lost 29–15 to South Africa in the 1998 Tri Nations from which they learned. They considered where they had gone wrong, regrouped and were ready for the World Cup when it arrived. 'The loss to South Africa triggered a positive response from the players,' said Macqueen. 'So much so, that I became grateful for the defeat.'

9. The captain

They had a fantastic captain in John Eales – a man who combined being a brilliant rugby player with being an outstanding man manager. He was an outstanding captain who had such a reputation for getting everything right that he was nicknamed 'Nobody' as in 'Nobody's perfect'.

10. Coach

There is no question that Australia had a great, thinking, intelligent coach in Rod Macqueen. He planned the World Cup campaign to start 18 months before the tournament, calling it 'the journey' and aiming for it to culminate in victory in Cardiff.

PART FIVE: 2003

The rugby world tilts
on its axis

24

Turning stones

Three billion fans, two million tickets, twenty teams, one Cup.

Headline in the Sydney Morning Herald

The sweep of marble floor in the reception area of the beautiful Brisbane hotel dazzled and gleamed like an ice rink in the stunning Australian sunshine. There were vast windows, grand pillars and a small forest of subtropical plants. It oozed elegance in that modern, summery, minimalist way of a million design magazines. Huge, squashy, butter-coloured sofas were everywhere. I sat in the corner of one, chatting to Clive Woodward about the England team's prospects in the 2003 World Cup. Yesterday Woodward had sat here, explaining the importance of homeostasis, biomechanics, nutrition, precision fitness and psychological state to Prince Harry. I wasn't interested in the physical aspects of the team, though. I could see they were fit and so could the New Zealanders, the Australians, the French and anyone else who had eyes. To be honest, for the £20 million that had been spent on the team – the hours, the staff, the luxuries, the equipment, the advice, help and support – the very last thing I'd expect them to be is unfit.

I was fascinated by what they had that made Woodward so confident they were going to win the 2003 World Cup. With a quarter-final ahead of them against Wales, a likely semi-final against the impossible-to-predict French, then a final against either New Zealand or Australia, victory was certainly not assured. Indeed, the weight of history combined to suggest that defeat was more likely. Northern hemisphere sides – even the most talented, did not have that magical 'something' that enabled them to win major tournaments – to win the killer matches. England had been the outstanding team from Britain and Ireland for years, but still they had managed to miss winning the Grand Slam on five occasions before they eventually won it in 2003. The losses, coming in the last game of the championships every time – to Wales, Scotland, Ireland and then to France – had appeared to indicate loud and clear that England didn't have the mental edge to win the big matches that really mattered.

> Those defeats were important [said Woodward]. We learned a lot from them. You can't win without defeats. Now, we're at the World Cup and we won't lose. We've done defeats, but we've also done winning, and we're very good at winning now.
>
> You could argue that the top four or five teams at the World Cup are roughly of the same technical ability, and have been coached as well as each other. What will determine the winner will be the team that can find little advantages in every area of play. It will be the team that has something that no other team has – the edge. We've spent seven years finding a way of doing all the small things better, all the things that will give us the mental edge. I have left no stone unturned, and neither have the players. No stone unturned. We've got advantages in every tiny little area of play and it adds up to quite a major advantage. That's why we will win the World Cup.

Woodward had spent sixty-eight matches in charge of the team by the time the World Cup came along. He was England's first full-time coach. The team had won 49 of those games, lost 17 and drawn 2. Over the four years since the defeat in the quarter-final of the 1999 World Cup to South Africa, they had won 35 out of 40 games. Ten of those were against southern hemisphere teams. England left for Australia having been unbeaten at Twickenham since 1999. They were rated number one in the world, and were vying with the All Blacks as favourites. They had beaten New Zealand away for the first time in thirty years, and recorded their first away victory over Australia. You couldn't argue with Woodward that his team knew how to win. But did they have what it took to win the biggest prize of all? Or, would they be gallant, respectful runners-up?

It's difficult to know where the story of the 2003 World Cup starts – does it begin with the appointment of Woodward? The appointment of Martin Johnson? Or does it begin with the defeat in the 1999 World Cup that prompted changes and developments? Does it begin with Woodward's time spent in Australia that gave him the certainty that England could beat them? Or, further back, on the day his father sent him away to boarding school to stop him from playing football, forcing the young boy to develop a determination and sense of purpose that continues to define everything he does? I wrote a biography of Woodward – 150,000 words about the man and his background, with views from psychologists and business leaders. When you analyse his background and everything he went through, it's as if he were destined to make it to the top. Perhaps England's World Cup victory starts with his birth.

But does that accord him too much of the credit? It may begin with Johnson's birth or the time he spent in New Zealand honing his rugby skills. Perhaps it starts with Jonny Wilkinson's decision to play rugby.

Perhaps a good start would be just over a year before the World Cup, when I sat down with Woodward to interview him for *The Times*. I had moved on from being Rugby Editor of *The Times* by 2003 and was the paper's Chief Sports Feature Writer. I did a weekly interview, talking to everyone from Sean Connery to Wayne Rooney. One of the fascinating things about the role was how successful sports people wanted to hear about others who had been successful in sport. Woodward more than anyone. He'd ask me to run through who I'd talked to and what they had said, what insights I had gleaned from them. What did I think made them successful? Why was Maurice Greene the fastest man on earth? Where did Ian Botham's confidence and inner strength come from? What motivated Steve Redgrave to keep going, and to keep fighting for more medals?

Was there anything the England rugby team could learn? What 'people' did successful athletes have surrounding them? Sometimes he'd jot notes down. Say what you like about Woodward, but he never missed a chance to unturn stones. He didn't know it at the time but, as we sat chatting in 2002, in the beautiful Pennyhill Park hotel – the England team's retreat, their base and their sanctuary – England were about to go through the most successful year ever recorded in the history of England rugby. Then they would win a World Cup at the end of it. From the point at which I sat down with Woodward that day, until the end of the World Cup, England would have a 95 per cent success rate, losing just one game (by one point). The sun was leaking through the oak-framed windows as we spoke, shadows spreading across the table and dancing across my notebook. Outside, the manicured gardens went on for ever – brightly coloured borders criss-crossing the lawns as an array of the finest privately owned trees in the country felt the warm summer breeze drift through their leaves.

'Beautiful, isn't it?' Woodward had asked.

I nodded.

'Yes,' he said, a touch of pride in his voice. 'It's all perfect. Just perfect.'

25

A year of triumph for England

Only the mediocre are always at their best.

Jean Giraudoux

E ngland were scheduled to play an incredible thirteen matches between autumn 2002 and the start of the 2003 World Cup, which meant that, if they made it to the World Cup final, they would have to play twenty times in just over a calendar year. Of those twenty games, three were in the 2002 autumn series, against New Zealand, Australia and South Africa, followed by the five matches of the Six Nations Championship, two away against New Zealand and Australia in June 2003. Then in August and September, there were the warm-up matches for the World Cup to negotiate – one against Wales and two (one home, one away) against France.

In the autumn of 2002, England played the three teams to have won every World Cup tournament ever staged. Week after week – first New Zealand, then Australia, then South Africa. They even played them in the order that they had won World Cups.

New Zealand were coached by John Mitchell, the former England assistant coach who had left the England set-up in 2000, a year after the team's exit from the rugby World Cup, to return to his native New Zealand. In 2001, he became All Blacks coach.

'The New Zealand team had been England's nemesis for so long,' said Woodward, 'that I really needed them to win this match.' They did. England won 31–28. An impressive scalp, even though many leading New Zealand players were missing from the side.

'A brilliant, motivating start to the World Cup countdown,' said Woodward.

Australia, the reigning world champions, came to Twickenham the following week. They had a new coach since their triumph over France at the Millennium Stadium. Eddie Jones – a confident, brash Aussie who was eager to express his opinions at every opportunity – had taken over from Macqueen. Australia had a classy back line and held nothing back against England, coming to Twickenham with a full-strength side.

England won by one point – 32–31 – thanks to a try by Dan Luger in the last few minutes of the game. It meant they lifted the Cook Cup again, and that they had won their last three games over the reigning world champions. It was one of England's best games at Twickenham, and their second victory in as many weeks. 'That one was important,' said Woodward. 'That was really impressive.'

Seven days later, and another Tri Nations giant flew into Twickenham from the southern hemisphere: South Africa, the team that England would face in the pool stage of the World Cup and the side that had eliminated them from the last World Cup. England won 53–3. The 50-point difference was the biggest margin of defeat ever suffered by a South Africa team, but the match will be best remembered for the fact that the South Africa players were reduced to underhand tactics in their efforts to win as their discipline and self-control evaporated with the mounting points tally. Woodward was furious. 'Something has to be done about this,' he said. But perhaps England had done enough on the pitch to warn the South Africans about what happens when discipline slips.

As the year ended, following their three successive victories, England became the world's number one team in the Zurich rankings. 'Christmas was nice,' said Woodward. 'I felt relaxed. Everything was completely on track.'

The Six Nations Championship had been a tough one for England to crack, but Woodward was determined that his team should go all out to win the 2003 Grand Slam on their route to the World Cup. After the four previous near misses, one would have forgiven him for down-playing the whole thing, and telling the players that the European tournament was meaningless – all that mattered was the World Cup in Australia. But, no, he told them that if they were serious about winning the World Cup, they would have to win the Grand Slam. 'I want to put pressure on them,' he said. 'Coping under pressure is what they will have to do in Australia.'

The first match of the Six Nations was against France, the reigning champions. Jason Leonard, winning his 100th cap, led the team out to a 25–17 victory. This was not England at their finest by any means, but it was a thundering victory from which France would take some time to recover. Wilkinson scored his 600th point for England, and the Grand Slam effort was very much on target. England continued their winning spree, with a 26–9 victory in Cardiff and a 40–5 victory over Italy. England managed to score thirty-three points in twenty minutes against the Italians, with the first scorer crossing the line after two minutes.

Italy's coach for most of the period between the World Cups was Brad Johnstone, the colourful former coach of Fiji whose one-liners had lit up press conferences at the 1999 competition and led to him being awarded the 'coach of the tournament' accolade. He had been intending to head back to New Zealand after the 1999 World Cup, when rugby officials in Rome called him and invited him to become the new coach of Italy. Within a week of the call, Johnstone took up the role, but found straight away that the blood 'n' guts attitude of the Fijians and New Zealanders that he had been used to working with was sorely lacking in the Italians.

On his first day, he was presented with a list of sixty names of squad players, but twenty-two of them arrived for the first squad session with letters from their clubs or doctors saying they weren't fit to train. Johnstone persuaded them all to get involved, and the team beat Scotland in their first ever game in the Six Nations in 2000.

But things had not been simple for the down-to-earth New Zealander, and a split developed between the coach and a core of the players, including the captain (Alessandro Troncon), who wanted to give priority to their clubs. 'I was trying to set new standards and I genuinely believed that Italy wouldn't be competitive internationally until they accepted these ideals,' said Johnstone. The rift between players and coach became well-known in Italian sporting circles, and was perceived as a battle between the clubs in the north and the foreign newcomer.

Johnstone was fed up with the culture in Italy, and the fact that the players seemed work-shy. On tour to Samoa he was confronted by the news that Andrea Scanavacca, a young fly-half, had suffered a panic attack in the night because he had woken to find a cockroach in his room. Scanavacca said he couldn't eat and never recovered from the trauma. He didn't participate in any of the games and when Johnstone got him back to Italy he dropped him.

This further antagonised the Italian clubs. Scanavacca was from the north like Troncon. The clubs issued a statement saying it was horrific for a poor player to be dropped simply because he didn't like cockroaches.

Johnstone was at his wits' end. He organised Test matches that the players refused to go to because they didn't like to be away from home. Against Namibia and Uruguay, for example, 27 of the 32 were unavailable. They put their club contracts, which were more financially rewarding to them, above everything.

Johnstone was eventually replaced by John Kirwan before the 2003 championships. Kirwan was a man who seemed to take to the Italian life straight away. 'I yell and scream like they do,' he said. 'I'm the worst of them. Totally, I'm a nightmare. Once they gave me the passport, that was it – started throwing my hands in the air, drinking red wine and flying off the handle.'

England won 40–9 over Scotland in the Six Nations, and by four tries to nil, heaping misery onto the shoulders of the Scotland players and their coach, Ian McGeechan.

The final match of the 2003 Six Nations was a showdown at Lansdowne Road, with both England and Ireland going for the grand slam. Ireland had undergone a considerable transformation since their World Cup defeat by Argentina in 1999 that saw them exit the tournament before the quarter-final. Eddie O'Sullivan was national coach and Keith Wood had overcome personal tragedy and injuries to make it back into the team as its talismanic captain. Under O'Sullivan, a former Munster player, and along with former rugby league player and coach Mike Ford, Ireland developed a complete defensive strategy for the team. This was a good Ireland side – the best Irish XV for years – with a strong pack and talented back line inspired by Brian O'Driscoll. By the time the 2003 tournament started, they were ranked number three in the world, behind England and New Zealand but above Australia, and had won eight out of ten matches played. They took a hammering against England in the Six Nations, though, losing 42–6. England won the Grand Slam in staggering style, sending a clear message out to the rest of the world.

And, just in case that message wasn't clear enough, England went on tour to the southern hemisphere in June, and beat both New Zealand and Australia. They won 15–13 against New Zealand – the team that had marched unbeaten through the Tri Nations. It was only the second time that England had ever won a Test in New Zealand. 'The World Cup,' ran the local headlines, 'has just got considerably harder.' England didn't play well, they had been reduced to thirteen men for ten minutes, but they had won. They followed this with a first victory over Australia, in Australia, just a week later when they beat them 25–14. It was the fifth victory over Australia in succession. Woodward's team was on fire. He was bursting with confidence. The Australians labelled him the new Douglas Jardine. They meant it as an insult. Woodward was delighted. 'By the time we left, they were saying I was the most disliked person to go there since Douglas Jardine . . . To be compared to Douglas Jardine, who I thought was quite a hero, was fine by me.'

Just three warm-up matches to go, then, before the World

Cup. The first, against Wales, featured a second string England team but they beat a disheartened Wales 43–9 to notch up their fourteenth successive victory. They scored five unanswered tries over the team that they would meet in the World Cup quarter-final. It made it ten victories to England in the last eleven games played against Wales. 'This victory shows what great strength we have,' said Woodward.

'That was a poor, poor performance and a very painful experience,' said Steve Hansen, Wales' coach.

With two games to go, Woodward shuffled his players round to have a look at everyone before the World Cup started. Ten changes were made for the first game, in Marseille. France put out a powerful side in front of a sell-out 60,000 crowd. In the previous three years, France had defeated New Zealand, Australia and South Africa in Marseille. They were determined to win, and they did: 17–16 against an England team that, bar three players, had been reserves. Laporte was delighted with France's victory. Woodward was disappointed that the winning streak had finished at fourteen games, but thrilled that the England second team had pushed France so close. England won the return match at Twickenham 45–14, and the team got ready to depart for Australia.

26

Old Soviet tractors

I think we will win all our matches.

*Georgia's captain Ilia Zedginidze sounds confident
before the World Cup*

England's biggest opponents in 2003 were always going to be the three southern hemisphere superpowers – New Zealand, Australia and South Africa, the teams to have knocked England out of the previous three World Cup tournaments. In 1991 they fell to Australia, in 1995 it was the turn of New Zealand and in 1999 it was South Africa. But there was another team needing a little attention from the England coaches: Georgia. Arriving at the tournament with little training after their camps in the Caucasus and in Canada were cancelled due to lack of funds (the government withdrew a promised £80,000 for Georgia's European Nations Cup matches, and World Cup warm-ups with Canada at the last minute), the players were forced to set up a makeshift camp in France. Georgia would be England's first opponents in the World Cup.

To their credit, they were an incredibly resourceful and determined team with a Svengali coach called Claude Saurel who had personally paid for all the team's tracksuits after taking donations from a couple of the other coaches. 'Otherwise – no tracksuit,' he explained. He also bought a video camera and computer for the team to help them improve the effectiveness of their training.

'Otherwise – no good training,' he said. And the world was getting the message – if Saurel didn't fund it, it didn't happen.

Saurel said that there was just one scrummage machine in the whole of Georgia, and an estimated 300 players involved in the sport. But what they lacked in personnel and equipment, they more than made up for with a blinding confidence bordering on what can only be described as an enviable detachment from reality. 'I think we'll win all our matches,' said skipper Ilia Zedginidze. 'Our determination is to win all, and after that we'll see what happens.'

In fact the whole of Georgia was convinced the team would do well. As soon as the players beat Russia to qualify, watched by 44,000 people (and by many more on television) a nation decided that the team was destined for greatness. In a poll, 42 per cent of the country's population believed that rugby would be the sport in which Georgia would excel. Their passion and conviction appears to be based on the fact that the national rugby team is known as Lelos, named after the national pastime of *lelo* which has much in common with rugby. 'They think we should be good side,' said Zedginidze, 'because of the name of our team – how can we be bad?'

The officials in charge of the ranking system clearly disagreed with the population of Georgia, though. Perhaps the esteemed men at the IRB had never heard of *lelo*. They ranked the team in seventeenth place. 'It cannot be,' said Zedginidze. But it was.

Georgia was the only side making its Cup debut in 2003, and their budget for the tournament was just £400,000. The players received £13 a day each. 'We are light years behind England,' said Gregiore Yachvili, the Georgian flanker, whose brother Dimitri plays for France (they were both born in France). 'We might not have tackle bags, body armour or a scrum machine, but at least we have a ball and a pitch.'

The Georgians had an astonishingly difficult time preparing themselves for the World Cup. As the tournament went on, they revealed that they had lost around 500 of the nation's rugby players in a civil war, five years before the tournament. 'All of these men have seen combat,' said Saurel of his team. 'Who knows, it might be just what we need to bring out the best in the team.' Saurel also revealed that instead of scrummage machines, they used old Soviet tractors to push against. 'They are hard to move. It serves us well,' said Yachvili.

Seventy-five of the Georgian players are based in France which causes yet more problems for the Georgian team organisers. In 2003, three of them were refused permission by their clubs to play in the World Cup. All of the seventy-five players were suspended by the French federation for the duration of the tournament. Another five were sacked. It made it a great financial hardship for Georgia even to send a team.

Saurel had started working with the Georgia team in 1997, after being asked to conduct an audit of Georgia rugby. He worked with the team and with the sevens team until 1999 when he was made, formally, the head coach. There was a surge in success for the national side once he started, culminating in March 2002, with qualification for the Rugby World Cup in Australia after drawing 12–12 with Russia. They expected to do well in the 2003 tournament, but the withdrawal of money for their warm-up games made it extremely difficult for the team, and the attitude of the French clubs made it difficult for the players. But despite their financial difficulties and their minnow status, Georgia revelled in the tournament, and soon embraced the whole philosophy of the rugby World Cup – closely observing the teams they sought to emulate. For example, when Woodward – desperately keen to make sure that his privately run training sessions for the team remained private – put up huge sheets outside the ground when he ran his training sessions, the Georgia team decided to do likewise. One of the funnier sights of the 2003 World Cup was when the coach of Georgia was seen hanging up sheets outside his team's training session to stop people from watching. Not one person had been to watch a Georgia training session – whether welcome or not – so the action was entirely superfluous, but the motivation sound enough: copy the teams who know what they're doing. 'If the big boys are doing it, so they are not watched, then so must we,' said the coach, as he pegged torn sheets to a makeshift clothesline. 'We must not be watched.'

Sadly, his efforts amounted to very little, as England beat Georgia 84–6 in their first game. Georgia, neighbour of Chechnya and birthplace of Stalin, did better in their second big game – against South Africa in front of over 34,000 fans. They lost 46–19 to what was a rather lacklustre second-string Springboks side, but the crowds were delighted. Georgia even managed to score their first try of the competition, as the hooker went over. 'Tonight you saw some of the true face of Georgia,' said Saurel. 'We came here . . . determined to do our best, give it a go and see how we go against the strong teams.'

England topped Pool C after beating South Africa 25–6, Samoa 35–22, and finishing off their pool games with a 111–13 victory over Uruguay. South Africa qualified behind them.

England against South Africa was the big match of the tournament, and the one that would determine which side had the easier journey through the rest of the tournament. Both sides had worked exceptionally hard since 1999. England under Woodward's regime, and South Africa under often bizarre military-like conditions. Before they arrived in Australia, SARPA (South Africa Rugby Players' Association) announced that they would be requesting an inquiry into the 'barbaric' military-style manner in which the Springboks were trained for the rugby World Cup. Photographs had emerged of the players standing naked in a freezing lake holding rugby balls in front of their private parts (the players were apparently ordered into the lake to pump up the balls under water.) There were further allegations that those who tried to get out were pointed back at gunpoint. The team was also ordered to climb into a foxhole where recordings of England's national anthem and New Zealand's haka were played while ice-cold water was poured over their heads. There was public outcry when news of the severity of the camp emerged, and calls for the resignation of Rudolph Straueli, the coach. Gideon Sam, the team manager, denied that training had been carried out at gunpoint or that players had been forced to crawl naked through the bush, but admitted: 'Sure, the guys were pushed hard, but that is what preparing for battle is all about.'

Before the tournament had kicked off, there had been controversy at the World Cup when New Zealand lost their status as sub-hosts thanks to disagreements between the International Rugby Board and the NZ Union, over sponsorship, advertising and ticketing. It left defending champions Australia to run the tournament by itself which actually made the whole thing much better for the two million spectators who passed through the turnstiles, and players who didn't have to go trooping off from country to country to play in matches. As with the 1995 World Cup in South Africa, the fact that the 2003 World Cup was in one country helped enormously. It was played out over eleven stadia in ten Australian cities.

Pool A contained Australia, Argentina, Ireland, Romania and Namibia. Australia and Argentina had kicked the tournament off – playing in front of 81,350, the biggest crowd in World Cup history. Australia had delighted them with the 24–8 victory.

'It's the pool of death is Pool A – no doubt about it,' said Ireland's coach, O'Sullivan. He had a point. With three of the top seven ranked teams in the world in the pool, and only two able to qualify for the quarter-finals, it would be keenly fought from the start. They began their campaign with a 45–17 victory over Romania. They beat Namibia 64–7. Against Argentina they came close to defeat, beating them by one point – 16–15. The final game of the pool was against Australia.

'It's Australia we're worried about, of course,' said O'Sullivan. 'They've had a below-par season, and that's never a good thing because they'll come out like a wounded animal with something to prove. It makes them more dangerous that they've had a bad season – I'd rather play them on form.' Whichever way Ireland had played them, their record against the reigning champions was not great, with Australia having emerged victorious from fifteen of their twenty-two meetings. In the event, they pushed Australia close, in a match reminiscent of their 1991 quarter-final game, Australia won by just one point – 17–16.

France and Scotland battled in Pool B, with Bernard Laporte brimming with confidence. 'We have beaten England twice in two years,' he told anyone who would listen. 'We're the only team that has done that. In the same time, the All Blacks and the Wallabies have both lost three times against them.' Laporte discreetly ignored the fact that France had relinquished their Six Nations crown to England and suffered a 2–0 series loss to Argentina before going down heavily to New Zealand. 'Ah, we picked a team containing players who were still recovering from injury and who are young,' he said. In Pool B they faced Fiji, Scotland, Japan and USA. France topped the group after a clean sweep of victories. They beat Scotland 51–9, Fiji 61–18, Japan 51–29 and USA 39–26. Scotland went through in second place.

Pool D contained New Zealand, Wales, Canada, Italy and Tonga. The group was topped by New Zealand, with Wales in second place. The All Blacks won all games in the pool, but were tested by Wales, despite the 53–37 scoreline in favour of the kiwis. There had been moments in the match when it had looked as if Wales might create an almighty upset. They led 34–28 in the forty-sixth minute in a match in which the New Zealand forwards were simply not as dominant as everyone thought they would be. 'I thought Wales played fantastic,' New Zealand captain Reuben Thorne said later. 'We wanted a real contest and they certainly gave it to us. Our defence was the area that let us down a wee bit. It was a real battle, just what we wanted going into the quarter-final. Now we can look forward to South Africa.'

The toughest quarter-final looked as if it was destined to be the one played between two previous winners of the trophy – New Zealand and South Africa. In the event, the match was far from close, it was dominated by New Zealand, as South Africa struggled for possession in the first half to trail 13–6 at the break, then they were undone by a powerful kiwi pack to go down 29–9 by the whistle. It was New Zealand's seventh win over South Africa.

France were too athletic, too fast, too well-organised and too eager for a bewildered Ireland who lacked the necessary firepower either up front or behind the scrum. The French set off at a furious pace from the outset and crossed Ireland's line within five minutes after Magne scored from Frédéric Michalak's high kick.

France stormed to a 27–0 lead, with Laporte's men seeming to lay down an ominous marker for the rest of the tournament.

French fans were delighted, unlike their English counterparts, who watched Wales and England battle in the quarter-final of the World Cup, as Steve Hansen's side moved to a 10–3 lead with forty-three minutes gone. Colin Charvis, Martyn Williams and Stephen Jones claimed three tries for Wales and although Will Greenwood came back, it was the twenty-three points from the boot of Jonny Wilkinson that proved to be the difference between the two sides. Woodward brought on Mike Catt to steady things down a bit, and in the end it was a comprehensive victory for England – 28–17.

Australia managed a scratchy 33–16 victory over Scotland in their quarter-final at Lang Park in Brisbane. The Wallabies were strong favourites going into the match, and were eventually too good for the Scots, scoring three tries to one. But the victory asked several questions of Australia, particularly of the backs who mis-fired. 'We can certainly play better,' admitted Eddie Jones. 'It was a very tough first half, 9–9. We can certainly play better than that.'

Scotland coach Ian McGeechan praised his side for what he said had been 'a tremendous display. We needed a few more points on the board in the first half and we are a bit disappointed in not making the semi-final.'

He may also have been a little disappointed in the weather. Scotland did some heavy-duty training for the tournament at the Edinburgh Botanical Gardens – locked in the greenhouses in preparation for the stifling heat of Australia. But, when they arrived, they found it was snowing in Canberra and the weather was unseasonably cold over the whole of Australia. Robbie Russell, the Australian-born Scotland player, at London Irish, said: 'I can't imagine what people must have thought of us – ped-alling away on our bikes in the greenhouses. All my teammates kept saying "you don't need to do it, Robbie, you'll be fine – you're from Australia", but I've been away a long time, so I joined in . . . just in case. We got here and ended up putting jumpers on! Playing for Scotland was a joy in 2003 though – just a really spe-cial time. I wish we could have gone further, but Australia were just too tough to get past.'

27

Tensions in the England camp and a display of cultural differences

I have yet to see any problem, however complicated, which, when you looked at it in the right way, did not become still more complicated.

Poul Anderson

Days before the World Cup semi-finals Sydney was subjected to a whitewash. There was white everywhere – the St George Cross fluttered from hotel windows, faces were painted white and the England rugby shirt was stretched across bodies of all sizes – mainly, it must be said, across expanses of pale beer belly. Travel companies reported that record numbers had traversed the globe to watch fifteen men in white shirts take on fifteen in the blue of France.

The England team decamped to Manly in advance of the match – to the Manly Pacific hotel where Woodward stayed for his first days in Australia some twenty years previously. He's a creature of habit in many respects, is Woodward, which is odd considering that one of his primary traits is being a massive habit wrecker – wielding an axe through bad habits, ingrained attitudes and stubborn unwillingness to change. It can make him appear mad at times – this swinging from liking nothing more than a cup of tea with his closest friends, to wanting to change the world. Never, I would suggest, has it made him seem more mad than in the week leading up to the semi-final against France. During one press conference, he berated a French journalist for being, well, French, by all accounts. Then, he changed his mind about something three times within the course of a sentence. I looked at my notebook afterwards and it was filled with crossings out. I'd put a big question mark by the side of it with Woodward's name in brackets as an explanation.

There was obsessive training, security checks, officialdom and a feeling of deep paranoia in Team England. 'He's lost it,' muttered the journalists.

'Is he okay?' I asked Dave Alred, Jonny Wilkinson's esteemed and highly respected kicking coach and a man with such an astonishing suntan all year round that he looks like he's stepped off the set of *Footballers' Wives*.

'Yes, he's fine,' said Alred, loyally. 'It's tough for him, though – there's a hell of a lot of pressure on him. You should see what goes on in our team meetings. Honestly, you couldn't make it up.'

With that, I decided that I would – and I penned a piece for *The Times* that was my tongue-in-cheek take on what probably went on behind the scenes in the England camp. It involved Woodward crawling up the walls dressed in nothing but his socks. I had a tremendous response to the piece – most readers saying how amusing they found it, which was lovely. Many saying how fascinating it was to read about what was going on away from the public eye. They had missed the fact that it was all just a little joke at how serious and slightly mad the England set-up was beginning to look. It made me smile that it was now all so utterly barmy in the England camp that you couldn't even parody it – people believed it was happening. Perhaps Woodward climbing up the walls in his socks wasn't actually as far-fetched as some of the notions he'd had over the previous seven years! Readers of *The Times* didn't seem to think so and they're an unusually discerning and sophisticated bunch.

So then, just days before the semi-final of the World Cup and having been told that I couldn't just make articles up every day, I had to get a few real interviews in the paper, I headed over to the Manly Pacific hotel and walked through the door. A line of officials greeted me. It turned out that getting into the England team hotel before the World Cup semi-final is harder than getting into the Met Bar. At least when they turn you away from the celebrity hang-out for wearing trainers, jeans or committing some other sartorial blunder, you can go somewhere else. Unfortunately, there's only one Martin Johnson, so there's only one place any self-respecting sports interviewer wants to be just before an England game.

'Pass?' I was asked, even though the guy on the door knew exactly who I was because he'd asked me to sign his copy of Jason Leonard's autobiography the evening before (I was Leonard's 'ghost'). I showed the pass, with the photograph melted into the laminated backing and making me look as though my face was four times as wide as it was long. He did a double take, checked the name again and allowed me in without so much as a smile. It was all very serious now in Team England. The management locked themselves away in the provocatively named war room all day and had all notes shredded before they were discarded. They insisted on a new lock on the war-room door, and only three keys for it. Cleaners were watched as they cleaned and hotel staff were told to keep out. This, as I say, was serious. I looked up the walls for signs of footprints.

In the hotel that day there was a respectful silence in the area where the press waited, sipping coffee and hoping that the players would arrive soon. It was as if we were all waiting for a wake to begin. The joy seemed to have disappeared from the team – drowned out by the seriousness of the occasion. Rugby in 2003 was a different beast entirely to rugby in 1987. I don't think Paul Rendall would have cared for it too much – the solemnity would have driven him up the wall. But then Rendall didn't win a World Cup, and that's what these guys were trying to do. Perhaps this was the price of success at the highest levels. The price, perhaps, of a professional sport?

I've known Martin Johnson for a long time. I knew him when I worked for the team in the early 1990s. I got to know his wife Kay well, too, when she arrived on the scene as his girlfriend and was so friendly and such fun. I went to their wedding. They're both lovely people. She hasn't changed at all over the years. Neither has he. But the world of rugby has changed all around them.

'Who are you waiting for?' I was asked.

'Johnno,' I replied. 'I need to have a chat with him for *The Times*.'

'Oh,' replied my inquisitor. 'Have you requested an interview?'

'Yep – I left a message on his mobile.'

'No. I mean did you put in a formal request with the PR people?'

No, of course not. It hadn't occurred to me that anyone would think I didn't want to talk to Johnson.

'I'm not sure whether it will be possible,' she said, walking away with a shake of her head. I did get my interview with Johnno because he came over and talked to me, but I was reprimanded for my failure to observe due procedure. Protocol regulations had been breached.

After ten minutes of talking to me, Johnson was called away to his next meeting. When the official came to get him, Johnson raised those big eyebrows, told me he'd see me soon and trooped off like a schoolboy called to the headmaster's office. I hope they win, I thought, as I watched his frame disappear. I hope this is all worth it for him.

The journey from the England team's hotel in Manly to the French players' base in Bondi Beach where I was planning to interview the captain Fabien Galthié is quite a journey. In fact, it turns out it's a journey to another planet. As I walked into the hotel (no pass needed) there were girls in bikinis checking into rooms. The public milled around and the French rugby players were lounging across sofas. I travelled to the hotel with a group of English journalists and we were all looking for different players to talk to. We spotted the French PR man and rushed over to detail our player requests and apologise most profusely for not having pre-booked interviews.

'Ah,' he said with a Gallic shrug. 'No problem. Just go – talk to the players you want to talk to. It is no problem. If you cannot find them, they will be in their rooms – just go get them.'

I found Galthié surrounded by French journalists and introduced myself. I explained that I wished to do an interview with him and he said it was no problem. The French journalists remained, and turned over the pages of their notebooks. I had no desire to conduct the interview for the entire French press, so asked Galthié whether I could have a chat to him on his own for ten minutes.

'Of course,' he said. 'We will walk.'

And so it was that I strolled down Bondi Beach with the captain of the France rugby team just a couple of days before the World Cup semi-final. What was captaincy like for him? I asked.

'Every man in my team must know he is loved by me. He must know how I feel about him,' said Galthié. Ah, but that Johnson could be so gushing. Imagine Johnson turning to Lawrence Dallaglio and telling him how he feels about him? It could happen, but not while the world's still turning. Galthié resembled the romantic lead from a black and white French film – all soft, brown, soulful eyes and dimpled chin; Johnson resembled The Terminator – all giant, dark black eyebrows and square jaw. Galthié told me how nice I looked; Johnson probably wouldn't notice if I went to interview him with my head on back-to-front. Different captains for different teams, different cultures.

As I walked away from the two vastly different experiences and headed back to my hotel in Sydney, it was easy to make unfavourable comparisons between the France camp and what the England players appeared to be enduring. In the England team hotel the tension was palpable and the hostility crackling in the air all around us. They spoke of winning being everything. They said 'we are here to win' so many times, you felt quite hypnotised by it.

For Galthié, though, winning had to be the result of a greater endeavour – not an end in itself.

The son of a cattle salesman who grew up in the countryside of south-west France, he said that it was his job to make sure the players were happy so they felt 'comfortable to make great play'. I wrote up my piece about these two very different captains and the two very different cultures, walked down to the harbour and sat by the water. I called Simon Barnes, my dear friend and colleague on *The Times*. 'Fancy a drink later,' I asked. I don't know why I felt the need to bother to ask, we drank together every night. 'Sure,' he said. 'Are you okay?'

'Yes,' I replied. 'But I have this horrible feeling that England are going to lose.'

We sat and chatted that night about what it takes to be successful, what the sacrifices are and how different leaders, different players and different times produce different cultures in teams. By the end of the evening, I was back on track. I believed England were going to win and all was going to be well with the world, but it had been a derailing experience. The joy in the French hotel had been a refreshing delight – the place had felt vibrant, youthful and energising, the local community was thrilled to have them there and they were a pleasure to talk to. Meanwhile in the Team England morgue things had been very different. How would this all translate on the pitch? It would be just two days before the world found out.

Before England's encounter with France, though, there was the small matter of the first semi-final, between Australia and New Zealand. The winner would be in the final, the loser would be ridiculed, mocked and scorned by their nation and doubtless their coach would be fired. It's tough at the top.

The winning team, in the end, was Australia, their 22–10 win confirming just how incredibly good they are at these World Cups. Their clinical demolition of the tournament favourites was staggering. They dominated the match from start to finish. From an interception try after ten minutes, to a penalty in the seventy-fourth minute – this was Australia's game.

And what an achievement it was for Australia, who were heartily beaten last time the two sides met in Sydney. With the pressure of the occasion acting like springs under the feet of the Australians, and weights on the shoulders of the All Blacks, the reigning World Champions shot to victory and New Zealand crashed out at the semi-final stage for the second tournament running.

For Mitchell, despite his efforts to hang on to his job, it marked the end of the road. The All Blacks had played twenty-eight games since he took over in 2001, winning twenty-three, losing four and drawing one. The truth is that his record stood comparison with that of any New Zealand coach in the history of the game, but the All Blacks failed to win the World Cup, and that, now, is the benchmark. New Zealand secured the Bledisloe Cup for the first time in five years, they won the Tri Nations and scored fifty points against South Africa and Australia in consecutive weekends away from home. But they didn't win the World Cup, so Mitchell returned to find that he would have to apply for his own job (the polite way of saying 'on your bike').

While the All Blacks prepared for a dismal third-place play-off, the question of which team Australia would play in the final was answered the next day, as England and France met in appalling conditions – with high winds whipping through the stadium and torrential rain cascading down. It was left to Jonny Wilkinson and Frédéric Michalak to battle it out. The England fly-half scored all of England's twenty-four points with three drop goals and five penalties, while Michalak managed just one kick from five attempts. It would be an England–Australia final.

'I told you,' said Woodward, and suddenly he didn't seem quite so mad after all.

28

Fifteen men, a maverick coach and a World Cup victory

I've lived in Australia and played with their best. They are human and their games and image have fundamental flaws.

Clive Woodward

It was Christmas 2003. There was frost on the ground, and my passes from the 2003 rugby World Cup, along with the cuttings of the articles I'd written, were consigned to a box somewhere in the attic. I was sitting, planning my interview series, when there was an almighty clatter in the hallway as a pile of cards fell through the letterbox. Among them was a large padded envelope containing a Christmas card from Clive Woodward. It featured the England team on the front, smiling as they clutched the World Cup. Their faces were luminous in the early evening light – glowing from the flashes of a million cameras. I opened the card and there was a message from Woodward offering his thanks for my support of the team. In the middle, there was an odd-looking, lumpy plastic contraption. 'Press here,' it said. I pressed the button and the dulcet tones of Ian Robertson burst into the room, brightening up the cold winter morning and taking me back there – to that moment, that second when Jonny belted the ball and England were the greatest rugby nation in the world.

'Martin Johnson has it. He drives. There's thirty-five seconds to go. This is the one . . . It's coming back for Jonny Wilkinson . . . He drops for World Cup glory . . . It's up . . . It's over! He's done it! Jonny Wilkinson is England's hero yet again. And there's no time for Australia to come back. England have just won the World Cup.'

It all came back. The squeals of delight from a normally silent press box, as we all jumped up and hugged each other as if we'd just kicked the ball over ourselves. We'd stood there watching, thrilled, as Woodward ran on to the field amid scenes of jubilation. Beaming, muddy, blood-encrusted faces filled the large screens around the stadium. Then the Webb-Ellis trophy was passed to Johnson – the magnificent captain. He lifted it and the cheer was so loud they must have heard it back in England. The players touched the precious golden Cup, then passed it to Woodward as the crowd roared their approval. He stared at its shiny surface as you might gaze upon the face of a lover, lost in thought and mesmerised by its beauty. Ticker-tape rained down. The players danced, smiled, hugged each other and scanned the crowd for loved ones. Woodward lifted the Cup into the air and the crowd cheered again. 'World Champions' screamed the large screens. There were white flags everywhere, noise everywhere and confetti raining down in the shape of the Webb-Ellis trophy. 'England are champions of the world', said the man on the loudspeaker. 'Congratulations to England. Clive Woodward and England have done it!'

When Woodward set out to turn England into the best rugby side in the world, not many people believed he would do it (your author included). He arrived hot on the heels of professionalism as the country's first fully paid coach, taking over from Jack Rowell and fighting the officials at the RFU who, he says, completely misunderstood what it would take to make England great. Woodward's first meeting with the England players was at Bisham Abbey – the same place that they had gathered over ten years previously to meet the first fitness adviser to the team. As soon as Woodward walked in, he recalled the musty smell, the old-fashioned rooms and his personal disappointment on never fulfilling his own potential as a player. He knew that he had to do things differently. I don't think that even he knew just how differently he would end up doing things!

'Nothing you've ever done in your international careers can prepare you for what lies ahead,' he told the players. Jason Leonard remembers looking over at Martin Johnson and the two men raised their eyebrows. 'I liked Clive,' said Leonard. 'He was refreshing and gave everyone in the team everything they needed to be the best they could, but I do remember on that first day thinking "here we go again". I walked out and said to Johnno "What do you think?" and he said "What do you think I think?" and we both laughed. It took a while to "get" Clive but we all worked it out in the end – if we gave everything we had, he would give everything he had, and if we all did that all the time we'd start winning things . . . He was a bit mad though, wasn't he?'

Woodward spotted the glances that the England players were exchanging but carried on regardless. 'From this day forth, it's vital we all start to think differently about how we play and how we train . . . We're going to throw away all that we've ever done before as an international team, and we've going to rebuild it all from the ground up with a new way of thinking . . . Whatever greatness you think you might have achieved in the past means nothing because I don't think England has ever produced a great side capable of dominating the world. My aim is to build a team capable of winning the World Cup.'

It is interesting to look back now at what Woodward told the players at Bisham Abbey that day because, despite the fact that he appeared to chop and change his ideas in the six years before England won the tournament, the things he told them when he first met them remained. The madness along the way appears to have been a by-product of his eagerness to achieve all his objectives as thoroughly and quickly as possible, rather than because he violently swung between fundamental ideals. He changed his methods rather than the ideals themselves, which remained pretty entrenched throughout his time with England and, indeed, remain the principles that he advocates for success at the highest level even today.

Once Woodward had started with England in September 1997, and persuaded the RFU to give him an office, desk and secretary, he had six immediate tasks:

To appoint a captain

He selected Lawrence Dallaglio, but the tabloid sting which robbed Dallaglio of the captaincy opened the door to victorious 1997 Lions captain, Martin Johnson, who, though a very different character to Woodward, formed an extremely valuable partnership with him.

> He's hugely important [said Woodward of Johnson]. I can't say enough about this guy. He plays in one of the toughest positions, and he's an awesome player. In terms of his captaincy and his leadership in keeping everyone calm, he's a very, very bright guy. To be able to be make the right calls, say the right things, do the right actions, under intense pressure as captain are immense. We put a camera on him sometimes and look back at it afterwards and realise what a gifted player he is – his body language is brilliant – he's totally in control, totally unflappable and always one of the best players on the pitch. He keeps everything together.

To create the right management and back-up team

Woodward would end up creating a management team that had more members in it than there were players on the pitch. I once joked that if they employed an eyebrow technician, the players would have a bigger entourage than Jennifer Lopez. 'Why, how many people does she have?' asked Woodward, only slightly in jest. The large group of managers became his trademark – with a coach or trainer for every conceivable area of play.

To create the right environment

To make Team England a fun place to operate, and one conducive to international sporting excellence, Woodward would develop a very strict 'code of conduct' and be clear with his players about what was expected of them, what they should wear, when they could use their phones and what time they should turn up for meetings (five minutes early).

A base for the team

Bisham had no on-site gym for weight training. Woodward moved the team from Bisham Abbey and the Petersham Hotel to Pennyhill Park Hotel where they could have luxurious surroundings, their own chef, rugby pitches on site and the best care and attention possible.

Stop the southern hemisphere obsession

'We need to stop being so comfortable in following others and aspire to be the leaders, the ones that everyone else wants to copy. Listen, I've lived in Australia and played with their best. They are human and their games and image have fundamental flaws. We can beat them,' he said. 'I just need you to believe that.'

Fitness

'I fully expect you to be in the best physical condition possible, ready to play your best rugby when you show up here. If you don't, you'll soon find yourself off the mailing list.'

Then he began to think about his own business successes in computer leasing, and how he might apply the business skills and expertise he'd acquired in that field to sport. Woodward was not the first person in rugby to do this – Macqueen's success in 1999 was founded on the strong business principles that had guided the Australia coach to success as a businessman. It could be argued, though, that Woodward was the first coach to bring radical business ideas into rugby.

When Woodward first started, he knew that his biggest problem would be time with the players. He had come in as the first professional coach and, while this gave him many advantages over his predecessors, it also made life more difficult in many respects, most of all because the players were contracted to the clubs so it was difficult to get any of their time for England training.

The team stayed at the Petersham Hotel in Richmond in the

week leading up to an international match, and there were no rugby pitches there, so precious time was being wasted travelling to the Bank of England training ground to use the pitches there.

He identified early on that winning had to be extended beyond the players, to winning in every respect, so the entire organisation and elite environment would become a winning organisation. That, he concluded, was the way to win long term, develop a winning habit and achieve victory in the biggest competition of all – the World Cup. 'Our goal is winning against the best teams in the world. What does our organisation need to have in place to do this?' he asked himself. He distilled all his thoughts on the subject into seven key, identifiable, measurable, short-term goals, and set about achieving them:

Coach the basic skills well

Woodward decided early on that he wanted coaches for every key area of play – not just backs and forwards, but attack, defence, scrummaging and line-out – in order to aim for that elusive total rugby. He wanted the best coaches and he wanted them full-time. The cost would be enormous but Woodward was determined – the coaches and players were what he described as 'critical essentials'. No short cuts could be taken.

Fitness needs to be outstanding

Dave Reddin, the fitness guy who had been working part-time when Woodward started, was signed up full-time. Woodward wanted him to devise personal training programmes for each player to make them the fittest and most powerful players in world rugby.

Medical/recovery

Woodward needed specialists who could work on preventive medicine with the players, not just on emergencies and medical treatment. He wanted to reduce chances of injury as well as get them treated when they occurred. He appointed Dr Simon Kemp and instructed him to overhaul the medical facilities for the England team.

Analysis and IT

Tony Biscombe was working with the team on an analysis of their performance, but, in addition to scrutinising England's game, Woodward asked him to look at what the opposition were doing and analyse their performance.

Management

Woodward wanted every little detail attended to so that all the fears and expectations of the players were addressed. He wanted to take away all worries and concerns about playing for England so they could concentrate on the game. There needed to be managers in place who would 'just sort it'.

Leadership

Woodward wanted to look at leadership differently, and to develop leadership characteristics in all players, all over the pitch.

Psychology

Dave Alred was a world-class kicking coach who understood mental motivation – Woodward needed him to be much more involved with the team in terms of preparing them psychologically for the game. Alred went on to assume that role and perform it with aplomb, signing himself up for a PhD in the subject. 'I believe the team that actually wins the World Cup will be the team that has the best mindset that encompasses new ideas and change. The difference between good teams and world champion teams is what goes on between its ears,' says Woodward.

The process of developing the right mental approach was summarised in the term 'change thinking' – this was the process of thinking laterally (outside traditional confines) and vertically (in detail).

There were two men who were crucial in helping Woodward as he aimed to change the players' mental states. The first was Humphrey Walters, the second was a crazy Brisbane dentist called Paddy Lund who ran what he described as the 'Happiness-Centred Business'. He made dramatic changes to his business practices after feeling desperately depressed about his life. On the brink of suicide, he knew things had to change. Being a dentist was driving him mad. He went into the office and looked through his files – he discovered that 20 per cent of his customers were bringing him profit, and 80 per cent were costing him money to serve. He decided to cut the losers straight away, and wrote to them explaining that they had driven him close to suicide and he wanted them to go somewhere else for future treatment. He wrote to the remaining 20 per cent and thanked them for their custom. He added that, because of them, he had not commited suicide. He asked them to keep coming and to refer friends. After that, he set about creating a lovely 'dental experience' with classical music, china cups and sophistication.

'It's important to realise how much your environment affects you,' said Lund. 'When I read about concentration camps, I found that almost everyone associated with them – guards, administrators, inmates – behaved badly towards one another. Very few people seem to be able to keep their morality in that situation – most act like animals. Our environment really does have an impact on us. It also affects people's perceptions of each other. It's hard to feel happy and valued in an unpleasant workplace atmosphere.'

So, Lund set about making the dentist's surgery into a nice workplace. He wrote to all his patients and said that he expected them to say 'please' and 'thank you'. He also composed what he describes as his CNE theory (critical non-essentials). I went to see Lund at his dental practice and spent the day chatting to him about the critical non-essentials theory. He explained that few people properly understand dentistry – they don't know whether a dentist has done something well or not, so they make the judgements on other things. 'If you are given tea served in a silver teapot, you think that the dentist must be a cut above the average. The truth is that you have no idea whether I am or not.' Lund maintains that if you had lipstick marks all over your teacup you would think that the dentist was sloppy and would assume that he didn't sterilise his instruments properly either. This is the foundation of CNE thinking – get the small stuff right or get it wrong, and people will make assumptions about you based on that. He says that, unwittingly, we make judgements about people in an emotional way rather than an intellectual one. 'People assume that Clive's players played rugby really well because they were treated in other aspects of their life as if they did. It's intimidating to the opposition team.' It gives a team the psychological edge, the winning mentality.

Humphrey Walters was quite a different character to Lund. No less lateral in his thinking but a little more businesslike in the traditional English way. Walters was a management consultant who had been involved in facilitating corporate change when Woodward walked into his life. What struck Woodward immediately was how he had the same principles, values and thoughts as Walters. The men shared a view of winning, and what it takes to be a success, but Walters had the crucial ability to see the situation with 'fresh eyes'. One of the first things Walters looked at was what he describes as 'the journey' – what the whole experience of playing for England was like for the players, not just the 'on the pitch' stuff.

'To be honest, I thought it was a bit of a joke,' says Walters. 'I waited at the England team hotel, and Jonny Wilkinson turned up but there wasn't even a room for him for the night. No one knew who he was. The first stage of the journey was horrible.' Walters reported back that, though these players were supposed to be the elite, they were being treated worse than a shop assistant turning up for a first day at work. Walters argued that since 90 per cent of a player's time with England was not spent on the field, how they felt about the experience, how motivated and inspired by it they were, would depend very much on what happened to them off the pitch as well. Walters told Clive about shops he had been into where they looked beautiful from the outside but the staff area inside was a shambles. 'Why treat staff like that?' asked Walters. 'What are you saying about your staff if you treat them like that? You're saying "we don't value you". I think we have to value the England rugby team.'

Walters also introduced Woodward to the concept of '6f thinking'. He showed him the following:

Finished files are the result of many years of scientif
ic study combined with the
experience of many years.

How many 'f's are there in it? asked Walters. Clive replied that there were three. Walters pointed out that there were, in fact, six, but most people just read over the 'f's in 'of'. The theory was that England rugby players needed to be able to see 'all the fs' where their rivals were only seeing three. The concept of 6f think- ing meant seeing things that others weren't seeing. England needed to be more observant, more focused and more determined to get everything right – every little detail needed to be perfect. England needed to change their mindset and do things differently (lateral thinking) but they also needed to do things in great depth and thoroughly (vertical thinking).

Walters and Woodward addressed the team and urged them to envisage their time with England as a white room with nothing in it. Then he suggested they now put into it everything they thought they needed to succeed, but make everything they put back as great as it could possibly be. So, do the players need shirts? Yes – so they have to go into the room. But are the shirts right? Are they perfect or could they be better? How about skintight Lycra shirts that opposition players can't grab hold of, and that allow players to slip through like eels? Would they be better? What would be the best shirt imaginable?

What about a changing-room? Yes – you need a changing- room – but is this changing-room absolutely the best it can possibly be? Could it be better? Cleaner, more inspiring, bigger, smaller? He urged the team and the management to consider everything and ponder the myriad ways in which they could be improved. In the event, they called a BBC make-over team in to work on the changing-rooms, and made a point of having the opposition room containing nothing but a mop and bucket.

'We did everything we could think of to make England better,' said Walters. Woodward and Walters put a booklet together called *To Be The Best*, in which they listed the key areas that they thought England would have to develop in if they were to be just that – the best.

At the top of the list was that England should have the most destructive defence in world rugby. In order to fulfil this, Woodward brought in Phil Larder just before England drew 26–26 with New Zealand. The match had been a key test for Woodward's England and the coach was pleased with some of what he saw. 'There were flashes of brilliance out there today,' he gushed. But he was not at all happy with other areas. He felt first that mentally they hadn't coped too well with the All Blacks, had built Jonah Lomu up into something massive, and had been absolutely thrilled with a draw. Woodward wanted an England team that was so confident the players expected to win against everyone and were always disappointed with a draw.

Second, and more immediately remediable, he thought that England were at nowhere near the same level of fitness as New Zealand. Reddin moved things up a notch or two in his efforts to make England the fittest and most powerful team in world rugby.

After the New Zealand game, Woodward began hammering home his critical non-essentials theory. He produced a charter for the players which outlined what was expected of them; it included dress code, standard of behaviour around the team hotels, changing rooms, when to use the mobile phone and how to relate to the public.

Before England left for their first tour of the Woodward era, the head coach brought in Brian Ashton to shore up and develop the team's ability to identify and capitalise on attacking opportunities.

With Ashton on attack and Larder on defence, Woodward had the two key coaches he'd been eager to secure. He brought in equipment for the players, signing separate sponsorship deals and agreements with companies in order to give the players what he believed they needed. Every player was given a laptop and lessons in how to use a computer.

Next, the team were taken to Lympstone in Devon where they met the Royal Marines and learnt two crucial lessons: first, that the best-laid plans go wrong, and you should be prepared for that; second, that teams are vitally important. The right team-mates mean your life will be saved. It's vital that everyone in the Marines is the sort of person you'd be happy to go into battle with. Woodward called it 'Jumping out of a helicopter'. Would you be willing to jump out of a helicopter with this man? If not – should he be in the team? He decided he would be more brutal, more determined, and he would get rid of the energy sappers or change them into energisers.

Despite all of Woodward's work, the team ended the 1999 World Cup at the quarter-final stage – the same place they'd finished in 1987. But he remained calm and philosophical, telling the world:

> I believe that all too often, in the business world particularly, managers and coaches make too much of defeat and too little of success. Normally in business, when you lose the big deal, you're hauled into the boardroom early on Monday morning for a bollocking and a huge enquiry into what went wrong. Whereas when you win the big deal, you're usually taken straight down the pub to celebrate. I think most managers have it all wrong. When you win the big deal, that's when you should be straight into the boardroom on Monday morning to analyse what happened, what went right and how you can learn from your success to do it again the next time. However, when you lose the big deal or the big game, the last thing you need is to dwell on the mistakes. That's the time to head down the pub. It's a management concept I call 'Success from set-backs and build on success'.

Woodward looked again at 'winning' and asked Biscombe, the analyst, to give him some feedback on how the team were doing throughout the course of a match. Biscombe said that the team were starting the match well – the first ten minutes of the first half was always great, but not so the first ten minutes of the second half. 'I knew that we needed to find a way to get the second half off to as good a start as we'd been getting the first half off to, so we decided to do "second half thinking" and come out for the second half as we had at the beginning of the match. The team changed their shirts, so they came out in clean shirts as they had in the first half.' 'The difference was bigger than you would think,' says Bernard Laporte, the France coach. 'Suddenly in the second half, there are players looking muddy, dirty, sweaty and tired, and there are the England players looking fresh and fit and bright. It made a big psychological difference to them so everyone soon started to do it.'

Sherylle Calder was the last member of the team to come on board. She was the visual awareness coach for the team and set about training the players' eyesight. Calder is convinced that the eyes are just muscles and can be trained. By putting the players onto a computer and doing various tests she produced training programmes for them. She also suggested that the players needed to develop the habit of continually looking around the pitch throughout a game. Woodward is convinced that it made a difference to his players. All these small improvements would add up to make a significant difference to the team. Did England win the World Cup because their eyesight was the best? Probably not. Because their shirts were clean? No. But the combinations of all these improvements made them significantly better – physically and – crucially – mentally. Quite simply, they felt like the best team in the world. They felt like they couldn't be beaten.

Another difference was made by Prozone – the most advanced sporting analysis programme in the world, featuring twenty cameras at Twickenham to capture images throughout matches and project them onto screens with the players represented by dots. It showed straight away who was out of position, and where the gaps, overlaps and spaces were, what decisions were made by the players and how these might have been different.

Prozone tracks every move and tackle and pass of every player from start to finish of a game. 'When we got it in 2001, it was being used by four or five Premiership [football] clubs,' says Woodward. 'The biggest thing in coaching is in the debriefing after the match. This system allows you to go way beyond what you do immediately after the game. You show players clearly how much they're working and not working. "From the moment you walk down that tunnel, we've got you. We know every step you make and how fast and how hard you are working." They know it too. They call it Big Brother.'

There were times when the pursuit of perfection took Clive to extremes. On one occasion he flew to Israel to talk to a man called Yehuda Shinar – an expert in understanding 'winning behaviour'. Shinar had identified eleven high-performance behaviours after investigations with over 3000 athletes. He had compiled a database of common characteristics in psychological conditioning, and had devised a computer simulator that could train anyone to master the skills of mental competitive advantage. By improving patterns of thinking, performance improved in every respect. Woodward was hooked. Shinar came to London and began working with the team. 'I think it might have been one thing too far,' says Johnson. 'Even though Clive was clearly hooked on the thing, we never really took it that seriously. It was like a computer game. We did it for a while, then it kind of disappeared.'

Woodward was eager to analyse exactly what it took to win, and whether you could train these traits away from the rugby field. He felt that there were three key areas which had to overlap in order to win a World Cup: teamship, leadership and partnership. He drew a Venn diagram with all three circles overlapping – the place they overlapped was where the team that won the World Cup must be.

Teamship was identified as leadership, coaching, fitness/ nutrition, psychology, medical, analysis and management.

Leadership was vision, culture, building teams, values, strategy and standards.

Partnerships were things like the relationship between the England team and clubs, the players' families, the RFU, sponsors, fans and referees. Steve Lander, an international referee, came to talk to the players before each match.

By the time that England left for the World Cup, they were in the best physical and mental shape possible. The average player was consuming around 6000 calories a day, 300g of protein and nine litres of water and sports drinks. Under advice from team nutritionist, Matt Lovell, the team were on a high protein diet that allowed no carbohydrates after midday.

Breakfast was egg-white omelettes with bacon or gammon steaks and porridge mixed with quinoa – a grain rich in protein. Lunch was fish or chicken with vegetables, potatoes and bread – the last carbs of the day. Dinner would consist of meat (chicken or fish) with vegetables or salad.

The whole squad had their body fat measured before and after each training session, of which there were three a day commencing at 7 a.m. For every kilo lost, the players were required to drink the same in water and sports drinks. Ice tubs were used as a way of halting the build-up of lactic acid and to aid recovery.

Woodward, says Johnson, spent hours working out what could possibly go wrong, and establishing a solution to the problem before it arose. For example, the team regularly practised defending with a man down. 'We tried to think what we would do when certain players got a yellow card,' said Woodward.

Virtually every minute of every day was mapped out for the squad. A full day's schedule was pushed under the door of each squad member on the previous evening. After the tour of Australia and New Zealand before the World Cup, Woodward took the squad to Perth, where they were to be based for the tournament. He wanted the players to assess the hotel, training facilities and stadium. He wanted nothing to come as a surprise.

In Sydney, it was injury time and the England players who had been dismissed for being old and unfit were on the verge of making history as the first northern hemisphere winners of the World Cup, after one of the most successful years in English rugby history.

Woodward watched as the teams kicked off after the penalty that had taken them to 17–17. Mat Rogers sliced his kick into touch after an attempted charge down by Lewis Moody, sending the ball out of play within thirty-five metres of the Australia line. This was England's big moment. They had control of the ball as the seconds ticked down. What would they do at the line-out? Steve Thompson walked to the front and prepared to throw the best ball of his life. It had to go long. It had to go to the back for Lewis Moody so the forwards could provide quick ball for the backs. If they did not do that, they would not get the vital score they needed in order to win. Could Thompson do it? Johnson nodded and Thompson called the move.

Woodward saw the line-out call and knew they were going for the zigzag move – a routine which would give them the best chance of a drop goal. The move was designed to get Wilkinson in front of the uprights. It necessitated the other players controlling the ball in contact and making quick breaks to take the team further up the pitch. But, before any of that could be achieved, Thompson had to get his throw-in absolutely right. All the pressure was on Thompson to get his throw spot on. He had been training with a visual awareness coach and had a full-time line-out coach to assist him. What difference would those small factors make now, under pressure, in the World Cup final? Could Thompson deliver? Yes. Clean over the line it went. Moody flipped it down to secure the quick possession they so desperately needed. The ball was in the backs and the posts were tantalisingly close. The zigzag move was on. Woodward leapt up off the bench and screamed with all his might at players who could not hear him.

From Moody who won the line-out expertly to Mike Catt who drove up field. Would it go to Jonny Wilkinson for the kick of his life? The players had been taught to think carefully under pressure. So they thought of the zigzag routine. Wilkinson needed to be closer to be sure of victory. Somehow, in the deafening din of the stadium, worn out and mentally exhausted, seconds away from victory or defeat in the biggest match of their lives, the players thought so correctly under pressure that even now, years later, their calmness seems staggering. They needed to get Wilkinson closer to the posts. He might have scored it anyway – we'll never know. But 'might' wasn't nearly good enough. Catt recycled. The ball was secured by Dawson, the scrum-half. Would he pass to Wilkinson? No. Don't take the easy option, take the right option. Dawson showed such courage, setting off through the smallest of gaps and making those extra strides, around a dozen of them, each one crucial in getting Wilkinson to within striking distance.

Dawson set the ball back again and in came Johnson. How appropriate that the greatest captain the game has ever known should step into the fray now, when needed most. Johnson took it on. The seconds ticked down. Time was running out. They had to get the ball to Wilkinson, but Johnson knew it had to be the right ball. They would get one chance. Johnson went up the side of the ruck and laid the ball down carefully. Then, Dawson. This was it. The clocks stopped ticking and hearts stopped beating as Dawson passed to Wilkinson. Millions of people all over the world knew what would happen next.

The world's greatest kicker stood in front of the posts. It was the moment that he had been training for and the moment that Woodward had been preparing for. The left-footed kicker lifted his right foot and shattered a million Australian hearts. The ball flew clean over. 20–17. Woodward prowled the touchline at the re-start – screaming at England to boot the ball into touch as soon as possible. Catt did not hear his words, but the England centre knew what had to be done – he blasted the ball away. The referee lifted his whistle to his mouth and the rugby world tilted on its axis. England had won the World Cup.

What made Woodward's preparation of England for the 2003 World Cup so special was depth and detail, coupled with a change in the way he thought about the game, using fresh and vibrant business techniques in rugby union. He brought people into the sport who had never worked with rugby players before, bringing a new perspective to the team. Woodward battled to make preparation thorough so that nothing would take them by surprise. He came up with the concept T-Cup – Think Correctly Under Pressure – in order to persuade the players to make the right decisions even under the most intense pressure (Prozone helped them with understanding what the right decisions were, and Sherylle Calder's work taught them how to see the options). T-Cup was also about not conceding needless penalties. When the opposition were pressured into making mistakes, there was Jonny Wilkinson on hand to turn their errors into points for England. If the T-Cup mentality evaded the players momentarily and the players found themselves in the sin bin, what then for England? Woodward would often get England to train with fourteen men, to make sure they were ready in case they might have a player or two sent to the sin bin. It happened in New Zealand on their summer tour, when, already down to 14, Lawrence Dallaglio followed Neil Back into the bin early in the second half. He figured his indiscretion was worth it because he believed England could hold out with six forwards against eight. They'd done it in training. There's no question that such confidence in decision-making was a psychological blow to the team's opponents.

Their work, through Larder, on their defence, left England incredibly adept at slowing play down when they needed to, infuriating rival teams. Woodward spent seven years employing any tactic possible to improve the squad. Tony Biscombe developed such a library on teams and players around the world that the coaches could access information on anyone or anything rugby-related and Biscombe could hand it to them. He followed not only the movement of England players, but the playmakers in the opposing team. Knowing which players kick or run more, to whom they passed, which direction and under what circumstances, how they handled harassment, what they were likely to do in different weather conditions – it all added up to quite a weighty information bank on opposition players.

'It was all the little things that made the difference,' says Dan Luger. 'Like the new shirts. It really became hard to hold on to a player in the tackle after they came in. The detail of the whole shirts thing was terrific. The forwards have a looser part on the shirts, so they can get a grip in the scrum. Everything is thought through.'

After England had won the World Cup, I went to watch Woodward giving a talk at Telford Conference Centre at which he addressed hundreds of teachers eager to find out what it takes to win in sport. What are the skills? The attributes – mental and physical. Woodward stood on the stage like a rock star while the audience screamed and shouted their appreciation.

'There are five things you need to do to create a winning mindset,' he said. Then he ran through the five things that he thinks are the most important characteristics. He says he has these five points on his laptop, his mobile phone and in his wallet.

1. Happiness
2. Lateral thinking
3. Critical non-essentials
4. Management and players (critical essentials)
5. No compromise

They form the basis of the reasons that England won the World Cup in 2003.

Why did England win?

1. They had a great captain
Martin Johnson was outstanding as England captain. Players ran faster, stood taller and acted stronger when he was around. When Johnno was playing, England's success rate increased dramatically. He had a colossal impact on the side.

2. Management
The Woodward management team was much derided because no coach had ever demanded such a large and wide-ranging group of experts, but having the coaches who taught the basic skills well, backed by an outstanding medical and recovery team, great analysis and IT back-up, and coupled with his more original staff members – like Sherylle Calder – gave England a real advantage.

3. The players

England had some of the greatest players in the world in their positions. They had the experience of men like Jason Leonard, coupled with the reliable kicking skills of Jonny Wilkinson. Across the field there were talented players, all with that 'team spirit' mentality. Like the Marines who he took the players to visit – Woodward wanted his men to trust each other implicitly. He assessed this by asking 'Would you be willing to jump out of a helicopter with this man?'. He says that he put 15 players onto the pitch that day who he would happily jump out of a helicopter with.

4. The environment was perfect

Woodward made sure that everything was all right. The journey was perfect ... from the hotel being the best and the travel being well-organised to the greatest of experts and the best food. It was all designed so players would have no excuse for not playing perfectly. In return, the players were expected to respond to this environment properly and to follow a strict code of conduct. Players had to be respectful and thoughtful, and behave in a manner appropriate to the greatest rugby players in the world.

5. An end to the hero-worshipping of the southern hemisphere sides

The shadowing of the great sides stopped. Woodward made the England players believe in themselves and their skills and abilities. His ability to do this significantly reduced the impact of the southern hemisphere sides.

6. Woodward thought differently

He broke the rules, thought laterally, and created a new approach. Eye trainers and Israeli experts on winning, laptops for the players, and new shirts at half time were part of this process. He left no stone unturned, as he thought of everything and tried everything.

7. The fitness of the players was outstanding

Dave Reddin was told to make the England players the fittest in world rugby. He did and it all paid off in extra time of the World

Cup final when, despite being told that they were old and past it, they proved they were fitter than their opponents and able to think more clearly than them.

8. There was leadership all over the pitch

There were energising, thoughtful and analytical players across the pitch. They weren't just good players, they were good leaders. Woodward and Johnson could not make all the decisions on the pitch. Faced, in any given moment, with a variety of options, Woodward needed players who could think on their feet and make the right decisions.

9. Defence

England had the best defence in world rugby, and Woodward was eager that defence should be an attacking platform.

10. Learn from success as well as setbacks but value the lessons of defeat

Woodward needed players to learn from but not obsess about the setbacks and really study when things went right – trying to recreate the feeling, learn what they did right, so that they could reproduce it. If you spend too long obsessing about the defeats, are you destined to repeat the patterns that led to them. Learn from the defeats and move on. Absorb the feelings, strategies and tactics that took you to victory.

PART SIX

Conclusion and 2007

CONCLUSION

1987 – gross revenue of £3.3 million and £1 million net profit. Around 600,000 people passed through the turnstiles. Global television audience touched 300 million.

1991 – rugby World Cup generated £23.3 million, with a profit of £4.1 million. Crowd figures topped 1 million and the TV audiences were up almost sixfold, to 1.75 billion.

1995 – rugby World Cup revenue at £30.3 million with profit of 17.6 million. Crowd figures stayed the same at around 1 million, but the TV reach had increased to 2.67 billion.

1999 – revenue was £70 million with a profit of £47 million. Crowds reached 1.75 million and 3.1 billion viewers watched on television.

2003 – revenue was £81.8 million with a profit of £64.3 million, the crowd was 1.8 million and 3.4 billion viewers saw the tournament on television.

The prediction from the IRB is that there will be 2.4 million spectators and 4 billion TV viewers for RWC 2007. The event is to be broadcast by 250 networks.

Percy Bysshe Shelley, the great romantic poet, suggested that poets of all ages contributed to one Great Poem perpetually in progress. His feeling was that individual poets, however much they were separated – culturally, historically, geographically or emotionally – from their peers, would offer their jewels of inspiration and in doing so contribute not just to the body of their own work, but to the body of the whole of poetry.

Now it may be considered a leap of some height and distance from the pens of the mightiest poets to the boots of the most sublime rugby players, but this sport of ours which catches a player at his physical peak – tests him, taunts him and either breaks or builds him – now has its own Great Poem.

The World Cup was feared and dreaded by so many because they thought that it would mark the end of joy, laughter and passion, and replace it with an acquisitiveness and lust for riches and fame that could erase the very essence of the sport. Not so. The World Cup has added to rugby's great big colourful mix and has given rugby a stage grander than any previously imagined. It turned out there was nothing to fear from the stage. It turned out, let's be honest, that our scruffy old players running around in our little am-dram production of a sport, were all Richard Burtons in disguise. They have excelled themselves in rugby's new theatre, and the World Cup, in its own way, has helped rugby to grow and excel.

There's no question that rugby has changed – as a result of, and through the period of, the Rugby World Cups – but nothing fundamental has really changed about the essence of the players themselves. They behave differently because the sport is different, but one feels that the same people who play today would have played twenty years ago, even though it was a different game. Rugby has not become football, and rugby players have not become footballers. Rugby's surface is undoubtedly shinier and its coffers fuller, the sport is better to watch and is watched in greater numbers. It is played by fit, strong athletes, but the players are the same as they ever were.

One must remember how important players are to a sport. They are all that sport is. Rugby is meaningless in any real sense. In fact, it doesn't exist in any real sense – it's just the interaction of fifteen players against fifteen players on a given day on a prescribed pitch under a set of laws that are applied by a referee. Then, rugby is created. They create it. Rugby is just people.

That's why, when I came to identify the top ten reasons why teams win World Cups, there were a lot of the items in the lists relating to people. I have been back through the reasons why teams win World Cups and established that, despite the way rugby has changed, there are similarities between strategies for victory which span the years.

The top ten reasons why teams have won the five World Cup tournaments to date:

1. Great players
You need to have some of the best players in the world if you are to have a chance of winning a World Cup. This extends to the bench and the rest of the squad. Lochore in 1987 and Woodward in 2003 stated unequivocally that the non-playing players were essential for team morale and creating the right team spirit. Dwyer said it in 1991 and Christie said it in 1995. Everyone involved with the team needs to be positive and confident – not just the XV who run out on to the pitch.

2. Good management/coach
All coaches of World Cup-winning sides have been masters at their art. They are all very different, but they were all the stand-out coaches of their eras.

3. A great captain
I do not think you can win a World Cup without a Johnson, an Eales, a Pienaar, a Farr-Jones or a Kirk. The captains themselves say that a captain is not that important. I think it is. For lots of reasons – most of them psychological – great teams need great leaders, and World Cup-winning teams need the greatest leaders of all.

4. Fitness and preparation
Yes, it's right up there at the top of the list. Teams that win World Cups are fit, arguably the fittest in the tournament they win. There is, according to the Australian Institute of Sport, a direct correlation between fitness in rugby and success in rugby. On the preparation front, it's important to remember that teams don't turn up at World Cups and 'wing it'. They are focused, determined and have done all they can to get themselves in the right shape to win. I think Australia have won twice because of this. Their preparation is meticulous and quite ruthless.

5. Belief

If you believe you can fly, it does not mean you will fly, but if you believe you can't, it means you never will. Belief is a complicated characteristic – so much more complicated and fundamental to success than many realise. Self-belief does not mean bursting into the room and running over hot coals, it means having a quiet, unshakeable confidence in your own ability and that of your teammates. It takes a lot of time to build but I'm sure, after writing this book, that it does turn finalists into winners.

6. Team spirit

I think members of teams have to *like* one another. It may sound obvious, but I think it's vitally important – more so than in other sports where there isn't the physical danger and direct man-to-man confrontation. When James Small was told he was tackling Lomu and saw the man mountain for the first time, it really mattered that other players came up and said, 'Just hold him till we get there.' 'Like' may sound a weak word – but it brings in the respect and trust that build team spirit and I think all winning teams have it.

7. Work hard

World Cup-winning teams work hard. Not what anyone wants to hear, of course. It would be much more magical to think that players were born with winged feet and the sublime skills to take them to the top, but they work hard. They work on their basic skills, their fitness and their studying of the opposition.

8. Big vision

The World Cup-winning rugby sides were all hugely different, but shared the fact that they had a clear understanding of what they were trying to do, and this vision was shared by all the players who understood fully what was expected of them.

9. A notable defeat prior to the wins

All of the coaches of the teams who have won World Cups say that great motivation and the ability to plot a path forward came from a significant defeat on the way – from 'Remember Nantes' in 1987, to 'those Six Nations defeats won us the World Cup' in 2003. It is not surprising that this is the case – in business there is a very clear link between success and failure. The top ten richest American businessmen have failed at least three times in business. If you look at the heads of business at the top of the Fortune 1000 companies in the United States, over 80 per cent have failed in their careers at least once. Failing at things is important to deal with, because it will happen, and it is how you bounce back from the failures that will define your ultimate success. The World Cup-winning sides did not enjoy failure but what unites them and sets them apart from so many teams is that they never believed the failures made them a failure. They still believed they would win in the end.

10. Critical non-essentials

I'm appropriating Woodward's language here, and they weren't always called critical non-essentials, but the various decisions made by coaches – to allow players to live in greater comfort and make them feel special – contribute to performance. There's no point beating players if you want them to win a World Cup. Players who win World Cups want to feel that they have fulfilled their destiny. You need to create the feeling in players that they are destined to win (which is also how they develop that elusive 'aura' that some teams have), and you do this by getting everything off the pitch right for them. External reward does not create internal motivation – that has been shown by studies time and time again, the world over. To motivate someone, you create in them the desire to succeed at all costs and you build in them the sense that they are destined to achieve it. This is done by environment, facilities, communication, coaching and success. You need to make the players feel that they are the best, long before they are.

Interestingly, since professionalism, the two coaches who have led their teams to victory – Woodward and Macqueen – both used business techniques to transform their teams into world beaters, and both stated 'defence' as one of the most important attributes of the teams.

A further question on the subject of winning World Cups might be – why don't northern hemisphere sides win more frequently? Those I talked to suggest three reasons:

1. A high level below international level is vital. Graham Henry, coach of World Cup sides in both hemispheres, said he thought this was a fundamental difference between the two halves of the world. He thought that northern hemisphere sides needed a Super 12-style tournament to raise the quality of their game. Will Carling agreed: 'Super 12 teams have better defences – they use their defences as an offensive weapon,' he said. 'You only learn to do that if you're playing at a high level every week.'

2. Australia's ability to succeed is based on the fact that they have new players coming through all the time – to win one World Cup then get to the final the next time is an astonishing achievement. There's no question that the Australian Institute of Sport plays a huge role in this. They work on bringing in new star players of the future all the time, while the Australia team management concentrate on turning the players they currently have into World Cup winners. 'If you want to win World Cups consistently, you need to get yourselves an AIS,' said Bob Dwyer. 'And you need one yesterday.'

3. Paradoxically, according to the AIS the reason that British and Irish teams don't do so well is that there are too many people involved. Officials at the Institute say that English selectors have too much choice because there are too many players in the system. They think that England should select a small squad and work with those players, giving them everything and not spreading resources too thinly.

'I know that a huge advantage for us is that we have a smaller player base – we can focus pretty early on, on a core group of players,' says Ben Whitaker from the AIS. 'In England, South Africa and New Zealand there are too many resources split, and there's a need to focus on a much larger group of players. We are able to say – here are the twenty young players and haven't got to worry about a group of 100 or more coming through. These are the ones who are going to win the World Cup – now, let's get on with it.'

Now, twenty years on from the first tournament, it's time for the World Cup again and, it seems it will be all about New Zealand and France. The two teams who made it to the first-ever World Cup final, in 1987, do look on paper as if they will rise to the top of the pile again. When they reached the final in 1987, it was in Auckland and New Zealand won. This time, if they meet in the final again, it will be in Paris. Does that mean it is likely to be France going for glory?

It's always a dreadful mistake to make such predictions, but just look at the draw. There are twenty teams competing in the tournament, split over four pools, with two teams from each pool going forward to the quarter-finals. As usual, the quarter-finals round consists of the first-place team in one pool playing the second-place finisher in another. So finishing top of your group is a clear advantage.

In the 2007 competition, Pool A contains England, Samoa, South Africa, Tonga and the United States, and Pool B contains Australia, Canada, Fiji, Japan and Wales. So, if England finish top of their pool, they are likely to face Wales in the quarter-final (assuming Wales do not beat Australia), and if they come second, it looks like an early clash with Australia. In Pool C, it is Italy, New Zealand, Portugal, Romania and Scotland and in the final pool are Argentina, France, Georgia, Ireland and Namibia. On form, New Zealand should finish first in Pool C, with Scotland in second place and France should top Pool D, with Ireland coming second. That would leave New Zealand with a quarter-final against Ireland, and France playing Scotland. As the on-form British Isles' team of the moment, Ireland could really do with topping their pool (i.e. beating France on 21 September at the Stade de France – quite a request!) to avoid such an early clash with New Zealand.

All this means that the likely scenario at semi-final stage is South Africa or England v France (again, at the Stade de France – scene of the 1998 football World Cup triumph). Then Australia versus New Zealand in the second semi. Does that not sound to you like a France v New Zealand final? Obviously, this is assuming that New Zealand break with tradition and play to a minimum of 50 per cent of their ability. If they don't, Australia – the vultures of the world game – will win.

And if it does come down to New Zealand and France – what a fascinating match that will be. The very interesting thing about these two teams is that New Zealand seem to have underperformed to their potential more than any others in the competition's history, while France have had stunning moments of over performance. New Zealand won in 1987, but it was France that played in the match of the tournament. In 1991, both sides went out of the competition after playing against the eventual finalists, and arguably the two best sides in the competition. In 1995, New Zealand were utterly outstand-ing – the best team in the competition, but they lost to South Africa in injury time by a kick. In 1999, New Zealand were still an outstanding side, but lost to a French team that excelled itself – their skills appeared from nowhere and, against all the odds, hurled New Zealand out of the competition, before losing to Australia in the final. It's as if all the fireworks and star play-ers are provided by New Zealand, all the razzmatazz and creativity by France, leaving them no time to focus on winning the thing, so allowing another team – usually Australia – to sidestep them on the line and lift the Cup. In 2003, both sides went out at semi-final stage to the two teams who would con-test the final . . . again. So many times the page boy, but never the groom. This time?

New Zealand have had a fantastic period since 2003. In fact, it would not be too much of an exaggeration to say that they have changed the face of rugby, and taken it to a whole new, higher level. Their lines of running, their offloading in the tackle, and the intensity and the skills of the players – notably Richie McCaw, the flanker, and Dan Carter, the fly-half – have been awesome.

Magnificent. They won the Tri Nations in 2006, and played seven other matches that year – they won them all.

And France? They go into the tournament as Six Nations champions and with home advantage on their side. The grounds they will play at are the ones that were used for the football World Cup in 1998. The World Cup which France won in thrilling style – remember the mad horn-blowing, singing and partying up the Champs Elysées afterwards? They estimate that there were a million people on the streets of Paris celebrating that night.

Olivier Magne recalls the moment vividly. 'The whole of France came out that night – not all literally onto the streets – many of them just in spirit but they were all there with the footballers and it lifted the whole country. There is not a person in France who does not dream of France winning the 2007 World Cup. Does it create pressure? Yes. Do we love to have some pressure? Yes. Will we win? I think so.'

The trouble with France is that they defy prediction. In 1999, they were hopeless leading up to the World Cup. During the World Cup itself they were so concerned about beating Fiji that Philippe Sella said on the flight down to Toulouse to play the Pacific Islanders, 'Let us sip a little champagne now because we might not want to do it tomorrow night.' Then they went on to beat Fiji by the grace of the referee who disallowed a Fiji try and gave France a penalty try, and looked destined to go straight out in the quarter-final. But they beat Argentina, then beat New Zealand to make it to the final.

It's hard to predict how well teams will do in the World Cup based on results from the Tri Nations, too, because New Zealand win so frequently, but do not achieve as well in the World Cups. New Zealand have won eight of the twelve championships that have taken place since the Tri Nations started. Also, the outstanding individual performances have come from New Zealand players. When you look at the top try scorers from the Tri Nations, the top four are all New Zealanders, as are three of the top five all-time points scorers in the competition.

New Zealand have won the Tri Nations for the last three years.

France have won three of the four Six Nations competitions that have taken place since the last World Cup. Interestingly, England won three out of four of the Six Nations before they won the World Cup in 2003 and France won two out of four before making it to the final in 1999. All wildly speculative this – but there is some sort of correlation, it would seem, between performance in the Six Nations and results in the World Cup.

1987 France Grand Slam (France make it to World Cup final)
1991 England Grand Slam (England make it to World Cup final)
1995 England Grand Slam (England gets to the semi-finals)
1999 Scotland win (but it is France who make it to the World Cup final)
2003 England Grand Slam (England win World Cup)
2007 France win

And what of the reigning world champions? It's been a tough four years for England. They returned with the Webb-Ellis trophy to national celebrations, meetings with the Queen and parties with the Prime Minister. Then, things started to go pear-shaped. Leading players announced their retirement from the game, there were injuries and a couple of players were dropped. They lost their third game of the Six Nations to Ireland (at fortress Twickenham) and the successes of Sydney seemed a long time ago.

Woodward left the sinking ship, feeling that he could do nothing while the RFU continued to limit funds and fail to back him in his ongoing battles with the clubs over access to the players. Andy Robinson, his deputy, took over but the chariot's descent was gaining momentum and there was little he could do to halt it in the short term. He presided over a string of defeats.

Rob Andrew, England's fly-half and the saviour of the England team in 1995, came in as elite rugby director (over Woodward who had been approached about the role, and who expressed an eagerness to return to the RFU). The defeats continued, with Robinson managing to guide the players to victory over South Africa in November 2006, in what was the first international victory for nine months, but it was too little too late and the English coach was told to pack his bags. Dave Reddin, the fitness guru who had been Woodward's right-hand man in 2003, was also dismissed – the last of the old guard to get his marching orders. Then, five days before Christmas in 2006, Brian Ashton was announced as the new coach of England.

Ashton's arrival as head coach coincided neatly with a return of Jonny Wilkinson to the side. The new England coach selected the old England fly-half and a 42–20 victory over Scotland ensued, largely due to Wilkinson's five penalties, two conversions and a try. They then beat Italy at Twickenham but were crushed by Ireland. The 43–13 defeat ranking as England's worst result against Ireland in the 132 years of competition between the two sides. France won the championship.

The World Cup committee predicts that 2.4 million spectators and 4 billion television viewers will watch the action from the tournament between twenty countries, in forty-eight matches, over the forty-four days. Forty-two of the matches will be spread between ten French cities, with four matches to be held in Cardiff and two in Scotland.

There will be one new team in the mix this year – Portugal playing in the tournament for the first time after qualifying with a 24–23 aggregate victory over Uruguay. It is unlikely they will topple any of rugby's superpowers, but just being in the competition is regarded as a huge achievement for the Portuguese.

Football is by far the biggest sport in Portugal, hogging the vast majority of the nation's media coverage. The country's leading daily sports newspaper *A Bola* is 80 per cent football, 5 per cent rugby, with the remaining 5 per cent shared between all other sports. When Portugal qualified, the sports editor said he would 'watch very carefully now the events in rugby. We will have much more rugby in the paper. Much more. I feel an enthusiasm for it.'

There are around 4000 registered players in Portugal, but the

Federação Portuguesa de Rugby, governing body of the sport in Portugal, says that the Portugese government has announced increased funding for the sport and new facilities inside the national stadium, so they estimate that this figure will go up, perhaps even double next season, if Portugal can make any sort of mark at the tournament.

Certainly, when they qualified, they partied with such intensity that six players clashed with police and were arrested and jailed. The president of the Portuguese Rugby Federation, Didio de Aguiar, said: 'The competition is very demanding, they had a free night and unfortunately they went out drinking. That was it.'

The Portuguese Six spent the night in jail but were released without trial. 'Just fun,' said the management. 'Just boys and their fun.'

World Cups have transformed rugby union, of that there is no doubt. They have given the sport a window that has opened eyes and opened up opportunities. It is now hard to imagine the sport without the four-yearly tournament. It is hard to remember back to a time when they asked: 'What do we need a fitness instructor for?'

'To be fair, though,' says Lawrence Dallaglio, 'if I'd been playing when Rendall did, I'd have been the same as him. We're all just kids really, aren't we? Messing around in this sport – trying to have fun while being the best we can.'

Rugby union, then: the sport that transformed itself utterly and completely over a twenty-year period, without really changing at all.

There is one player whose antics, reputation and charisma have come to define all that is best about the sport. Jason Leonard played in four World Cups, bridging the years between amateurism and professionalism. He changed as the sport changed around him, to cope with its new intensity, but never really changed all that much at all . . . really. A man with both feet on the ground and his pint raised in the air – Leonard is the most capped World Cup player ever, so it is to him that I turn to guide the book to its conclusion.

CURTAIN CALL

A final word from the World Cup's most experienced player

L adies and gentlemen, please be upstanding for Jason Leonard – the man who has played in more World Cup games than anyone in the history of the sport. The man known variously as 'Fun Bus' and 'The Scourge of Barking Barmaids' was first capped for England on the 1990 tour of Argentina, and his last game was against Italy in the Six Nations, fourteen years later. He won 119 caps (five for the Lions), during an international career including four Grand Slams, two World Cup finals, twenty-two World Cup appearances, and three Lions tours.

THE WORLD CUP TOP TEN
of players to have played in four tournaments

THE MAGNIFICENT SEVEN

1. **Jason Leonard (England) – 22 games**
   (the only one to have won a World Cup and to have reached the final on two occasions)

2. **Brian Lima (Western Samoa) – 16 games**
   (will become the first player to participate in five tournaments if he plays in RWC07)

3. **Fabien Galthié (France) – 15 games**
   (captained France to the final in 1999, and captained them in 2003)

4. **Gareth Rees (Canada) – 13 games**
   (the only one to have played in RWC87, the first World Cup tournament, in which he was the youngest competitor – and captained his side in the World Cup)

5. **Al Charron (Canada) – 12 games**

6. **Carlo Checchinato (Italy) – 10 games**

7. **Pedro Sporleder (Argentina) – 9 games**

THREE HONOURABLE MENTIONS
The following men travelled to four World Cups, as part of their country's squad, but didn't make it on to the pitch in the 1991 World Cup, thus only played in three World Cup tournaments.

8. **Yukio Motoki (Japan) – 9 games**

9. **Dave Lougheed (Canada) – 8 games**

10. **Tsutomu Matsuda (Japan) – 8 games**

Important he may be, but how many telephones does Jason Leonard need? The man's only got two ears and they're so smashed up and cauliflower-like in appearance, it's hard to believe he can hear anything through them. Nevertheless, he has three phones – all bleeping, jumping and vibrating on the table in front of him as he prepares to talk to me about his experiences across four World Cups. 'That one gives me my emails,' he says, pointing to a BlackBerry with fingers the size of iced buns. His hands are like large tennis rackets – big enough to take out an entire opposition front row at twenty paces.

'And this one – this is for work calls,' he says of the black one. 'This silver one is for social calls.'

I notice that it is the silver one that is jumping more than the others are. In fact, unless I'm mistaken – the others aren't jumping at all.

'No,' agrees Leonard. "Cos they're not switched on.'

'You don't switch the work phone on?' I ask.

'Not all the time – people call on the social one. It's not really work is it? Rugby. It's all social anyway.'

Could this be the most delightful thing about Leonard, and the thing that has come to define him over his decade and a half of competing? While other players exude seriousness – they are such a mess of concentration and commitment that they can't sleep at night, Leonard reminds you how simple life can be. 'I'm as competitive as the next bloke, but I never saw any point in getting wound up about it all. I trained hard, then I went out there and gave it all I had. I came off afterwards and, win or lose, I had a couple of pints with the guys I'd played against. Where's the stress in that? It's been a bloody good life and I've had a bloody good laugh.'

Leonard was working as a carpenter when the 1987 World Cup came around – having followed his father's footsteps into the building trade.

The final was on early in the morning, and I was working in this big office in central London – refurbishing it. The furniture arrived and there was a very flash television there – all boxed up. I was doing some chippy work in the director's office, and the TV needed to go in there, so I took it out, sat down in the bloke's executive chair that I'd just put together, put my feet up on the desk and watched the match on his big television. Actually, to be honest, I must have done it quite a few times because I can remember watching other matches in 1987; I don't think I was doing too much chippying, to be fair. I saw the semi-final between Australia and France. I remember watching England lose to Wales, too, and seeing how devastated the players were. I thought: 'Cheer up, lads – it's the best thing. If you'd won, you'd have to play against New Zealand and you really don't wanna be doing that.' They looked awesome in '87.

It's interesting to think that there might be some guy somewhere in the city sitting in the chair that Leonard put together before the 1987 World Cup. 'Nah. That chair wouldn't have lasted four years,' he says. 'Probably collapsed under him after about a week.' Leonard was playing U-19s rugby at the time, with no idea that he would play in the next four World Cups and become the most capped rugby player of all time. 'I had this manager when I got my first cap – he was a friend who worked as an accountant so said he'd look after me. I told him I'd pay him. He said, "Don't worry, son – you keep winning the caps, and I'll keep looking after you for nothing." Poor bastard didn't realise I was going to earn so many – he thought I'd get a couple and that would be it. He looked worried when I got to ten, but he still had no idea that I'd get over a hundred. He worked for nothing for fifteen years. Ha!'

He does a nice line in self-deprecating wit, does Leonard. There are numerous tales – now almost mythical through years of telling . . . Like the time that Jack Rowell decided to take him on: 'Jase. You've got to prove to me that you're more than just a crafty cockney collecting caps,' said Rowell, soon after he took over as England manager. Leonard just shrugged and ignored him. The next day, Leonard won his thirty-sixth cap and Rowell approached him. 'So, what did you think about what I said to you last night?' he asked. 'What?' asked Leonard, innocently. 'About you being a crafty cockney collecting caps.' 'Nothing,' said Leonard. 'I just thought if you try to say it quickly three times, it's a bit of a tongue twister. You try it, Jack.'

Rowell was forced to back away. The comment, designed to imply that Leonard lacked soul and commitment and was just hanging on in for the ride, hoping to get as many caps as possible without putting in too much hard graft, was never an accurate or considered reflection of Leonard's motivation. The man does hard graft like the best of them, and the simple truth is that he is the last person in the world who would be motivated by collecting caps. He never has an idea how many matches he's played in. He collects memories, experiences and friends – not caps and not statistical evidence of his achievements. Trust me, I wrote his book, and I spent much of the time asking him how many matches he'd played, how many years, how many club games, how many internationals . . .

'I don't bloody know,' he'd shrug, lifting his broad shoulders to his chin, past the place where most people have a neck. 'Ask my mum. She has a scrapbook.'

Perfect – a mum with a scrapbook! Every ghostwriter's dream. I called his mum and asked whether I could borrow it, just to flick through the cuttings.

'Sure,' she said.

I asked her whether she could bring the scrapbook to a rugby function that we were both due to be attending. 'I can't carry it,' she said, alarm ringing through her voice at the very suggestion. 'I'll have to get our Jason to bring it.'

England's celebrated 6 ft, seventeen and a half stone prop forward could only just lift it. It turned out that Maria Leonard's scrapbook was less a book and more a suitcase packed full of cuttings. It was the greatest research tool that a writer could ask for; a physical manifestation of the longevity and impact of Leonard's career, and the endless pride of his mother.

Leonard began playing rugby after being taken down to his local rugby club, Barking, aged fourteen, by Mickey Eyres, his PE teacher at Chadwell Heath School. Eyres either spotted the potential in the boy, or he tired of young Leonard ruining all the school's football matches by chopping down and taking out all the attackers. 'All I can remember from my time playing football at school was people shouting at me "you can't do that, you can't do that" as I stood at the back – flattening players before they had the chance of scoring against us,' says Leonard. 'I was the original Enforcer!'

Actually, it will surprise no one to hear that Leonard was something of a tough guy at school. In his first year at Chadwell Heath he instigated a daily challenge whereby he clenched his stomach muscles and invited children to punch him to see whether they could hurt him. He'd do it every day and a bunch of his friends made a fortune. He had no idea that they had been charging people to punch him until decades later. So, he endured all the physical pain and none of the material gain – a little bit like rugby union before professionalism.

Leonard took to rugby immediately. He was a natural. They put him straight in the U-16 team, despite him being fourteen, and with no experience of the sport, and by the time he was fifteen, he was in the U-19s. He captained the U-19s by the time he was sixteen and ran around Barking telling anyone who would listen that one day he would play for England. But it wasn't all natural ability that got him to the top. From a very early age he worked hard on his fitness and he watched other props – trying to absorb as much of their knowledge as possible. 'He was like a sponge,' recalls his dad. 'He'd watch and watch and learn and learn until there was no one at Barking who could teach him anything.' The young Leonard prided himself on training more often, and harder, than any of his contemporaries. On one occasion, he made the decision to try and 'up' the intensity of his training, so carried a bus-stop sign, complete with concrete base, in his arms as he ran the four miles home from the club. He arrived home exhausted and dripping in sweat. 'Mum went mad,' he admits, 'and Dad threw the thing outside and told me to calm down and not train so hard. It's funny but all I remember of the incident now is that all the bus drivers in the area were looking very confused when they went past our house – not sure whether to stop or not.

'At Barking, I was just loving the rugby so much that nothing else mattered. I wanted to train and train and be the best I could. I thought the club was brilliant, and in rugby I had found something that I could be good at and enjoy. Great fun, great mates, great sport.'

One of the reasons that rugby fans have taken Leonard to their hearts so much is because he did always seem to be enjoying it all. Britain is still a country of people weighed down by notions of Corinthian spirit who do not readily take to sportsmen who appear to squeeze the joy out of sport in the name of success in it. With Leonard, the hard work was always masked by an incredible fun-loving veneer. Many people will know that Leonard has a reputation for his big nights of drinking and curries, but he was always an athlete during the season, and the nights of excess, though they littered his career, were the exceptions rather than the rule. I can remember staying in Leonard's house, around the mid-1990s, because he was going away and wanted someone to keep an eye on his cats (honestly!). I went to the cupboard to get something to eat (like a biscuit of some description) and was hit by the brutal reality of what it is like to be an international player ... nothing but isotonic drinks, bananas, protein shakes and vitamins in there. I called him on his mobile. 'Where do you keep the crisps?' I asked. I'm sure he hung up.

I remind him of this incident as we're talking and he says he remembers it clearly. 'By 1995, we were all really focusing on our diet and cutting out junk, which was good because before that the guys had been eating nothing but crap. But, when you look back, we were being really amateurish about it, and not eating the right stuff at all – we were making it up as we went along. When I started playing for England, I was sixteen stone and a bit, by the time I finished, I was nineteen stone, much faster, more flexible, more powerful, and I could run further. That's what thirteen years of rugby did for me.'

*

Leonard's first foray into World Cup rugby came in 1991, when he was the baby of the side.

'I was quite relaxed about it all because things seemed to be going well for us – in my first year we had won the Grand Slam. I thought that it was always going to be like that. I didn't realise you should treasure those moments of victory because they're actually quite rare. We played good rugby all the way through, beating France in the quarter-finals in a fierce game. We lost the final, of course – which was massively disappointing; I'm the only one of the 1991 final guys to go on to win it in 2003, so I'm pretty lucky.'

Leonard says the contrast between the 1991 final and the 2003 final is the real story of how much rugby and World Cups have changed. Two finals featuring England and Australia, one of them held in England, and one in Australia. But that, apparently, is where the similarities end.

In 1991, we thought we were doing as much as we possibly could – we thought we were so professional. We couldn't imagine there was anything else we could do. Looking back now, of course, there was lots that we could have done. We hadn't even skimmed the surface in terms of preparation. As a professional, I can see how amateurish it was. Fitness, the game analysis, diet and lifestyle weren't a big deal in '91. All they said about our diet was that we had to eat more carbs. Bloody hell, I used to take on board some quantities of pasta. When we got a proper diet and fitness guy in, he said: 'What are you doing? You're eating enough carbs to run a marathon every day. You need protein to repair muscles.'

The difference between 1991 and 2003 was astronomical. In 1991 we really wanted to win, in 2003 it felt like all our lives had been on hold for seven years, gearing up to this moment when we simply had to win. I think other teams felt the same way – that winning was all the more important because the rewards of winning were greater and the consequences of defeat were worse.

Leonard says that there is no question that the World Cup changed the way all the players viewed rugby. As soon as the 1987 World Cup was over, the players began to think about 1991 then, after 1991, the focus quickly moved to 1995 and the players found themselves in a four-year cycle of training and preparation. Then came the end of amateurism. 'Professionalism really changed everything, but it took us all a few years to realise what being a professional meant, and that it meant lifting your game mentally as well as physically. We learnt that being a professional is about being a craftsman – that's a continual process, never-ending. If anyone thinks they're the finished article, they're heading for a fall. You can always be better and you can always work harder.'

When I worked with Leonard on his autobiography I was given something of an insight into this. He's the most laid-back man in the world but, boy, does he put the work in when he has to. Training every day, fitness work and an individual gym pro-gramme in any spare moments. I thoroughly enjoyed working with him, though. He was the consummate professional and became fascinated with the process of putting a book together – asking endless questions like a six-year-old on a school trip until he was content that he understood what was happening. He started off being amazed at the level of detail that goes into choosing the right word, and avoiding confusing sentence construction. By the end, he was correcting the grammar, rear-ranging the clauses in the sentences and questioning my use of the reflexive pronoun. He was an absolute delight . . . except on one occasion – when I mentioned producing an all-time Drinking XV for the book. Oh, how I wish I'd never made that suggestion. I thought it would be a bit of fun. I never meant it to be so serious . . . I should have known better. We put the first draft together – fifteen names, all of them big drinkers except for Rory Underwood (chosen because he doesn't drink at all, and thus could drive the motley crew around and remember which hotel they had to go back to). Leonard chose Dewi Morris for pure comedy value, illustrated by the time, in February 1992, when England played France and Morris was screaming at the referee for giving penalties to the French. 'Monsieur, Monsieur. Le ballon, le ballon,' cried the suddenly bilingual Morris. 'It's all right, Dewi, I can speak English,' said Hilditch, the Irish referee . . .

'An Englishman needlessly talking French to an Irishman. Pure class,' Leonard said. 'Put him in the Drinking XV.'

We were all finished and I started writing up the chapter that evening, then, as I was about to hang up my pen for the evening, Leonard called me. 'I can't miss Skinner out,' he said in a blind panic, referring to the former England flanker, and drinker of legendary standing. 'I'll put him at fly-half.'

'You can't', I retorted. 'Skinner can't play fly-half.'

'Course he can,' said Leonard. 'He'll be fine at fly-half.'

So the phone calls continued, as Leonard tried to squeeze about forty men into a team for fifteen. If he'd had his way, there would have been no backs in the side.

'Replacements!' he declared – bellowing down the phone one morning, in a Eureka! moment. 'We'll have loads of replacements!'

'We can have some,' I tried. A small part of me had fantasised about Jason genuinely picking the fly-half he most liked drinking with, the scrum-half, etc. through the team. Suddenly, he had the three blokes he used to drink with at Barking coaching the side, three props on each wing and a fifty-strong scrum. I don't think there's a replacements bench anywhere that would have held the heavyweight drinkers that he selected to sit on it for the duration of the match.

Then, perhaps inevitably, the call came. 'I was thinking, Ali,' he said. 'How about if we actually went on tour? We could all jump into a coach and head off somewhere . . . play some matches! That would be good, wouldn't it?'

I think that might have been my turn to hang up.

As well as having a reputation for being good fun and liking a drink, Leonard is also known as one of sport's 'good guys', a decent man as well as a talented player. There have been a couple of occasions on which he has behaved like the living embodiment of decency. In 2000 when England lost 19–13 to

Scotland as they were on the verge of a grand slam, the England players stomped off the field before Scotland were presented with the Calcutta Cup, in a manner which displayed a surprising lack of good grace; Leonard alone stayed and shook hands with the Scottish players even when he must have felt like crawling into a hole and not facing anyone. Then there was the time in 2003, witnessed by Gareth Rees, the former Canada captain, when Leonard showed the human touch and humility in victory.

> I remember it so clearly [says Rees]. The English boys were getting their medals when Jason saw Ben Darwin who had been injured earlier in the tournament. He went over and shook his hand. He stayed there a while, checking the guy was okay. You know this was Jason's glory moment. After all the disappointments and all the hard work – he had won the World Cup. His teammates are all leaping up and down and screaming and shouting, and Jason's chatting to an injured player. He realised what was important when he saw Ben and went over. Others were revelling in what they'd achieved, while he was being selfless and checking on a mate. It was a lovely moment, but not that unexpected – that's just what Jason's like.

Leonard worked with a variety of coaches in his World Cup career, starting with Geoff Cooke, a man for whom he has an enormous amount of respect. 'Geoff Cooke was a revelation. He rewarded players with loyalty for the first time, so you could have one bad game and keep your place which was excellent because it allowed players to take risks to be the best they could, instead of trying to stay out of trouble.'

There was also Dick Best. 'A great coach. He was brought in to give the team a hard edge. When it came to the forwards, there was a great technical aspect to his coaching that you don't very often get at international level.'

And Jack Rowell: 'He allowed the people who run the game to run it . . . the spine of the side – 2, 8, 9, 10: these are the decision-makers – Moore, Richards, Morris, Andrew. They were allowed to get on with the job of organising and running the team on the pitch.'

And then, of course, there was Clive Woodward:

> He was very much a facilitator – not really a coach, more a manager or you could describe him as a broker – between the players and the RFU. He always wanted players to play and not worry about anything – wives, kids, etc. He wasn't inspirational, and many of his team talks were instantly forgettable, but he created a no excuses environment . . . players had nothing to use as an excuse – travel was all sorted, kit was where it should be, hotels were perfect, travel arrangements were the best. Clive took the excuse culture out of England rugby. He allowed a group of great, hard-working players to win.

Leonard retired soon after the 2003 World Cup and today works for a construction company as well as being a regular on the corporate dinner-party circuit, and a frequenter of players' testimonial years. For Simon Shaw's testimonial evening last year, there was a *Generation Game* evening in aid of the NSPCC at which contestants could try their hand at the Art of the Pint Glass with Jason Leonard. Then, a *Mastermind*-theme evening for Phil Vickery, led leading players to answer questions on their specialist subjects. Leonard's specialism? 'Porn stars from 1978 to 1985.'

Leonard is dressed casually today, as I interview him in a gym that we both go to in west London. We usually meet in the coffee bar and chat for hours instead of working out. In jeans and a big baggy navy-blue jumper, he looks very much the retired rugby player, as he lounges on the sofas. It's a far cry from his days with England when he'd be dressed up in a blazer or in that rather hideous grey England suit which was to sartorial elegance what Leonard is to synchronised swimming. 'The jumper hides the stomach,' he says, patting what is, let's be fair, much more of a stomach than he ever had when he chased an oval ball while dressed in skin-tight white Lycra for a living. Though he was always barrel-shaped, of course, leading one fan to shout out, while he was receiving treatment for an injury on the side of the pitch: 'Oi Leonard, you don't need a physio, you need a midwife.' As we're chatting, the work phone begins to ring.

'See!' he cries. 'It does ring.'

He looks quite impressed with himself, not least because he thought the thing was switched off.

He answers the phone proudly, and chats to a journalist who wants to hear about his modern incarnation as a committee man. 'See how media-friendly I am these days,' he says.

It wasn't always the way, I remind him. Such as the occasion when I was covering a Harlequins match against Northampton as rugby editor of *The Times*. Leonard was sent off, and all the press were eager to talk to him afterwards because his red card might have implications for forthcoming England games. We hunted everywhere for him. I had taken my parents to the match with me and I rushed out to apologise to them for taking too long, but explained that I must get some quotes first.

'Don't worry,' they said. 'We'll wait here.'

So, I tore back into the press room. No sign of Leonard. I banged on the changing-room door – no sign of Leonard. I teamed up with the reporter from the *Sun*. 'You go that way, I'll go this way,' he said. We were like Cagney and Lacey – hunting through the clubhouse with our notepads cocked. There was no sign of him, anywhere. I decided to call it a day, go back to rescue my parents and call him on the phone later on to get a quote.

'Sorry I've been so long,' I explained to Mum and Dad, who were sitting on the stone-cold steps at Northampton rugby club, sipping tea out of plastic cups.

'That's okay,' said Mum. 'We were being entertained.'

'By whom?'

'Jason Leonard.'

'What?'

'He came over. While you were off, chasing around for your quotes. We were talking to him for half an hour. He seems very nice. He was a bit upset about being sent off.'

BIBLIOGRAPHY

Jeremy Guscott	*The Lions Diary*	Michael Joseph
Mark Ring	*Ring Master*	Mainstream
Ron Palenski	*Encyclopedia of NZ Rugby*	Hodder Moa Beckett
Stuart Barnes	*Rugby's New Age Travellers*	Mainstream
Bob Dwyer	*The Winning Way*	Rugby Press
Edward Griffiths	*One Team, One Country*	Viking
Barry John	*The King*	Mainstream
Derek Wyatt	*Rugby DisUnion*	Victor Gollancz
Ian Jones	*Unlocked*	Celebrity Books
Richard Bath	*General Encyclopedia of Rugby*	Carlton
Peter Jackson	*Lions of England*	Mainstream
Will Carling	*My Autobiography*	Hodder & Stoughton
David Kirk	*Black & Blue*	Hodder Moa Beckett
Peter Jenkins	*World Cup Glory*	Sandstone Publishing
Matt Dawson	*Nine Lives*	Collins Willow
Stephen Jones	*On My Knees*	Mainstream
Stephen Jones	*Midnight Rugby*	Headline
Graham Hutchins	*The Road to Cardiff*	Harper Sports
Rod Macqueen	*One Step Ahead*	Random House
Dean Richards	*Deano*	Victor Gollancz
Kyran Bracken	*Behind the Scrum*	Orion
Jason Leonard	*The Autobiography*	Collins Willow
Neil Jenkins	*Life at Number 10*	Mainstream
Brendan Fanning	*From There To Here*	Gill & Macmillan Ltd
Peter Fitzsimons	*The Rugby War*	Harper Sports
Jeremy Guscott	*At The Centre*	Pavillion
Gerald Davies	*Rugby's Battle of the Giants*	Generation Publications
Brian Moore	*The Autobiography*	Partridge Press
Andy Haden	*Boots n' All!*	Blandford Press
Richard Hill	*The Autobiography*	Orion

Bob Howitt	*Rugby Nomads*	Harper Sports
Phil Shirley	*The Unofficial Biography of Jonah Lomu*	HarperCollins
Rory Underwood	*Flying Wing*	Stanley Paul
Jeff Probyn	*Upfront*	Mainstream
Will Carling	*Captain's Diary*	Chatto & Windus
Ieuan Evans	*Bread of Heaven*	Mainstream
Clive Woodward	*Winning!*	Hodder & Stoughton
Gary Teichmann	*For The Record*	HarperCollins
Jason Robinson	*Finding My Feet*	Hodder & Staughton
Graham Henry	*The X Factor*	Queen Anne Press
Rory Steyn	*One Step Behind Mandela*	Zebra Publications
Ian Malin	*Mud, Blood & Money*	Mainstream
Peter Jackson	*Lions of Wales*	Mainstream
Frank Keating	*Band of Brothers*	Michael Joseph
Francois Pienaar	*Rainbow Warrior*	Collins Willow
Donald McRae	*Winter Colours*	Mainstream
Official Account	*World Cup 2003*	Orion
Ian Robertson	*World Cup 1995*	Hodder & Stoughton
Edward Griffiths	*Kitch – The Triumph of A Decent Man*	CAB
Jeremy Guscott	*The Autobiography*	Headline
Robin McConnell	*Inside The All Blacks*	HarperCollins
Sean Fitzpatrick	*Turning Point*	Penguin
Jonny Wilkinson	*My World*	Headline
JJ Stewart	*Rugby: The All Blacks' Way*	Crowood
Jonah Lomu	*The Autobiography*	Headline

INDEX